Praise for *The Product-Minded Engineer*

Being product-minded is what separates decent software engineers from great ones at startups and Big Tech. This book is the missing guide on how to get better in this highly impactful area: how to get more "product-minded" and help your company, your team, and yourself succeed.

—*Gergely Orosz, author of* The Pragmatic Engineer

In this wonderful book, Drew Hoskins encourages software developers to adopt a product focus and teaches us the skills to do so. This material is particularly valuable to those of us who develop software artifacts that are *not* generally considered products, such as libraries and in-house applications. We who develop such software generally don't have product teams to fall back on, so it's up to us to learn these essential techniques.

—*Joshua Bloch, Carnegie Mellon University, author of* Effective Java

In an age where AI handles the syntax, engineers who master user empathy and product thinking will define the future of software. Drew Hoskins provides the definitive guide for making that transformation—blending deep technical wisdom from Microsoft, Facebook, and Stripe with practical frameworks that turn engineers into product-minded builders. This is the book that finally bridges the gap between writing code and creating impact.

—*David Singleton, cofounder and CEO of /dev/agents and former CTO of Stripe*

The artificial split between product and engineering wastes so many hours and opportunities. When delay is expensive, avoiding a handoff is valuable. If your programmer can make good enough product decisions for now, you increase your chances of survival. This book condenses the skills necessary for good-enough-for-now decisions.

—*Kent Beck, creator of extreme programming and test-driven development and author of* Tidy First

The Product-Minded Engineer is one of those books that belongs on every software engineer's shelf. Drew Hoskins draws on his real-world experience to unlock the secrets to creating software that users will love.

—*N. Scott Storkel, 35-year software engineering veteran*

I'd highly recommend this book for engineers looking to amplify their impact in building industry-leading experiences. This book levels up engineers at any stage of their career with an appreciation and foundation for product-focused thinking, providing a comprehensive toolkit for how to apply that thinking day-to-day with measurable results.

—*Kimberly Hou, engineering manager, Stripe*

Reading this book, I frequently found myself thinking back to past experiences where this book would have applied—both from the perspective of being a user of a product and from the perspective of being on the team producing one. The product-minded approach the book advocates is something most engineering teams can benefit from adopting—and I expect I will be recommending this book frequently to others going forward as well as returning to it myself.

—*Peter Schuller, Staff+ engineer, Meta*

For an engineer who has so far succeeded at staying in the code on their projects but finds themselves no longer able to do so, this book provides a singular reference for achieving basic literacy on product-oriented engineering decisions and the impact of product development on engineering teams.

—*Chelsea Troy, Mozilla, University of Chicago,* chelseatroy.com

The Product-Minded Engineer

Building Impactful Software for Your Users

Drew Hoskins

O'REILLY®

The Product-Minded Engineer
by Drew Hoskins

Printed in the United States of America.

Published by O'Reilly Media, Inc., 141 Stony Circle, Suite 195, Santa Rosa, CA 95401.

O'Reilly books may be purchased for educational, business, or sales promotional use. Online editions are also available for most titles (*http://oreilly.com*). For more information, contact our corporate/institutional sales department: 800-998-9938 or *corporate@oreilly.com*.

Acquisitions Editor: Louise Corrigan
Development Editor: Angela Rufino
Production Editor: Ashley Stussy
Copyeditor: Dwight Ramsey
Proofreader: Rachel Rossi
Indexer: Judith McConville
Cover Designer: Susan Brown
Cover Illustrator: José Marzan Jr.
Interior Designer: David Futato
Interior Illustrator: Kate Dullea

November 2025: First Edition

Revision History for the First Edition
2025-11-10: First Release
2026-01-30: Second Release

See *http://oreilly.com/catalog/errata.csp?isbn=9781098173739* for release details.

978-1-098-17373-9

[LSI]

Table of Contents

Part I. Develop

Part II. Deliver

Part III. Discover

Preface

Northern sea otters, such as the one featured on this book's cover, are like software engineers, except more adorable. They wield tools—mainly rocks to break open seashells. They also collaborate—they form large "rafts" of many otters, clutching one another's paws so they can stay afloat and avoid drifting apart.

Sea otters are also *liminal* creatures, meaning they float on the boundary between air and sea, belonging fully to neither. These marine mammals must get oxygen from the air, but their food comes from the ocean. They have paws like a land mammal, but their flippers adapt them for the sea.

Engineers are liminal creatures, too, except we inhabit the space at the border between systems and users. The software, with its databases, protocols, call stacks, and containers, is like the ocean. When we dive deeper to the ocean floor, we come to rest on the hardware that supports it all.

But users are our oxygen and our sunlit sky. We see farther by their light, and we must always stay afloat to do so.

Why This Book Exists

Thinking about software products boils down to two topics:

System thinking
: Considers topics like algorithms and data structures, programming languages, fault tolerance in distributed systems, memory constraints of firmware, and so forth.

Product thinking
: Comprises understanding users, their background knowledge and needs, their sequences of actions, and group dynamics—plus the design techniques and information architectures that serve them.

Software engineering education is mostly about system thinking. University computer science curriculum, coding bootcamps, and software engineering literature focus on algorithms, data structures, programming languages, system knowledge, and design patterns. Outside of the odd Human-Computer Interaction elective, we mostly learn about product design and our users slowly, by osmosis. Why?

It's true that system thinking is our most differentiated skill—product managers, designers, and user experience researchers can't do it. But ask any of those people and they will tell you they wish their engineers had more product skills. They are stretched thin across many products, and communication and alignment are challenging. We can control our product's destiny much better by drawing on deep knowledge of our users rather than trying to interpret a PM's hastily sketched requirements document that doesn't talk about any edge cases.

Some of us could get away without product skills when software engineering was a frontier discipline. Even the basics took unusual talent, grit, and dedication to master. So few people knew how to code effectively that the most urgent task was to train a generation of coders and software designers. The tools and languages were so difficult to use that mastering and using them was a full-time job.

That's changed. Developer technology, spearheaded by the open source ecosystem, cloud computing, and deep capital investment in developer tools companies, has improved dramatically over the last two decades. AI coding assistants and agents now do a lot of heavy lifting for us, taking care of small details so we can focus more on other topics. Topics like product thinking.

This book exists to supplement the rest of your education, blending your existing engineering skills with user empathy and product skills. For example, we won't be designing data structures or algorithms here, but we might choose one based on users' needs.

Armed with these skills, you could become better in engineering roles:

- Prioritize your efforts better based on your impact.
- Work more effectively with product managers and designers.
- Make better-informed engineering design decisions.
- Write more useful and maintainable code by treating your teammates as users of your abstractions.
- Wake up most days excited to serve the people who use your product.

Or you could level up in roles that require a mixture of product and engineering skills:

- Become a product/engineering hybrid, helping with product decisions as well as execution, simultaneously optimizing for engineering and product goals in a way that pure engineers or pure product folks cannot.
- Start a company as a technical founder with product sense, better able to navigate the diverse challenges that start-ups face.
- Become or improve as a tech lead, leading your teammates with sound reasoning based on user outcomes.

Who This Book Is For

This book is for professional software engineers of all stripes who have mastered the basics of writing and shipping code but yearn to make a bigger and more consistent impact. Topics will engage folks from a year into their careers to seasoned engineers. The user-focused skills learned here apply equally to serving coworkers, members of an open source community, and paying customers, whether the users are consumers, professionals, or other developers.

I have included a wide variety of examples, from user interfaces to developer platforms to infrastructure, all of which I consider to be products. Even a modest function is a miniature product, communicating with its users through its interface and fulfilling their needs.

Yes, even infrastructure engineers build products; it's just that their most direct target users are typically other engineers, along with the end users those engineers serve. Adding to the challenge, infrastructure engineering teams usually lack product managers and designers, counterintuitively making certain product skills such as use case awareness even more important to success.

Structure of the Book

Chapter 1 contains introductory material and is a prerequisite for the rest of the chapters.

You can then read the remaining chapters in any order, based on your interests or timing. However, I've placed them in the order I recommend if you have no special preference.

Those eight chapters are divided into four parts themed after phases of the "double diamond" model of software product lifecycles. Let me briefly digress about this.

The Double Diamond Process Model

This book isn't primarily about software processes, and I won't be trying to sell one to you. However, understanding the Double Diamond Process Model will help you navigate this book, and if you're like me, it will expand your conception of what it takes to create great software.

Many effective software lifecycle practices can be boiled down to these four basic phases:

Discover
: Determine who we're serving and the problems they need solved. This phase is about investigation, creativity, and exploration.

Define
: Architect a product that will solve those problems. This phase is about winnowing down our options into a focused plan.

Develop
: Choose and flesh out an implementation. In this phase, we search for the best way to implement and polish the high-level product we've defined.

Deliver
: Build it, validate what you built, get it out to customers, and collect their feedback.

Visualize the four combined phases as in Figure P-1.

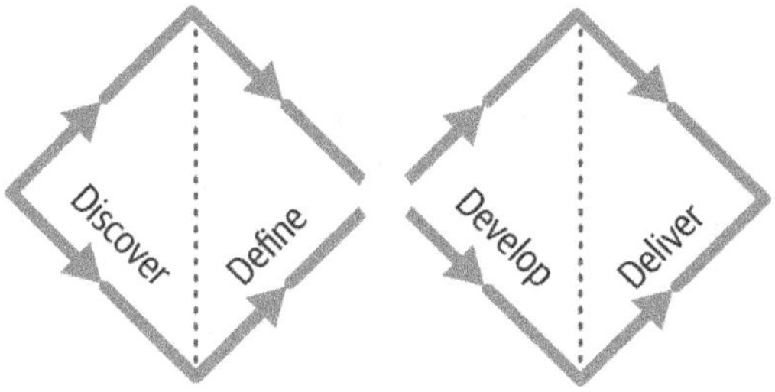

Figure P-1. The British Design Council's depiction of the Double Diamond process model

They're represented as arrows guided along two diamonds. In the Discover and Develop phases, the arrows diverge because we explore many different threads; whereas in the Define and Deliver phases, they converge as we try to weave a tight product from those threads.

Don't take me to mean that there's a neat progression through these phases in a software project. Cycles nest within cycles as you drill into subfeatures, you'll learn new things and backtrack, and so forth.

The back-and-forth between creativity and focus is enlightening. If you're ever frustrated with a colleague who seems to be defocusing things with creative ideas when you're trying to get things shipped, maybe you're mentally in a different phase from them. The same might be true if you feel that someone is shutting down your good ideas. Take a moment to make sure you are aligned on whether you're, say, in Discovery or Development.

This model also opens our minds to the entire product lifecycle, from the moment the problem is first posed to when it's shipped and we're getting feedback. Don't jump straight to a solution, and don't assume that you're done when the first version of your feature ships.

The seasoned product-minded engineer shapes their product's destiny through all four phases of the lifecycle.

The Parts

Product thinking comes up all the time for engineers, so throughout this book, we'll touch on all these phases and show how to use product thinking to achieve great outcomes in each one.

Roughly, the parts of this book cover the Double Diamond phases, rotated to start halfway through the product cycle. First, we start with the Develop and Deliver phases because these are commonly experienced by engineers of all levels. Then I will hop back to navigating the Discover and Define phases, which tend to be the domain of senior levels and above.

By the time we reach Parts III and IV, Discover and Define, the decisions we'll be making, although often made earlier in the product cycle, will be more challenging and require more context. But, if you'd rather read the parts in phase order, go for it; just know that you're tackling more challenging material first.

The Chapters

- Chapter 1 introduces the core concepts of personas and scenarios that I'll use again and again throughout the book and equips you with a touch of user psychology.

Part I, "Develop"

- Chapter 2, "Guiding Users Through Your Product" is about communicative, intuitive product surfaces. You'll help your users discover, understand, and use your product through effective naming and carefully revealed hierarchical design.
- In Chapter 3, "Errors and Warnings", you'll write actionable error messages and architect your code to make errors programmable and useful.

Part II, "Deliver"

- Chapter 4, "Experiencing Your Own Product" discusses some of the most effective ways to dogfood your product, for example to write documentation, scenario tests, and friction logs.
- Chapter 5, "Keeping Up with Users" will teach you to "design for change" and then iterate toward success based on user feedback and metrics.

Part III, "Discover"

- In Chapter 6, "Understanding Your Target Audience", you'll meet your customers and learn what they're looking for, and share that understanding across your whole team.
- Chapter 7, "Discovering Your Product Through Simulation" helps you turn user scenarios into product requirements and prioritized plans.

Part IV, "Define"

- In Chapter 8, "Interaction Design", we get into the details of feature design, helping you to design products that are used only for their intended features and not for unsafe ones.
- Chapter 9, "Product Architecture" applies product thinking to system concerns such as throughput, data consistency, and latency.

Content Notes

Here are a few notes before you start:

- This book includes code listings. I've chosen Python because it is both commonly known and relatively straightforward to understand. I will occasionally explain syntax that might be unfamiliar.
- Every chapter concludes with thought-provoking exercises and sample answers to those exercises. Please do them! Product thinking takes practice.
- I have worked at Microsoft, Facebook, Stripe, and Temporal. Some examples in this book are drawn from my experiences at these companies, some from products I worked on myself. I chose them not as an endorsement of these companies, but because this firsthand knowledge allows me to provide the nuanced detail a book on product thinking requires, and to do so accurately.
- I've spent most of my career building products for developers. While I cover a much broader range of products in this work, and have sought many inputs in order to make my advice universal, there may be a bias toward techniques that are more relevant when serving technical users rather than consumers.

Conventions Used in This Book

The following typographical conventions are used in this book:

Italic
: Indicates new terms, URLs, and email addresses.

`Constant width`
: Used for program listings, as well as within paragraphs to refer to program elements such as variable or function names, databases, data types, environment variables, statements, and keywords.

> This element signifies a tip or suggestion.

> This element signifies a general note.

> This element indicates a warning or caution.

O'Reilly Online Learning

O'REILLY®

For more than 40 years, *O'Reilly Media* has provided technology and business training, knowledge, and insight to help companies succeed.

Our unique network of experts and innovators share their knowledge and expertise through books, articles, and our online learning platform. O'Reilly's online learning platform gives you on-demand access to live training courses, in-depth learning paths, interactive coding environments, and a vast collection of text and video from O'Reilly and 200+ other publishers. For more information, visit *https://oreilly.com*.

How to Contact Us

Please address comments and questions concerning this book to the publisher:

O'Reilly Media, Inc.
141 Stony Circle, Suite 195
Santa Rosa, CA 95401
800-889-8969 (in the United States or Canada)
707-827-7019 (international or local)
707-829-0104 (fax)
support@oreilly.com
https://oreilly.com/about/contact.html

We have a web page for this book, where we list errata and any additional information. You can access this page at *https://oreil.ly/the-product-minded-engineer-1e*.

For news and information about our books and courses, visit *https://oreilly.com*.

Find us on LinkedIn: *https://linkedin.com/company/oreilly-media*

Watch us on YouTube: *https://youtube.com/oreillymedia*

Acknowledgments

Here's a wholehearted thank you to my friends and stalwart alpha readers, Carmen Krol and Peter Schuller, who subjected themselves to the entirety of the rough early draft and gave fantastic feedback.

I'd also like to highlight my beta readers, Kimberly Hou, Scott Storkel, and Chelsea Troy, who plowed through the entire beta and were honest with me.

Thanks to other contributors, Adam Hupp, Ben Lavender, Paul Nordstrom, Jason Rosenfeld, Jeff Schoner, Venkat Subramaniam, and Mark Wong, who all made positive impacts on the book.

Other thanks:

- Anthropic for creating my research buddy, Claude. There are a lot of topics in this speedrun through product thinking, and I needed a knowledge boost on many of them.
- Louise Corrigan for believing in me and suggesting that I write on this awesome topic.
- My patient and knowledgeable editor, Angela Rufino.
- Joshua Bloch, Don Norman, and Steven Clarke for setting me off on this product-minded journey.

- Charles Zedlewski for suggesting that I give product management a try after so many years as an engineer. It would have been hard to write parts of this book well without this experience.
- Gergely Orosz for his inspiring blog post, *The Product-Minded Software Engineer*.
- Patrick Collison, for introducing me at O'Reilly, and for running a company full of product-minded engineers.
- Peter Dimov, for teaching me to embrace my calling as a product-minded engineer.

CHAPTER 1
The Foundations of Product Thinking

> *Here we go yo, here we go yo*
> *So what, so what, so what's the scenario?*
> —A Tribe Called Quest

If there is a core primitive of product thinking, it's the *scenario*. It's simply a user story structured to be useful for product design.

Here's a scenario about passwords:

> Darla is a retired baby boomer who began using computers at the age of forty-five. She is setting up an account at her local tea shop, so that she can order online. When it asks for an email and password, she chooses her daughter's birthday followed by her son's first name so that she can remember it. She has about thirty online accounts, so she uses the same password for most of them because otherwise, it would be impossible to remember, and she's been advised not to write down her passwords.

You can guess what happens next—her tea shop has a data breach, and her password—the same one she uses at her bank—gets leaked. Perhaps someone on the dark web buys her login and takes her money.

This nightmare scenario highlights a problem with passwords, but not one *in* the product, per se. You'd never get to it by simply considering the signup interface itself, the encryption protocol, the secure storage, and so forth. But by writing a complete story that incorporates predictable human frailties, the security problem becomes obvious.

In this section, we'll break down and analyze the components of an effective scenario and teach you how to craft a good one. Loosely speaking, a scenario has a plot and a character. I'll first flesh out those concepts and then give tips on how to build good ones.

But first, as in most chapters, I'll introduce a case study to guide the discussion.

Case Study

Tea++ is a 300-store cafe chain. The chain has expanded too rapidly and is barely staying afloat, so the company's goal is to find quick fixes to increase orders and avoid closing stores on a shoestring budget.

Tea++ has a popular mobile app that supports an ordering experience, and via the feedback widget, users have been asking for a "favorites" option so that their preferences can be remembered for quicker ordering. The software team figures this might be an easy way to increase orders.

The First Attempt, with No Scenarios

Let's visit Bob, a mobile app engineer. He doesn't use user scenarios at work.

Bob looks over some user feedback that came in through the app's feedback widget. Coffee drinkers are tired of respecifying their customizations each time they order, and they don't like digging through their recent orders. Sometimes, the item they want is buried within an order that had several other items, and it's tedious to split out.

Bob works up a mock that works well within the app structure (Figure 1-1). He'll add a menu item for Favorites to the bottom of the app and add a new page that lists users' favorites. It has a + button in the upper right for adding a new favorite.

Figure 1-1. Bob shows his proposed mobile app changes. New elements are shaded.

Happily, this will be easy to implement because the favorites list uses existing menu widgets. Once drinkers click *Order*, they'll be dropped into the existing shopping cart experience.

The new favorites database table will be sorted by most recent purchases, and Bob specifies the (SQL) database schema and notes that it will be indexed by recency for quick querying.

```
Table: favorite_items
- created_time : timestamp
- updated_time : timestamp (Index)
- item_id : long
- milk_customization: varchar
- sweetness_customization: varchar
- special_instructions: varchar
```

Bob also proposes that they replace the new product advertisement on the home screen with favorites, but the "New Products" team shoots the idea down because they need a place to drive awareness of their seasonal specials. He grudgingly cuts it out of his design.

There's a big review meeting, and everybody likes the design, in particular because it's cheap to implement. One person notes that the Starbucks app has "heart" buttons on recently ordered items and in the shopping cart. Why not have a similar button that adds items to Favorites?

But Bob pushes back, noting that this button will double the time-to-implement since it's a more invasive change, for example, adding a new database query on several pages. The team agrees, and the project is built and shipped as designed.

Meh Results

Reviewing the data a few weeks later, there's good and bad news. The good news is the favorites feature shipped without major bugs. Unfortunately, only six percent of active users use favorites, and orders increased by only 0.3%.

Tea++'s app is well-instrumented, so Bob digs into the data and finds that few people click into the Favorites menu, and most of those who do leave immediately. The ones who have no items in Favorites are overwhelmingly likely to leave rather than click the + button.

Bob thinks back to the "heart" button idea and meets with Carlos to propose adding that to increase conversion. Unfortunately, the team priorities have shifted to monthly subscriptions, and there's no time to build it anytime soon. Everyone is stressed about the chance of store closures, and Carlos seems a little annoyed with his proposal. Bob leaves angry, feeling like he is not being allowed to finish his product.

What Went Wrong?

Bob did many things right. He listened to user feedback. He tracked a metric. He collected user interactions and studied them. He cut scope and made an efficient, achievable, and stable design.

But his proposal was weak. The questions he elicited from his team during the design review were interesting but weren't the most fundamental.

First, he skipped the Discover phase, the first of the four phases I mentioned in the preface, instead jumping straight to database design.

Put another way, his proposal took a project where the most challenging parts were product decisions and the way those choices interacted with implementation constraints, making it seem like the implementation concerns were the most important bits. He wasn't lucky enough to have a teammate who could see the problem.

Let's see a developer who uses scenarios to think through user needs.

A Second Attempt with Scenarios

Six months later, Bob's still working on subscriptions when Alice, a more senior engineer, is brought in to build the Starbucks-style Heart button that Bob regretted not building.

She doesn't stop there—she *also* builds a concept of favorite stores. Now, users who frequent a particular store can skip a few clicks in the checkout flow—something that Bob hadn't even considered since he had been asked to focus on favorite drinks.

Thirdly, she A/B tests a change where the new product promotion on the home screen is replaced by a huge pair of "order now" buttons, plus a peek at the top of a third button to indicate that scrolling is possible (Figure 1-2). It's similar to the design Bob had thought of, but he hadn't been able to convince the product marketing team to give him the screen real estate.

Over time, Alice's experiment demonstrates that these changes combine to increase conversion by 3.8 percent. Since mobile orders account for half of Tea++'s revenue, this is enough to make a substantial impact on the bottom line! Armed with this data, Alice can convince the marketing department to drop their new product ads down in the list below the top two favorites and to roll out her test to everyone.

Bob wasn't very involved in her planning and wonders how Alice had such good intuitions for what to build. And how did she convince people to let her do it?

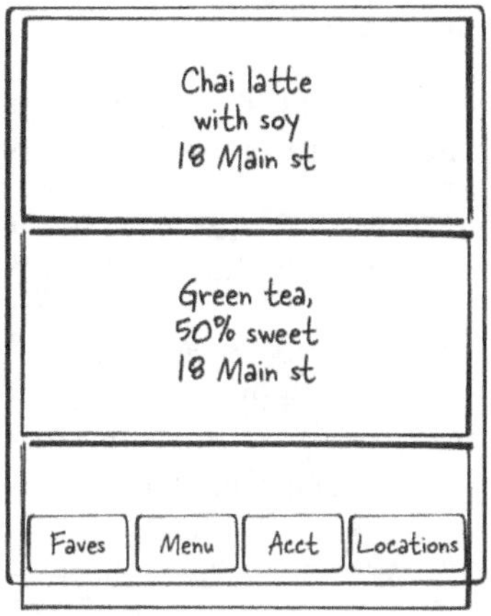

Figure 1-2. Alice mocks up a scrollable quick-ordering screen with "order now" buttons

Scenarios as Stories That Inspire

One of the uses of scenarios is to communicate and inspire.

When Bob asks Alice how she did it via a direct message, she replies with an inspiring story:

> Eliana is a busy professional who gets a chai latte with soy milk every morning on her commute. One morning, she forgets to enter the order before she goes. While she's driving, she presses the voice assistant button on her car's steering wheel and says, "Order my usual from Tea++." Her voice assistant, Siri, replies, asking her to confirm the amount and location, and she agrees.

Bob is confused. "Okay...But that's not what you built?"

"I know. Carlos thought it was too expensive to build," she laments. "He's probably right. But I wanted to set a high bar to show the potential. And I wanted to show a story that would be common, but where a favorites flow wasn't just convenient but made the difference between the user getting her tea and not."

"It sounds cool, but I didn't think we had that kind of time, either."

"There's value in a dream," Alice says. "Favorite Drinks and Locations will make it easier for users to use voice commands later, if we ever build it."

During Discover, it's essential to explore various possible storylines.

Scenarios That Capture User Interviews

If you've done some user research, scenarios can be fictional composites of what users are telling you. This can succinctly communicate common situations.

"I mean, I could easily make up some story that made my version look good," counters Bob. "Is ordering while driving really that important?"

"I kinda wish we had location tracking data to figure that out," Alice replies. "But mostly, I interviewed a dozen of my friends and acquaintances and asked them in a silly level of detail about their coffee ordering experiences. And yes, commutes came up. Eliana is a stand-in for *busy, scatter-brained person on a crazy morning.*"

We'll talk about user interviews in Chapter 6.

Scenarios That Highlight Product Gaps

Scenarios can be used to show a missing feature.

"That was my *after* story," Alice says. "Do you want to see my *before* story?"

"Um, sure."

She DMs it over:

> Eliana is a busy professional who gets a chai latte with soy milk every morning on her commute. One morning, she forgets to enter the order before she goes. While she's driving, she comes to a stop sign and opens the Tea++ app, then clicks on Favorites. She finds her latte at the top of the list and clicks "Order now." A car behind her honks, so she moves forward and focuses on driving. But she needs some caffeine, so when she gets to the freeway on-ramp, she pulls over to the shoulder. On the shopping cart page, she selects "Order and Pay." This page asks her to choose a location. Once the map loads, she jabs her finger at the Main St. pin and clicks OK, which routes her to the payment screen where she uses Apple Pay to complete the transaction. She puts her phone down, checks for oncoming cars, and merges back onto the on-ramp.

"I guess that explains why you built Favorite Locations," he said. "Did somebody ask for that?"

"One user asked why they had to select a location every time. And when I went through this myself, imagining I was in my car, I realized that the Heart button wasn't necessarily the most important thing."

Bob takes a deep breath. "I see. Well, anyway, kudos for getting the Heart button added," he offers. "I tried to convince Carlos to fund it, but he wanted me on subscriptions."

Scenarios That Highlight a Frictionful Experience

You can set up stories that demonstrate the pain of using the existing product. In this example, Alice sets up a little farce.

"I had a scenario for that too," said Alice. "This one came indirectly from user feedback. Here's the *before* story."

> Eliana is a lactose-intolerant, new Tea++ customer who remembers liking the drink she ordered previously. Intending to reorder, she sees the Faves menu, but she has never put anything in it. She sees the + button but can't remember the drink name or her customizations, so she clicks into Recent Orders and notices it was called the Tiger Chai Latte, which she customized with soy milk. She had also ordered a pastry, but she doesn't want that this time. Annoyingly, Reorder tries to foist that upon her, and she sees no way to select out the latte. She exits and goes into the usual ordering flow. When she gets through her customizations and orders, she looks for a Favorites button at the end, but she doesn't find it. Well, at least her latte is on the way—maybe another time.

Bob winces once again. "That's why I wanted to build the Heart button," he says.

Alice smiles. "Let me confess something," she writes. "I was originally trying to get Carlos to let *you* build the button. I sent him this story. Three weeks later, he asked me to look into it, but he told me to look for other low-hanging fruit first. That's how I came upon location favorites and replacing the ads."

I'll talk about capturing user feedback in Chapter 5, which can be turned into stories like this, as well as user quotes.

Scenarios That Validate the Feature You're Planning to Build

One of the most frequent uses I see for scenarios is to simulate how users will interact with the product you're designing.

For example, here is Alice's *after* story, which includes not only the Heart button, but Location, Favorites, and the front page placement, all working together:

> Eliana is a newish Tea++ customer who remembers liking the drink she ordered before. Intending to reorder, she clicks into Recent Orders and notices it was called Tiger Chai Latte. She clicks the heart next to it. This reroutes her to the Favorites menu, which lists it at the top, and she clicks the "Order now" button next to the item. She is presented with a location selector which defaults to Main St., her previous store. She clicks that and uses Apple Pay to complete the transaction. Because she has been to the same store twice, a pop-up appears asking her if she wants to make the Main St. store her favorite. She clicks Yes.

> The next time she's thirsty, she pops open the app, and there at the top, above the seasonal specials, is "Tiger Chai Latte from Main St." She clicks it and goes straight to the payment screen.

"This story was one of my north stars," she explains. "It gave me conviction that I was building and advocating for the right things, and helped Carlos buy in as well."

Scenarios like this that guide your product design are called "north star scenarios" and are discussed in Chapter 7.

Scenarios as Tests

Alice and Bob didn't talk about it, but when she was writing automated tests, she wrote "scenario tests" which exercised not just the individual app pages but also made sure they linked up properly to make sure that a user could complete common flows.

Scenario tests are highlighted in Chapter 4.

Searching for the Key Answers

In seeing Bob's initial design and looking at the mockups, you might have felt unequipped to critique it or that you lacked context. Perhaps you had some ideas on how to improve it based on prior experiences. Perhaps you were focused on the database schema, questioning certain details.

Alice's stories focused our minds on more important questions:

- Could they build a voice assistant?
- How common is ordering before or during a commute?
- Is the favorites feature working well for users?
- What else is causing friction in the ordering flow?

These are productive questions. They would help a team narrow down and prioritize different features. She both made me unhappy with the current app and set a high bar for ease of use, and her team could measure their ultimate solution by how close it got to achieving that mark.

In the process, she was able to highlight three of the most important fixes.

So, What's the Scenario?

Now that Alice has thoroughly motivated scenarios for us, let's break them down and help you build them yourself.

A scenario is a user story designed to elicit critical thinking about a product. It consists of two main parts: a character and a simulation of their actions as they discover and navigate a product or feature to solve their problem.

Let's start with character. A character consists of:

Persona
: Background information including the skills and faculties they possess

Motivation
: What they want or need from your product in the moment they're using it

Here's part of Alice's north star scenario:

> Eliana is a newish Tea++ customer who remembers liking the drink she ordered before. Intending to reorder, she clicks into Recent Orders, notices the heart next to the Tiger Chai Latte and clicks it. This reroutes her to the Favorites menu, which lists it at the top, and she clicks the "Order now" button next to the item.

See if you can spot the motivation and the persona. I'll dive into each of those.

A Motivation

The first rule of thinking about users is understanding what they want.

In fiction, a character's desires carry us through a story. We root for the hero to achieve their goals and feel it when they are thwarted. Famously, musicals often start out with a song dedicated to establishing the character's motivation, called the "I Want" song. In *The Wizard of Oz*, it's Dorothy's *Somewhere over the Rainbow*. In *Hamilton*, it's Alexander Hamilton's *My Shot*.

When motives are poorly written, we complain that characters don't do what they "would do."

Scenario users need motivation too. That helps us feel tension and release when the product works as intended to achieve their goals and helps us evaluate whether their actions pass the smell test. If money is involved, do we feel they have enough motivation to buy our product?

Let's drop the motive from the scenario and see how it works.

> Eliana is a newish Tea++ customer <snip>. She clicks into Recent Orders, notices the heart next to the Tiger Chai Latte and clicks it. This reroutes her to the Favorites menu, which lists it at the top, and she clicks the "Order now" button next to the item.

Would Eliana really take these actions? We don't know. Why did she specifically go into Recent Orders and not the Favorites menu? Did she set out to favorite something and magically guess that Recent Orders was where she could favorite things? We wonder if Alice, the story's author, is a puppeteer controlling Eliana's actions to serve her point. We also question if the feature is really discoverable.

When we see her mental state—that she can't quite remember the name of what she ordered, but remembered it being good—we understand why she went to Recent Orders.

Authoring a motivation

Make sure that your motivation is enough to get the character to use your feature.

If your product is rough, your users will often need a fairly intense motive to use it. Here's a *before* story that Alice could have used to criticize the existing design:

> Eliana is a lactose intolerant, newish Tea++ customer who remembers liking the drink she ordered before. Intending to reorder, she clicks into Recent Orders and notices it was called the Tiger Chai Latte. She has a little extra time and knows herself well enough to know she's obsessive once she likes something, so she heads to the Favorites menu, clicks the + button, and then searches for "tiger," clicks the search result, replays her customizations—with soy milk, medium—then clicks OK. Then she clicks "Order now."

This version highlights that it would take a diligent, avid customer to use the current favorites system, whereas Tea++ is trying to *reduce* the need for a heavy motive to order their drinks.

Forcing yourself to provide a clear user motive that carries through their actions in this way can highlight bad product design.

Be careful—when writing motives, it's easy to impose "straw man" motivations on your users that simply say, "<person> wants to use <my cool feature>" without explaining their underlying need. Take "Eliana wants to look at her recent orders." That's not her goal; it's a means to an end. But what end?

If you're not familiar, a *straw man argument* ascribes beliefs to someone they don't actually have, to serve the interests of the ascriber. These come up frequently in politics, when we are quick to imagine bad motivations and arguments for policies and politicians we don't like. Similarly, a *straw man user* is a fictional character who takes unreasonable actions, often because that's what we need them to do for our product to seem to succeed.

> Avoid creating straw men for scenario characters.

If you find yourself with a weak motive, look deeper into the character. You could call this a *root cause analysis* (RCA). A root cause is the *why* or the *so that* the user is taking a particular action: Eliana remembers that she liked a drink she ordered before. She can do this because she's a repeat customer.

> Do a root cause analysis of your users' motivations.

If you're not sure, you may want to talk to some users, or your local product manager or tech lead to figure it out.

In my root cause analysis, I moved beyond Eliana's immediate motivation into her persona when I said she was a repeat customer. In so doing, I touched on the character background, so let's talk personas now.

A Persona

If the first rule of understanding users is to know what they want, the second is that not all users are cut from the same cloth. They have different backgrounds and experiences that impact what they want out of our product.

This character background is called a *persona*. Personas are a critical tool for building quick empathy for your target audience. They can be used to communicate with your team and reach alignment. They usefully highlight contrasts between sets of users.

A persona is typically anchored by a demographic.

We saw in Alice's voice-commands-in-the-car scenario that Tea++'s core audience is commuting professionals. (With that in mind, the cafes are along roadways and near train stations, and Tea++ crafts premium drinks with higher prices.)

Such a persona comes with a set of means—the skills, knowledge, and proclivities that such a person would bring to use the product. This can also be narrowed down by the scenario, for example by pointing out if it's a new user.

For example, in Alice's north star scenario, Eliana's persona is of an early repeat customer who is not yet habitual, from which we assume that she's not an expert in the menu or the ordering flow.

If we strip the persona:

> Eliana <snip> remembers she liked the drink she ordered before. Intending to reorder, she clicks into Recent Orders, notices the heart next to the Tiger Chai Latte and clicks it…

This story, lacking hints about the means, makes it hard to understand whether this scenario is relevant to our business strategy. Is Eliana somebody Tea++ should care about? Only when it's framed in terms of a user who might or might not become a habitual customer do we see the value.

The persona also helps us understand who this feature *isn't* for. The "Favorites" feature is not very useful for users making their first order, so it shouldn't be relied on as part of any new user acquisition strategy. And it should not be prioritized if Tea++ cafes are designed for tourists who visit once.

Authoring personas

For starters, it's good for a team to agree upon one or more *target audiences*, which are the personas your app will be used by and perhaps marketed to. I'll guide you through defining a target audience in Chapter 6.

If you don't know your target audience, talk with the team. Your scenario's persona should be within the target audience.

You'll also often want to make your persona multifaceted to capture more about the skills, knowledge, and motivations that a user has.

Here are some common facets:

- Where are users in "the product funnel"? Are they signed up or not? Ever notice how websites make sign-up very prominent, but bury the widget for sign in for existing users? This comes from a recognition that existing users do not need to be as coddled as new users.
- Casual users versus power users. Suppose power users are 10% of your audience, and you ship a feature that solves a pain point that everyone experiences but is difficult to use. If your feature is too challenging for the other 90% of users to discover or to bother with, then you've effectively only solved the problem for ten percent of the folks who need it.
- Two sides of a marketplace, such as drivers and passengers, or free users and ad buyers. The two sides often have extremely different needs and should not be thought of as an undifferentiated blob of users.
- Coders in different programming languages. If your developer SDK is useful both for machine learning data pipelines authored by Python developers and authors of control planes written in Go, you might want to flesh out different aspects for Python than you do for Go.

So Eliana is a "commuting professional/new user."

Personas highlight the contrasts and complexities of building products that cater to multiple groups and are an excellent way to think more precisely about users. I'll discuss personas in more depth in Chapter 6, showing you how to talk about them and integrate them into your team's prioritization and design thinking. In the meantime, I'll refer to them frequently.

Determining a persona's means

Knowing a user's means will help you help them attain their goals.

Your persona will have certain powers—busy professionals often have a little extra spending money and tend to be computer-literate, but lack time, for example. Retirees on fixed incomes are the opposite.

In addition to these persona-specific means, you can use a few universal human attributes that apply almost no matter what. In fact, let me accuse you of having these characteristics:

First, you want to devote as little brain space to the product you're using as possible:

- You don't understand the implementation and can't read the author's mind.
- You would prefer to avoid reading the documentation if you can avoid it. You'd rather intuit from the product itself what to do.
- With perhaps one or two exceptions that are near and dear to you, you don't generally survey the entire set of functionality in an application or framework. Instead, you prefer to quickly seek and find the tool for your current task.

And, you have other faults and limitations:

- You multitask and are frequently distracted. You want to be able to make progress in one or more small "work steps" and be reminded to come back to things you didn't complete.
- You take the shortest path. You want to complete tasks quickly and are unlikely to do extra work unless you see a clear payoff.
- You want to avoid risk. You don't want to show up and find your tea order was never fulfilled or have to miss your train.
- You forget things. You may need redundant clues or reminders when you come back to things months later.

Here's a version of Alice's *before* story that skips the forgetfulness and the fact that people are busy:

> Eliana is a lactose intolerant, newish Tea++ customer who remembers liking the Tiger Chai Latte and knows she'll be ordering it a few times more. She clicks over to the Favorites menu, clicks the + button, searches for "tiger" and chooses the drink. Then, she replays her customizations—with soy milk, medium—then clicks OK. When it appears in the list, she clicks "Order now."

This is the kind of story that leads to a product that doesn't get as much uptake as we expected because users are turned off by it for mysterious reasons.

One way to remember these universal characteristics is to *shoe-shift*; that is, to put yourself in your user's shoes and think about what you would know and how you would behave.

One key is to develop *selective amnesia*, losing the knowledge you gained from developing the technology yourself.

But how? Are we forever tainted with forbidden knowledge that can't be unseen? Do we need to rely on feedback from new users to have any hope of empathizing with them?

Happily, no. While doing user research and testing with novice users shouldn't be overlooked—and we won't—in practice, not every decision can be made with full data. So, you must shoe-shift from the comfort of your own desk and with your own thoughts.

To shoe-shift, I try to detect any time I access knowledge and memories I gained while developing the product. If I access "forbidden knowledge," I proceed as if I didn't know it.

For Alice's part, she "forgets" that there's a concept of a favorite location when crafting her user stories. That's why she presents them with a pop-up to set their favorite location when she detects they are a repeat customer there.

I use shoe-shifting and selective amnesia to empathize with users all the time and will return to it frequently in this book, such as when writing "friction logs" in Chapter 4.

Character summary

A scenario's character is a combination of a persona, who has a certain set of broad goals and means, and a motive for using your product. Now, let's turn our attention to the plot.

A Simulation

The *simulation* is the plot of the scenario, taking the character, in detail, through all the actions they need to complete the task. The purpose of a simulation is to draw the designer's attention to important details that will affect the user experience.

A good simulation is like an elegant mathematical proof where every step is justified and follows logically from the previous step. It challenges the design rather than pandering to it. A bad simulation handwaves or is self-serving by highlighting only the good parts.

If this way of thinking is unfamiliar to you, you're not alone—most schools and coding bootcamps don't teach user simulations. Agile methodologies emphasize scenarios—they call them user stories—but give scant attention to the simulation aspect. However, the next time a seasoned engineer you respect is talking over a tricky design with you, pay attention. You may notice comments like "what if X happens?" or "what if the user was Y?" It's likely that this engineer is doing mental simulations even if they are not typing them out as formal scenarios.

I meet more engineers who are highly trained pattern-matchers. They see problems that seem similar to ones they've seen in the past and call up solutions, as Bob's colleague did when he remembered that Starbucks had Heart buttons similar to their proposed Favorites feature. These solutions form a growing repository of wisdom that they can bring to bear in new companies.

Use scenario simulations to supercharge your inner pattern-matcher. It's going to focus your attention where it's most needed, and then your pattern-matcher can go wild.

For example, here's Alice's most comprehensive north star scenario that highlights all three features she's adding:

> Eliana is a newish Tea++ customer who remembers liking the drink she ordered before. Intending to reorder, she clicks into Recent Orders and notices it was called Tiger Chai Latte. She clicks the heart next to it. This reroutes her to the Favorites menu, which lists it at the top, and she clicks the "Order now" button next to the item. She is presented with a location selector which defaults to Main St., her previous store. She clicks that and uses Apple Pay to complete the transaction. Because she has been to the same store twice, a pop-up appears asking her if she wants to make the Main St. store her favorite. She clicks Yes.
>
> The next time she's thirsty, she pops open the app, and there at the top, above the seasonal specials, is "Tiger Chai Latte from Main St." She clicks it and goes straight to the payment screen.

This highlights many features, along with their interactions: Recent orders, Favoriting, Ordering, Location selection, Location favoriting, the payment flow, and the home screen.

Personally, I read it and am thinking: What about the order flow? What about tipping? Should the system remember the user's tip amount preference to avoid some clicks and to set up for future voice commands? Alice never touched that, but maybe she should have. Personally, I didn't notice it until I added the plot point about Apple Pay while I was editing.

When later she gets down to more detailed design, she'll flesh out these high-level steps with more details and perhaps some prototype screen diagrams to make it into a storyboard. I'll discuss such "user flows" in Chapter 7.

Authoring a simulation

When I write a simulation, I want it to be complete, so I am sure I'll think of any gotchas. I often start with the feature I'm trying to build, for example the Heart button:

> Eliana is a newish Tea++ customer who remembers liking the drink she ordered before. In the Recent Orders tab, she notices it was called Tiger Chai Latte. She clicks the heart next to it. This reroutes her to the Favorites menu, which lists it.

Then, I push myself in three directions:

- What happened before, and what brought the user to that moment? How did they learn what to do?
- What happens next?
- Should I flesh out the detail of a step?

> Tell the complete story. Don't just focus on the feature you're adding.

If I get stuck, or find myself making things up completely, I may need to talk to users or look at metrics, talk to a PM, or consult other teams so I can be on firmer ground.

Sometimes, I conclude that I shouldn't be building this feature—it's not going to make the impact I want. Other times, I realize I need to do more than just the one feature, or I need to go talk to another team about improving their piece. In any case, I've learned something useful.

Teams that don't focus on entire flows end up with products that are crufty and incoherent. You've probably encountered login flows that are triggered by a deep link to a website, and been frustrated that, once you log in, the site has forgotten the original deep link. Such teams are probably not using scenarios to design their software.

Another technique when authoring scenarios is to look for "plot holes."

One type of plot hole is a skipped step. Above all, your product is the user's journey. Users don't merely "use" your product, they move through it. They discover it, think of it, learn it, use it, and experience the consequences. Narrow focus on the interface itself—the part we can see—gives us tunnel vision.

A classic blunder is to leave out a discovery mechanism. Like, maybe Tea++'s stores never mentioned that there was an ordering app, and only 10% of the users that could have found the app did—only those who were curious enough to search their phone's app store.

Another kind of plot hole is an edge case. You will need to write up different stories for different cases. Like, what if a user frequents two different stores, one in the morning and one in the afternoon? Alice should probably address and prioritize that case, but in a different story.

> Look for skipped steps and edge cases as you author scenarios or review others' scenarios.

How to Use Scenarios?

Scenarios should thread through every aspect of software development, from initial discovery, as Alice did here, through implementation specs. Thus, much of this book will rely on the power of stories.

- When developing, you'll use scenarios to pick good names (Chapter 2) and design hierarchies of errors and good, actionable error messages (Chapter 3). And you'll turn them into scenario tests (Chapter 4).
- You'll gather them from your users as feedback after you ship (Chapter 5) and when starting out via "customer discovery interviews" (Chapter 6).
- When designing, you'll form a product roadmap based on a prioritized compendium of scenarios and creating more detailed user flows (Chapter 7).
- They will also guide detailed interaction design (Chapter 8) and architectural decisions, for example being used to generate load simulations (Chapter 9).

While working with scenarios takes practice, we aren't starting from nothing. After all, we learn stories from a very early age. We are hard-wired to read and understand them. As product-minded engineers, we must also learn to generate or critique them.

When Alice explained how she'd used stories, she used the word *conviction*. She felt this when she had crafted the right scenarios and developed confidence that her product was going to work. She could bring that feeling to conversations when she could resolve trade-offs by thinking through the relative likelihood of different stories. She could ship with conviction because her tests exercised the scenarios that mattered most. She could draw lines from those scenarios to all the components that needed implementing to make them work.

Chapter Summary

I surveyed the fundamentals of product thinking for engineers and gave the following advice.

- Scenarios are a combination of a simulation and a user profile. Use complete scenarios to understand your users and their situations and guide product choices.
- Simulations are a powerful way to direct your attention to what matters. Think beyond the interface and consider the user's journey.
- Personas make sure you are connecting with your product's target audience.
- Shoe-shift and practice selective amnesia to empathize with your users as a daily practice.
- Use scenarios throughout the product lifecycle. As your design progresses toward implementation, make your stories more detailed.

These fundamentals will be used throughout this book. You are welcome to skip around after this point, but I will start with how products communicate to users, diving into topics such as naming and information architectures, which represent the most common of all product decisions. Practicing these is a great route to making product thinking instinctive.

Exercises

In these exercises, we will pretend that we work on Wikipedia.org.

1. List at least two personas of users who use Wikipedia and give descriptions of each. Ensure that you consider what those users value. (My answer will cover two broad personas.)
2. Wikipedia wants to improve the health of their articles, particularly in less popular languages. Today, users must click an "Edit" link to edit content. Should Wikipedia provide a slick inline editing experience that eliminates this friction?
3. Pretend like you're designing Wikipedia's search feature from the box at the top of every page. Using one of the personas from Question 1, write a one-paragraph scenario showing a reader using the "typeahead" feature, which displays likely search results in-line, so you don't have to load a separate search page. Use the scenario to highlight the problems that the implementation will need to solve.
4. Pretend like you're designing Wikipedia's "Watch this page" feature, which will let editors subscribe to learn of changes to a page. Using one of the personas from Question 1, write at least two one-paragraph scenarios to help your team think through the ways that people will use it. (It's okay if you have never used this feature—imagine how you think it should work.)

Answers

1. Reid the reader is a task-oriented reader of Wikipedia articles. Reid values the factual and unbiased information that Wikipedia provides, and prizes the transparency, particularly for political content. He wants to find and read content quickly and then move on with his day.

   Eddie the editor is a historian who creates Wikipedia articles in his area of expertise and also reviews others' content. He feels like a steward of the content, so he keeps up with changes that others make to his pages to make sure the content and citations are correct. He wants to feel part of a community, so the health, inclusiveness, and reputability of his collaborators make all the difference to Eddie.

2. No. Wikipedia's primary goal for its main article pages should be to serve the Reid persona, since Reids outnumber Eddies by three orders of magnitude. Reid likes quick page loads, which in-line editing would likely make challenging. And he doesn't want his random keystrokes to start editing the page. Eddie, meanwhile, is a fairly dedicated persona who will not be put off by a touch of extra friction.

3. In this scenario, I chose to highlight search ranking, spelling corrections, and the case when none of the typeahead results contained what the reader was looking for.

   Reid wants to find out who wrote *Paradise Lost*. He clicks into the search box and types "Paradice Lost"—he doesn't know how to spell it— and notices the top result is "Paradise Lost. Epic Poem by John Milton" with a thumbnail of the cover art. He sees a few other disambiguations—like, apparently, a British gothic metal band—but the top one was correct, as the links were ranked by popularity. Had he instead wanted to know the metal band's seventh album, he could have clicked on a magnifying glass at the bottom with the caption "search for pages containing *paradice lost*."

4. I've written a few scenarios that touched on ease of viewing edits, unsubscribing, or notification channels. You might instead have looked at how your user would get in touch with somebody whose edit they disagreed with or some other topic I didn't think of.

   Eddie has heavily edited a page on the architecture of ancient Mesopotamia and is feeling a bit nervous about its reception. He wants to see if anybody else edits the paragraphs he's added. He clicks the "Watch this page" checkbox in the editing form next to the "Submit" button, then clicks submit. He later adds a few more edits. Now the checkbox is already checked, and he leaves it that way.

   Later Eddie finds an email in his inbox telling him of some changes. The email clarifies that the changes are not to any of the sections he's edited, so he ignores it. But then, a few days later, somebody actually edits his section, and he gets another email. He clicks into the link in the email and finds himself at a side-by-side comparison of the "before" and "after" which jumps to and highlights the change. He sees that the change simply rewords some of his text for clarity, and he's happy.

After a few months, Eddie feels like all the emails are for edits he doesn't care about—it's a long page. So, he clicks "Change or unsubscribe to notifications for this page" at the bottom of the email. The page offers him a couple of checkboxes he had never noticed. He can uncheck "receive notifications for sections I didn't edit" and "receive notifications for minor edits." He realizes that he would gladly stay subscribed to changes to just his sections, so he unchecks the first box.

PART I
Develop

In the next two chapters, I'll teach you how to use product skills to execute with excellent judgment and thoughtfully create polished products.

I'll cover key user scenarios such as discovery, usage and understanding, and techniques for naming, commenting, erroring with good error messages, documenting, and testing.

These topics are the bread and butter of a coding software engineer's work life, and they offer an accessible and frequent basis for practicing product thinking.

CHAPTER 2

Guiding Users Through Your Product

It is the duty of machines and those who design them to understand people. It is not our duty to understand the arbitrary, meaningless dictates of machines.

—Don Norman, in *The Design of Everyday Things*

The user of your product is your hero. As in a work of fiction, you are rooting for the hero to get to the end and accomplish their goal.

Unlike a fiction author, the product designer's goal is to make the user's journey easy. Guided by scenarios, you'll provide signposts at the right places and the right times to help them on their path.

In his classic book, *The Design of Everyday Things*, Don Norman refers to such signposts as *signifiers*. Signifiers are clues in your interface as to what the feature does. There are innumerable examples of signifiers:

- A name or icon to signify a purpose
- A bounding box around a button to signify you can click
- A downward-pointing caret to clue a dropdown menu
- A radio button, signifying that at most one option can be selected
- A set of checkboxes, signalling that multiple options can be chosen
- An underlined blue hyperlink, showing that the target is a web page with the text clarifying the relevance or name of that page
- An error message suggesting what a person should do

and so on.

This chapter explores the concept of signifiers and their role in the user's journey. Through them, you'll learn to craft polished interfaces.

To start with, I'll introduce a case study about hierarchical menus, which has all sorts of opportunities to geek out about signifiers.

This will be one of two lenses through which to explore the advice in this chapter. The second way will be in sidebars like this:

> ### Coding Practice
>
> In these blocks, you'll see tips for applying product thinking to your day-to-day coding. After all, functions, classes, and the like are miniature products whose users are your teammates and collaborators. Good names and comments will make code reviews and code maintenance much more efficient, and along the way, you'll practice product-thinking skills.

Through those two lenses, I'll look at the three main phases of the user's journey: discovery, understanding, and usage.

Along the way, I'll illuminate topics such as ontologies, hierarchical design, and trading off consistency with specificity.

Finally, I'll zoom out and consider the user journey as a whole, taking into account cases where we need to trade off between the different phases or when we need to consider our design more broadly.

Case Study Introduction

In the mid-2000s, Microsoft faced a massive problem with its Office suite—Word, Excel, and PowerPoint. They were too complex for users to comprehend and locate everything they needed. By 2003, Microsoft Word had 31 toolbars and 19 task panes in addition to drop-down menus. Figure 2-1 shows a screenshot from a typical session, according to Product Manager Jensen Harris's presentation on the subject.

Through interviews with hundreds of users, they discovered that users struggled to discover features and develop a sense of mastery over the software. Heavily demanded features would be built, but users weren't finding them.

With Office 2007, Microsoft introduced its "ribbon" menuing system into its Office desktop applications, shown in Figure 2-2, along with contextual menus that popped up when you highlighted text, as in Figure 2-3.

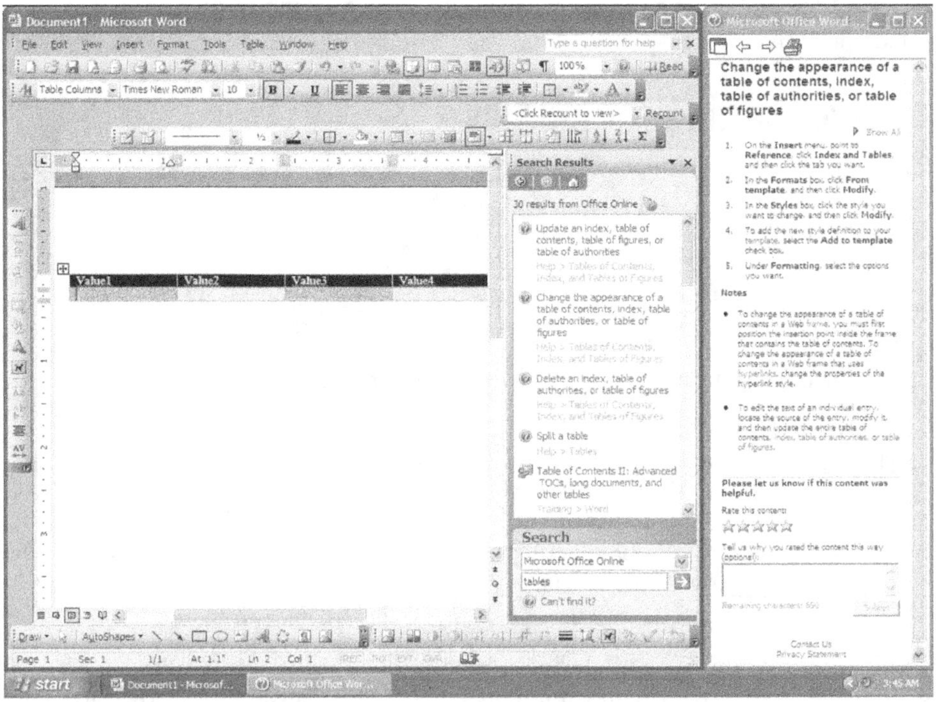

Figure 2-1. A messy screenshot of Microsoft Word 2003

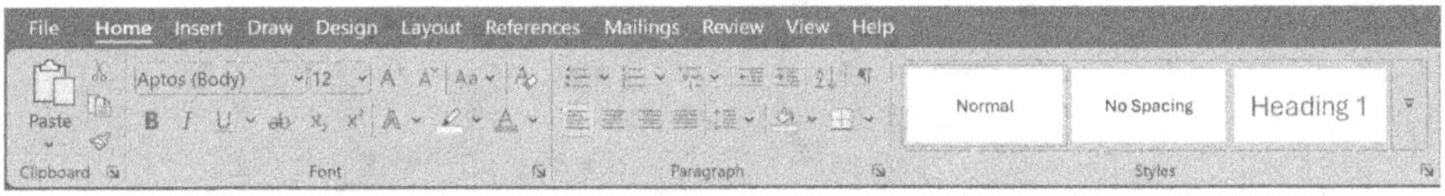

Figure 2-2. The ribbon in Microsoft Word for Windows in 2025

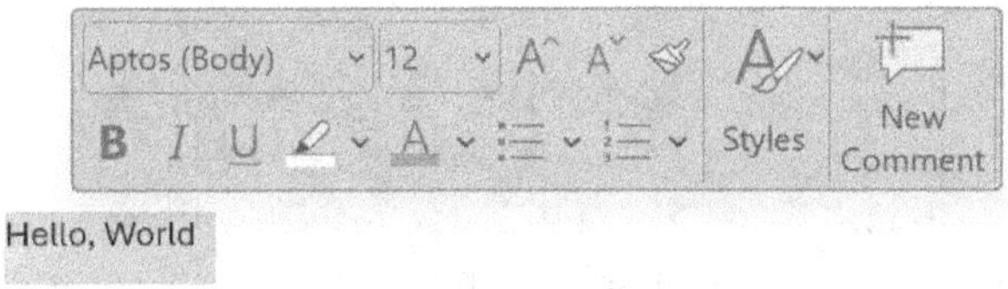

Figure 2-3. A contextual pop-up in Microsoft Word for Windows in 2025

In designing the revamp, the team collected usage frequency on thousands of features and grouped them into a new hierarchical menu design that also provided new ways of presenting features to users. These changes made these highly complex applications more approachable for many users and have so far stood the test of time.

Learning how and why provides us with clues for guiding the user journey in our own applications.

Scenarios in the User Journey

The user journey usually progresses through three main types of user scenarios: Discovery, Understanding, and Usage.

Discovery
: The user has a problem they want to solve but doesn't yet know how to solve it.

Understanding
: The user encounters a feature and wants to learn what it does and how it works.

Usage
: The user wants to employ the feature for its intended purpose while avoiding using it unsafely.

If you're tasked with shipping a feature, you must take ownership of all three of these. It's your team's responsibility to make your feature visible, help users understand it, and guide them through its safe use. Miss any of these three, and your feature will not make the impact it should.

As discussed in Chapter 1, you should be able to tell a plausible story that takes users through all three phases without plot holes. Making sure you cover all three main scenario types is a good way to eliminate plot holes. And as you cater to each scenario, flesh out more stories that cover the details.

The Discovery Scenario

How will readers find your abstraction? Engineers frequently overlook this part of the user journey, but it's often the most crucial aspect—your product is useless to people who don't know it exists. That's why online ads are such an enormous business—they solve discovery problems.

When considering discovery, remember that users will come from various directions. For a feature like superscripts in Microsoft Word, users can learn about it by reading the buttons in the ribbon, using a search bar, consulting online documentation, lists of hotkeys, or interacting with a chatbot. When you think users want your feature, all of their investigations should lead to it, so mentally run through as many simulations as you can. How would users approach it? Look for plot holes or implausible leaps of logic.

In this section, I'll discuss the knowledge users bring to the table, then explore the tools that help them find features, and conclude by guiding you in designing your features hierarchically so that you're not overwhelming users upfront or hiding things and making them unfindable. To guide you through it, I'll introduce Product Discovery Mapping, a useful design technique that will also visually illustrate what I'm discussing.

Product Discovery Mapping

A Product Discovery Map (PDM) can help you plot out the journeys a user will take through learning your product. Suppose you're reviewing your product implementation and trying to make sure that users can find all the key layout features they need to make newsletters in Word. Such users will want to make multi-column layouts, use landscape mode, embed images within the text, and will likely combine those techniques.

Let's focus on discovering the "Continuous Section Break," which you are pretty sure users don't come in understanding. Figure 2-4 shows the Layout menu in Microsoft Word with the Break dropdown menu expanded.

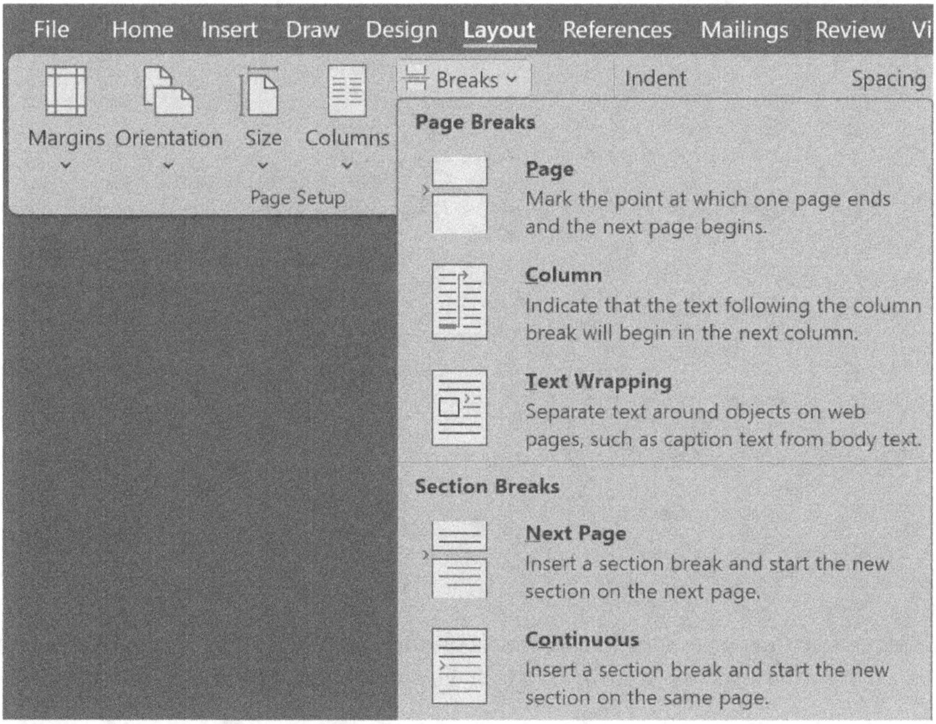

Figure 2-4. The Layout menu in Microsoft Word

Here's a user scenario for Yves, a casual user persona who uses Office occasionally for marketing community events.

> Yves is making a monthly newsletter for his local church. He wants a two-column layout, with the name of the newsletter centered at the top. He types out the name of the newsletter and centers it from the Home tab. Now what? He sees the Layout tab and notices a "Columns" widget. He clicks and selects two columns, but his title shifts over to the left column, which he didn't want. He undoes that and sees a prominent "Breaks" button, and based on the descriptions in the dropdown, learns how to use Continuous Section Break.

These scenarios can get long-winded quickly if you're shipping many features or trying to test the usability of a large product. A Product Discovery Map is a shorthand representation with three key components:

- Each map or graph is designed for a specific customer persona who is navigating your product, much like navigating a maze.
- Each node is an element of your product.
- Each edge is how that knowledge is discovered by that persona, as in Figure 2-5 showing Yves's journey.

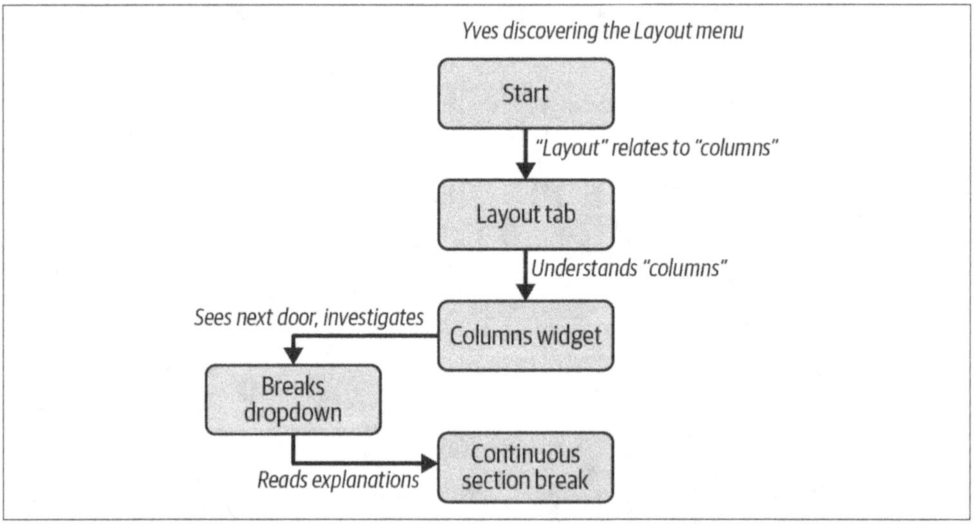

Figure 2-5. A PDM for Continuous Section Breaks

This map assumes that Yves knows what columns are but doesn't know what section breaks are, yet shows one way for him to navigate to the right feature successfully.

You can put a bunch of flows into a single map, making it quicker and more visual to conceptualize a part of your product.

The thinking and collaboration you'll do as you build and review the map is the important part. Is the naming helpful enough? Are you happy with the leaps you're asking the users to make? Is the number of steps it takes to get to features appropriate to their frequency of usage? Are features that are likely to be used together also grouped together?

Leverage Users' Knowledge

In Chapter 1, I said that personas have means—what skills and knowledge did they bring to the table?

The set of names and concepts that your product presents, along with the relationships between those concepts, is called an *ontology*. The ontology is a graph, and the better a user knows a product's ontology, the deeper their understanding and the more effective their usage.

The easiest way to make things discoverable is to use names and concepts already in users' ontologies. That is, don't reinvent the wheel.

In the Layout menu example, Yves knew "Column," but from "Continuous Section Break," he only came in knowing about "sections." Notice from Figure 2-4 how much more careful Microsoft had to be with the design for breaks than for columns. They had to provide detailed explanations and diagrams to compensate for unfamiliar naming.

Coding Practice

Be careful with opaque codenames. Those names are not in users' ontologies. If people are searching your company's codebase or documentation for a distributed cache framework, they might search for "cache," but they won't know in advance that your project was called, say, "Phoenix" because it rose from the ashes of a previous distributed cache. If you want your abstraction to be branded, try something like "SuperCache"—a bit of branding, a bit of discoverability.

Opaque codenames can be useful in some situations, like for confidentiality or when it is sufficiently unique and hard to describe that straightforward names would be misleading. Just be aware of the discoverability you're giving up, and make sure to leave other breadcrumbs, for example with comments, so people can find it.

Sometimes, the ontology depends on the user persona.

When I worked at Stripe, my dad—an accountant, barely a programmer—read through the documentation of Stripe's online payments and billing APIs. He gave me grief because he had been searching for proper, precise accounting terms like "receivables."

I informed him that this was an intentional decision. These APIs targeted generalist programmers and strove to use terms that people who had never taken an accounting course would be comfortable with.

But this also illustrated that if Stripe wanted accountants to be able to use it, it had work to do.

Offer Multiple Routes to Discovery

Of course, languages have synonyms and related concepts, but you've generally got to pick one for your ontology. Find ways for users who may come in with different guesses to find it.

For example, the Ribbon offers a handy command search box that supports some fuzzy matching. If I type the word "Margin" into the box, it gives me commands with the word "Indent," as shown in Figure 2-6. I can even interact with those commands inline in that menu.

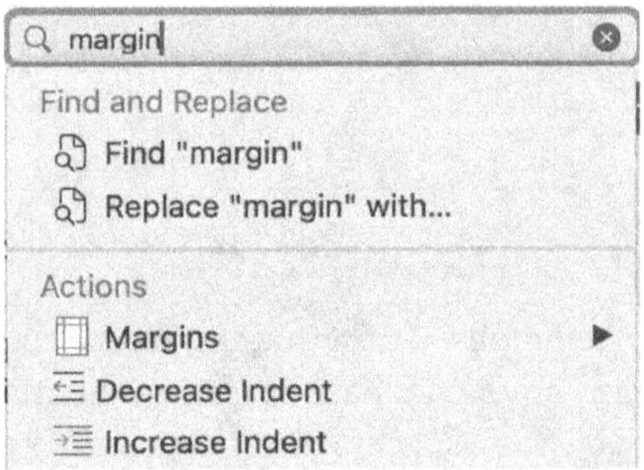

Figure 2-6. A search for margin in Word

Coding Practice

Use comments to add more ways to find your abstractions. For example, if your base class is called "Plugin," describe it with a synonym like "Extension" in your comments.

This generalizes:

> Give your users multiple ways to find a feature to cater to their different means.

Take a complex app like Word. Before the big redesign, discovery was a mess. Users needed to figure out which of the myriad menus, toolbars, or task panes was best for their task. If they needed a toolbar, only icons were there to guide them; if menus, they had to look over long lists of words and phrases with no particular rhyme or reason to the sorting order. The categorization of features often seemed arbitrary—what goes in the *Tools* menu as opposed to the *Format* menu? Why is *Find* in the *Edit* menu even though it's a read operation?

A mediocre Help widget provided the main alternative to this mess.

Since the introduction of the Ribbon, the menus have much better signifiers.

- Commands are grouped into a smaller number of tabs, and more screen real estate is given, making it easier for Yves to scan the Layout tab to find something for his use case.
- Break, as a common and recommended command, is made larger and put near related commands.
- Break and Continuous Section Break are represented by both icons and text. Different users might find one or the other more easily.
- There is a search box, useful if Yves knows the word "section" but doesn't know what menu it's in. This fixes a fundamental problem with traditional menus.

Figure 2-7 maps the variety of useful ways Yves could discover Continuous Section Breaks.

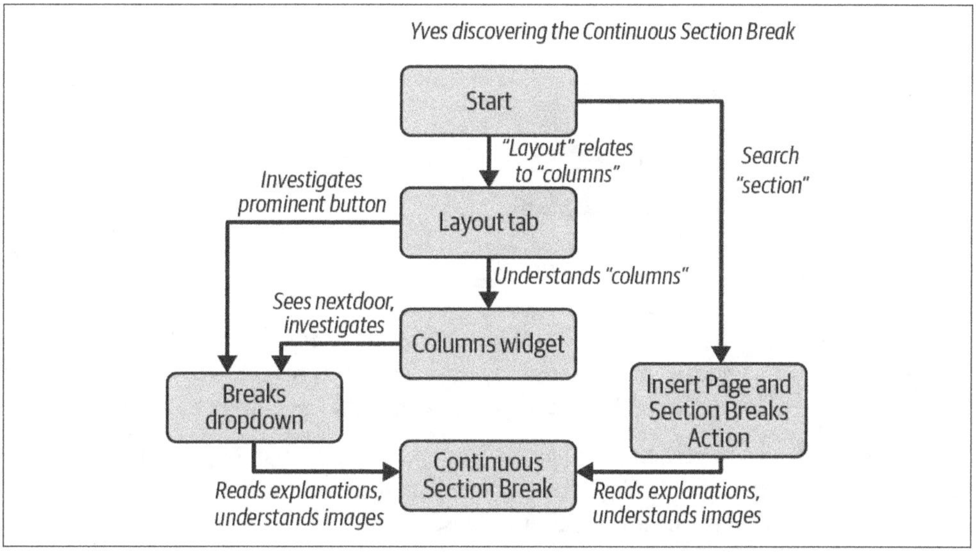

Figure 2-7. Multiple routes to discovering Continuous Section Break

Here are a few common routes users take to discover your product:

- Searching
- Asking a chatbot
- Scanning your app visually, or clicking around, looking for names and other signifiers
- Using a screen reader (for visually impaired folks) or listening to a voice menu
- Consulting how-to guides or other documentation

Try not to rely solely on documentation. In a consumer application, you likely won't rely on it at all.

Gracefully Reveal Complexity

Nearly all successful apps gain a lot of features. Even Google, with its famously simple search bar, now has many tabs and tools to accompany search results.

To navigate this proliferation of functionality, designers *gracefully reveal complexity* to users.

Take the ribbon. Even with its improvements, there are still too many commands and target personas to make approachable menus, so Microsoft created a notion of a contextual menu. This appears only when appropriate. Figure 2-8 shows the Shape Format tab, which does not clutter up the UI unless you've clicked on a shape.

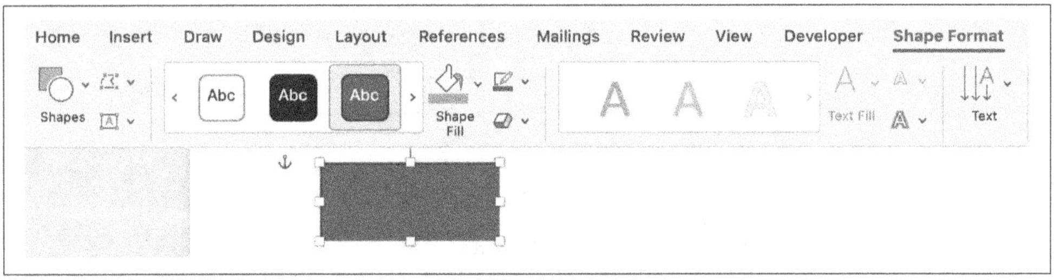

Figure 2-8. A contextual menu in the Ribbon

With its nine default tabs, the ribbon is bordering on being overwhelming, which is easy to spot in this Product Discovery Map. This graceful reveal avoids it becoming a problem by moving the Shape Format down in the graph, as shown in Figure 2-9.

Word also achieves a graceful reveal via context menus that pop up next to your mouse cursor when you highlight text, affording you common commands like bold and italics. Such menus announce themselves, making them quite discoverable; and they present few options, meaning users can easily scan for the needed tool.

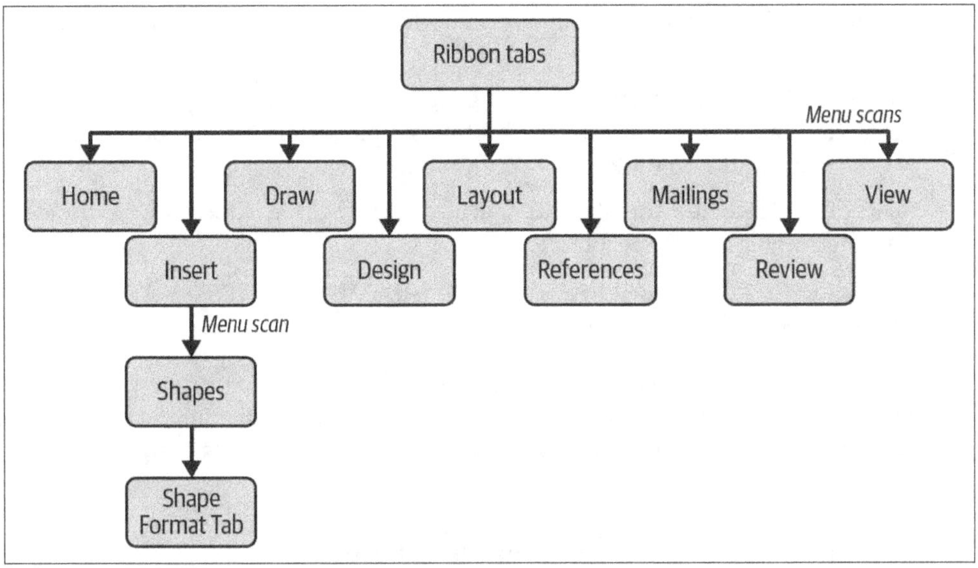

Figure 2-9. A PDM for discovering the Shape Format tab

Multipersona Design

A primary reason apps become complex is that as they grow, they attract different personas who use them for various purposes.

Microsoft Word serves a diverse range of personas, from novelists who need chapter navigation, to marketers who want charts and diagrams, to visually impaired people who need screen readers and dictation.

Most successful apps therefore have at least two different interfaces. Ideally, each interface is revealed gracefully as the user needs it.

Most apps have power users, perhaps 5–20% of the audience, who are highly active and immersed in it. Such users want more powerful primitives that allow them to customize their experience. This is often because they have additional incentives to use your products and get to know them thoroughly. A Word power user being paid for their work is more likely to use macros and track document changes than a student writing poems for high school English.

Look around and you'll see this dual interface, dual persona approach everywhere:

- Wikipedia pages have a small "edit" button that's easy for readers to ignore but useful for contributors.
- Websites with mega-prominent "create an account" for newbies and tiny "log in" buttons for existing users.

- Modern operating systems with user interfaces for the masses and command shells for the IT professionals.
- Progressively typed programming languages such as TypeScript, wherein type annotations are optional for people writing simple scripts but can be required by larger organizations to build more robust codebases.
- No-code or low-code frameworks that are easy for non-coders but allow programmers to write custom code.
- Clicking buttons for casual users, with keyboard shortcuts provided for habitual power users.

As a designer, one of the most important and freeing observations you can make is realizing you've reached the point when you should have multiple interfaces, allowing you to start optimizing for each persona independently. This opens design space and gives you more opportunities for problem solving.

Turn Unknown Unknowns into Known Unknowns

So far, I've mostly assumed that the user is aware that your app has certain functionality and it's just a question of how long it takes them to find it. But what if they don't even know the feature exists? This is particularly common for novel or innovative features, or for new users who lack a solid understanding of the domain's ontology. An Excel function to do some magic bookkeeping may be familiar to all seasoned accountants but be unknown to an undergraduate accounting major.

Thus, think of your product as a mysterious forest that the user is journeying through. Leave them a trail of breadcrumbs to help them navigate.

For example, lately I have seen little chatbot widgets pop up in several applications. Microsoft Word has a "Draft with Copilot" context menu next to my cursor. I wasn't aware Word had this. I'm not entirely sure what the chatbot can do for me, but at least I can explore it. An unknown unknown has been turned into a known unknown.

Think carefully about what you're leaving out in a menu. Users may not be aware that they can find any missing commands elsewhere. While Word presents all of the Breaks in the Layout tab, it has put only the "Page Break" command in the Insert tab, as shown in Figure 2-10. This design risks users who don't see the Layout tab assuming that Page Break is the only option. The tradeoff is that Page Break is more discoverable than it would be if it were buried under a vaguer "Break" command.

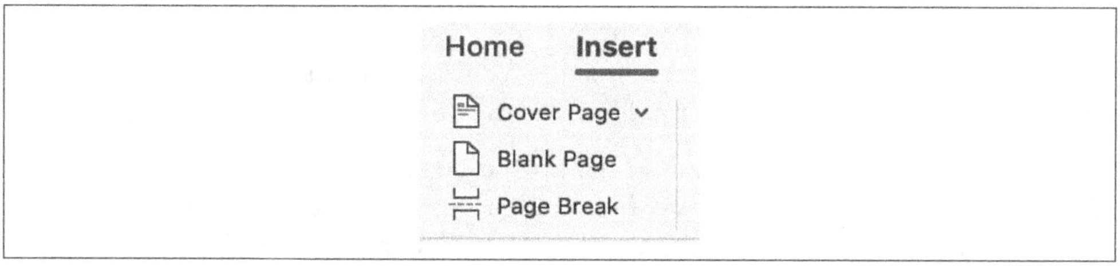

Figure 2-10. The Page Break command within the Insert tab

The Understanding Scenario

Once a user has discovered the feature they need, they now must understand what it does in more detail.

I'll start with the most common way to facilitate users' uptake of important concepts —picking great names. Next, I'll present other signifiers that you can use when names aren't enough or when you want to cater to other learning styles.

Picking Understandable Names

A name is your opportunity to put one or two thoughts in your readers' heads. In addition to aiding discoverability, a good name should also facilitate understanding. Users don't necessarily want to know what the feature is; they want to know, "How will it help me?" Often, the answer to those two questions is the same, but not always. Being product-minded means thinking through your impact on the reader rather than simply describing the system.

Perhaps the most important rule of picking a name is: Avoid the Curse of Knowledge.

> The Curse of Knowledge is a cognitive bias that causes system designers to struggle to anticipate difficulties users with less understanding might face when interacting with their systems.

Shoe-shifting is the best way to avoid this curse. Consider your target persona's existing ontology, or better yet, ask someone from that demographic how they would interpret your name.

Classic Naming Advice Revisited

Most people have heard advice for naming—you know, the short strips of text that could fit neatly in a bulleted list or on an inspirational laptop sticker. Let me reword a few of these using a user-centric lens.

Avoid ambiguity (instead of "be self-explanatory")

If you're choosing only one of these maxims to write on a sticky note and attach to the side of your monitor, "avoid ambiguity" is the one.

It's shockingly common for names of features to be ambiguous to readers who aren't infected with the Curse of Knowledge. To prevent this, shoe-shift into your users' heads, and brainstorm other interpretations of your names. (Or, again, ask them.)

When I was writing up the Layout case study, and I was playing the role of Yves making his church newsletter, I became frustrated by an ambiguity. I ran across this Align button in the Layout tab, shown on the right in Figure 2-11.

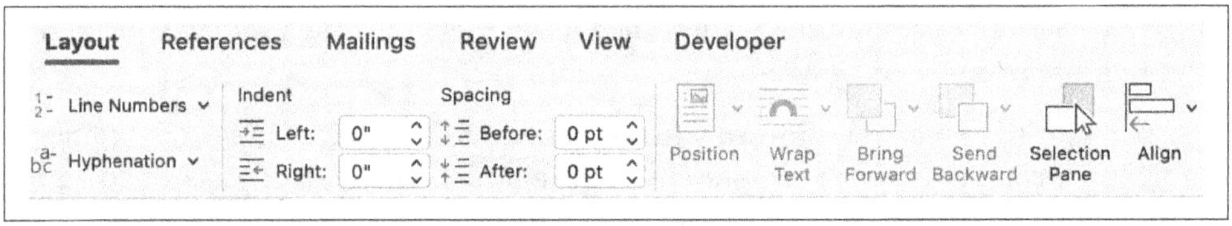

Figure 2-11. Part of the Layout tab in Word

What's your theory for what this does?

I thought that I would use it to center the newsletter title. However, when I expanded it (as shown in Figure 2-12), everything that looked useful was grayed out. I tried a few tricks to make it work, but to no avail.

Figure 2-12. A mysterious dropdown menu

If *Align* refers to something more specific than general text, images, or charts, it should say so!

> ## Coding Practice
>
> Here are a few ambiguities that commonly need clarification in codebases:
>
> *Roles and relationships*
> : When there are two objects with different roles, like parent/child or sender/recipient, clarifying "which one?" questions are critical.
>
> *Types, for variables*
> : This clarifies what it is on every line of code where it's used.
>
> *Units, for measurements*
> : You don't want readers to confuse pounds for newtons or millisieverts for sieverts, ending up causing damage to Mars orbiters or radiation burns.
>
> *Parts of speech*
> : Is `persist` a boolean requesting to write some state to disk, or an actual function to do so? If the former, `should_persist` would be better.

Trade off consistency with specificity (instead of "be consistent")

Consistent naming helps users who can learn a concept in your ontology once and then apply it repeatedly. When naming a new feature, always look around your existing product for prior art to match.

Yet, consistency often trades off against specificity, and specificity is often the best way to reduce ambiguity. In the example above, "Align" is perfectly consistent terminology, but it's not specific enough.

Being specific can also be more idiomatic. Say you're designing a feature for your streaming music application that shows lyrics as the song plays. Even if your product consistently uses the word "Track" to refer to a music file, you nonetheless might want to say "Song Lyrics" rather than the awkward "Track Lyrics."

Another common case where consistency bites during a naming decision is when something related was named poorly a long time ago, and you must choose whether to be consistent or pick the right name from first principles.

For some engineers, consistency can become dogmatic because they can reason about it without even considering the users' perspectives. Your local tech lead, who's not focused on your feature, may not have thought through your current scenarios or empathized with users, but will always be able to opine about consistency.

One way to combat this bias is to brainstorm your most understandable, most specific name idea, as well as one that maximizes consistency with the existing product. If those exercises end up with two separate names, you can discuss trade-offs. This will ensure you're both empathizing with users and testing your names against the existing ontology. As you weigh options, shoe-shift—thinking through the user journey of discoverability, understandability, and usability. Here are a few heuristics:

- When in doubt, be consistent, lacking a compelling reason to do otherwise.
- Account for your Curse of Knowledge. As a system designer, you often have much more comprehensive knowledge than your typical user. New users using only a subset of the product may not even see enough of it to care about consistency.
- Ask about the relative sizes of the audiences—maybe that old name was only used by a few power users, or is a legacy feature, but your new product has much broader ambitions. Perhaps it's worth sacrificing consistency to do the right thing going forward.
- In a multipersona application, it mostly matters what each persona experiences. It would be perfectly legitimate for Microsoft Excel to provide a single formula with two different names, one targeted at accountants and the other at software engineers. Or if your app supports iOS and Android, it's important to be consistent within each, but consistency between the platforms is of lower priority, given that users don't switch very often.

Only use acronyms and abbreviations that are ubiquitous for your target persona (instead of "avoid acronyms and abbreviations")

Acronyms are terrible for understanding scenarios because nobody is going to guess what the letters mean, and they are also challenging to discover.

But your target persona may be used to a specific term. Don't start spelling out "HTML" any time soon. "CPU" is best suited for an audience of software engineers, but try a term like "processor" for a more general audience.

If you're not sure, survey your target users to learn how they interpret your proposed term.

Convey only what users need to know (instead of "be concise")

Concisely, concise means "brief but comprehensive." This makes some sense. When learning, users struggle to read word salads, yet they don't want you to leave out important details.

But comprehensive of what? I would rephrase it to put more emphasis on the reader and what will help them.

I once played an online game called "PHP Diplomacy"—an adaptation of a classic board game named after the programming language the port was written in. Non-programmers were likely confused by the name. Come to think of it, I think all the people I played with were also software engineers.

By shoe-shifting, you can see what's just an implementation detail. Because names only have a limited number of slots to convey information, each irrelevant thing you remove gives you extra room to express something meaningful.

Suppose you're building an API for long-running operations: your users will enqueue requests on the queue, and then your system pulls from the queue and executes the operations. They can block waiting for the request, or they can fetch results later using a handle.

It would be natural to call the asynchronous request API `enqueue_request`. This seems fine at first, but then what do we name the function that both enqueues it and awaits the result? `enqueue_and_wait_for_request`? When we sense that this is awkward, we can ask: Which parts of this name does the reader need to know to use it properly?

The most relevant fact is that it's asynchronous—the responses may be delayed. The word "enqueue" is more specific than necessary.

It may not seem like a big deal, but when you remove the implementation detail of "queue," you unlock simple, evocative names like `start_request` and `execute_request` for the asynchronous and synchronous versions, respectively. Concise. Discoverable.

Coding Practice

If you find yourself wanting to put terse function and variable names into checked-in code, remember the words of Guido van Rossum, creator of Python: "Code is read much more often than it's written."

There are far more frequent scenarios in which a function's name is read and understood—code review, debugging, learning the codebase, searching for the right place to edit—than when it's typed—adding a new feature and writing a test. And those benefit from autocomplete.

Readers will keep coming throughout the lifetime of your codebase. If you're building something that may have enduring value, do it justice with a clear name.

Giving Redundant Explanations

Picking a name that's both discoverable and aids in unambiguous understanding is a challenge, and sometimes there's no hope of perfectly conveying everything users need to know. So it pays to provide redundant mechanisms for conveying your intent to users.

Take the Word ribbon, which makes effective use of icons to convey functionality. In Figure 2-13, witness these formatting commands in the Home tab, which are carefully designed to improve understanding in a way that words like "multilevel list" and "justify" do not.

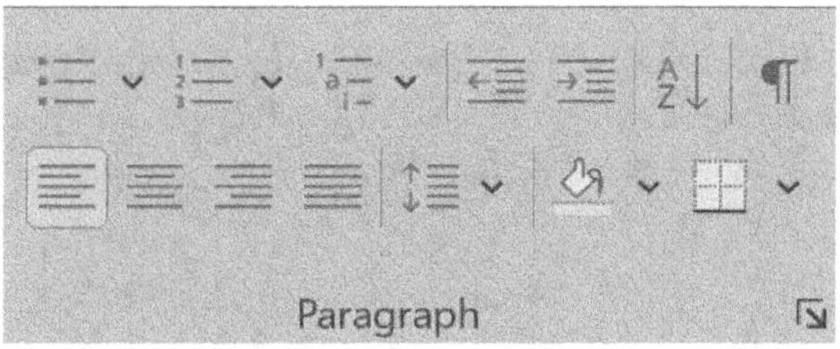

Figure 2-13. Icons for formatting commands

Here are a few ways to improve understanding without relying solely on nomenclature:

Combine images and words
: Images can show visually what the words are trying to convey, as we saw in the section break descriptions (Figure 2-4). And remember that not all users will be native speakers of the language they are using your product in. "Column" may seem like a basic concept for an English speaker but may not be in the others' vocabularies.

WYSIWYG (What you see is what you get)
: Users don't need to understand, because the effects of their actions are immediately displayed. Microsoft Office for Windows, in addition to being a WYSIWYG editor, also provides "Live previews" showing the effects of switching styles on the current document.

Rephrase
: Use synonyms or rephrasings to describe functionality in tooltips and documentation. Rephrasing a concept in different terms helps users triangulate the intended meaning and gain confidence.

Always remind users of the context
: People have fairly small short-term memories and may forget where they were. For example, if the user is in the middle of an ecommerce workflow to purchase an item, remind them of what they are purchasing on each screen in case they leave and come back.

Coding Practice

Redundancy can be useful in code, documentation, and other information-dense situations. When we think of user scenarios and human beings with limited working memory, the case becomes clear.

For example, in this code snippet, do you notice anything?

```
def email_lunch_invitation(sending_user, recipient_user, message):
  recipient_organization = recipient_user.get_organization()
  title = f"{sending_user.name} from {recipient_organization} " \
    "has sent you an invitation to lunch!"
  send_email(
    sending_user.email_address, recipient_user.email_address, title, message)
```

Did you spot the bug when computing the `title`? Do you think you would have if I had used the name `organization` rather than `recipient_organization`?

Here are some scenarios where a little extra redundancy can help:

- The reader is reviewing code, spot-checking for quality.
- The author of the function could accidentally misuse the variable, as above.
- The programmer got to the line of code via a breakpoint, go-to-reference, find all references, a debugging call stack, or a lint rule, and hasn't read the whole function.

If everything we need to know about a line of code is on that line, life is good.

The Usage Scenario

When, at the end of the reader's journey, they start taking action, there is more danger. Safety concerns abound. We'll discuss keeping your users safe more broadly when we introduce the concept of affordances in Chapter 8, but let's taste it here, experiencing how signifiers can guide people to do the right thing in the absence of other protections. Good names can railroad them into intuitively doing the right thing, staying on the tracks without realizing they were ever in danger of straying.

Think through usage scenarios and alert your users to possible safety concerns.

Here's an extreme example. Inside one web company in the early 2010s, a special configuration variable was copied to all machines that served web traffic. It contained a regular expression that was applied as a find/replace operation to every page of outbound HTML just before it was sent to users' browsers!

To make an urgent patch, say, to remove a problematic HTML tag, an engineer could add a regular expression to this variable and deploy it instantly to the whole fleet.

Does that seem dangerous? It was, exceptionally so, and was intended only for emergencies. If your regex-altered HTML caused parse errors, the whole site could cease to function. Accordingly, it was dubbed `TAKE_DOWN_THE_SITE`, named not after what it did, but what would happen if one misused it.

While extreme, the name shows awareness of safety issues in a way I begrudgingly admire.

A more mundane way to signal danger is to stick things under an "advanced" menu. This both lengthens the discovery journey, limiting the users who will find it, and signifies that there may be some unexpected effects of using it. Microsoft Office does this, for example, by requiring an opt-in before showing the "Developer" tab on the ribbon, confining tools like macros and VB scripts to those personas who are more likely to benefit from them than to mess up their settings.

To figure out whether you need to signal danger, generate simulations in which users go wrong and see how names could make those stories implausible.

The opposite of hiding dangerous features is to draw attention to concepts, for example, by forcing users to make choices. When selecting Break in the Layout menu, Word doesn't default to the most commonly used command, a Page Break. It instead forces me to choose which kind I mean, which in turn educates me about my options and prevents me from mangling my documents.

Coding Practice

Require parameters where the user needs to make a choice they may not realize they need to make.

Leave breadcrumbs in comments on your abstractions. For example, if there are two ways to accomplish something and a user finds one of them, point people to the alternative they may not know about, especially if that alternative is more recommended for most users.

Optimizing the Whole User Journey

As the `TAKE_DOWN_THE_SITE` scenario illustrates, by sacrificing discoverability and understandability to improve usability, there are sometimes trade-offs between optimizing for discovery, understanding, and usage.

A clear simulation of the user journey helps make these trade-offs.

For example, if my advice not to make up obscure acronyms is so good, why do Unix and Linux have popular, obscurely named commands like `ls` and `cd`? Are they just old and bad?

Well, no, not entirely. Arguably, these are still appropriate names because the common commands are typed much more than read. You learn them once—or twice if you forget, but you don't want to type `list_files` rather than `ls` a half dozen times a day. Furthermore, they are targeted at habitual and technical users. The usage scenario trumps discovery and understanding, and so the rules are thrown out.

But when designing for marketability, you may have to prioritize discoverability and search engine optimization. The name "Liquid Death" for a sparkling water drink is, thankfully, only 50% accurate and not very precise, but it sure does market itself. In this user journey, the name catches the shopper's eye, then they look at the subtext to see what it really is.

> Decide the relative importance of discovery, understanding, and usage for your feature.

The Limits of Signifiers

Not every problem can be fixed with signifiers, although you may not always know that in advance. You might set out to find the perfect name, only to discover, as you think through the user journey, that there's not a good name that conveys what your target persona needs to know. Maybe it's too complicated or includes a safety gotcha.

Take browser cookies and all the pop-ups you see around the web, alerting you that the page may be recording your data. It's challenging to convey to non-technical users exactly what's going on and exactly how intrusive it really is. In other words, the legislators who mandated that websites communicate about cookies, and the websites trying to comply, are attempting to address a problem with signifiers, which is, in reality, a more fundamental design challenge.

Valiant attempts have been made, for example, to distinguish between "essential cookies" and marketing-driven cookies; however, users still lack a clear understanding of the cookie ontology. The result is that most turn off all cookies, even if some would be beneficial or would support the internet economy at no personal cost.

A deeper issue is that cookies were intended as a low-level programming abstraction rather than a user-facing feature. Better abstractions, such as ones that would provide more granular and user-understandable categories, have been proposed. Alas, likely due to a collective action problem, as of 2025, the problem remains largely unsolved.

Trying to name and organize your product is a great thing to do earlier in your product cycle, as it forces you to pay attention to the whole user journey and often leads to fruitful design insights. Stay tuned for Chapters 7 and 8 where we will dive deeper into product design.

> ### Coding Practice
>
> If an abstraction is awkward or unsafe to use, and you can't fix it, don't try to hide it. Let the name be ugly and attract attention and scrutiny. Maybe your code reviewer will have a better idea. Or maybe somebody will come in later and improve it. I once saw a private class variable named, tongue-in-cheek, `_do_not_use_or_you_will_be_fired`, for which I developed a grudging respect.

Chapter Summary

We followed along with users as they discovered, understood, and used our products. Additionally, in a sidebar, we focused on making day-to-day decisions in naming code and building coding interfaces as a means of practicing product skills.

I landed on the following advice:

- For discovery, choose names that are already in users' ontologies or are consistent with other names. Provide signifiers that help users navigate your product, gracefully revealing more complex functionality. Take time to chart Product Discovery Maps if it helps you to visualize your users' journeys.
- For understanding, avoid ambiguity above all, while providing a consistent experience for each type of user. Embrace the diversity of your audience and their perspectives by providing redundant "ways in" to understand your product.
- For usage, leverage names to highlight possible gotchas and "danger zones" when people use your functions.

For multipersona applications, don't be afraid to provide different ontologies and discovery routes for each persona.

Finally, while this chapter is in the Develop phase, remember that naming and organizing the most important concepts in your product ontology should occur earlier, as it can provide valuable insights into the overall design process.

Exercises

In these exercises, I will name something *foo* or *bar* and your goal is to pick a better name. (Since *foo* contains zero information, think of your job as maximizing the *foo-distance*!) Of course, there will not be "correct" answers, but think about Discovery, Understanding, and Usage scenarios. I want these questions to feel like real-world exercises, which means you may want to do some light design thinking or use the internet.

1. Your database allows people to subscribe to change events when data in a particular table is altered. If they subclass `DataChangeSubscription` and register it with the database, their callback will be run each time after the database transaction is committed.

   ```
   class DataChangeSubscription(ABC):
     # subscriptions apply to a certain database table or collection.
     @abstractmethod
     def foo() -> TableType:

     @abstractmethod
     def bar(old_record, changes: Dict[str, Any]) -> None:
   ```

   What would you call these two methods that people need to implement when they subclass `DataChangeSubscription`?

2. You're building an app for beer connoisseurs to review beers. They click on a beer and are presented with a free-form text field called *Foo* where they can input their impressions. What to call it instead?

3. New users of your product complete a survey and signup flow which you are trying to optimize, so you want to track an aggregate metric, `foo`, which will keep track of how long they are taking. What to name it?

4. You work on a small social network, and recently you committed a change that regressed the performance of your product. You called this function:

   ```
   mutual_friends = await current_user.getMutualFriends(friend_user)
   ```

   In fact, you called it many times in parallel, once for each friend, which turned out to be more expensive than you realized, involving some computation and some privacy checks that you didn't expect. You don't have time to optimize it. Is there anything you can rename it to prevent others from making this mistake in the future?

Answers

1. For foo, `table_type` is fine, but consider `table_type_filter` for extra clarity. This makes it clear how the table type is used. For bar, try something like `on_record_changed`. The "on_" prefix uses a widespread nomenclature for event handlers, "record" (singular) clarifies what changed, and "changed" (past tense) clarifies that the commit already occurred. If you later add a callback for *before* the change is committed, you could call it `on_record_changing`. Also, I chose the word `changed` for consistency with `Changed` in the class.

2. After a bit of user research (or asking a chatbot), you'd discover that beer aficionados use the term "tasting notes" for descriptions of beers. You could use a generic term like `description` or `review`, but "Tasting Notes" is likely to get your target persona waxing poetic about "aroma" and "mouthfeel," which is what you want.
3. Think of the scenario of teammates reading graphs as part of your team's dashboard. What questions will they have? One is, what are the units: milliseconds, seconds, or minutes? Their second question might be, which metric are we tracking: average, median, or p90? So, you might name it something like `user_signup_seconds_to_complete.p50`.
4. `getMutualFriends` should somehow indicate that it's expensive. Perhaps just call it `computeMutualFriends`, which might have been enough to get you thinking about cost. Or, if the name is easy to change later, `computeMutualFriends_Expensive`. Perhaps in the future, the overt ugliness will inspire somebody to cache it or make it cheaper.

CHAPTER 3

Errors and Warnings

"PC Load Letter?" What the @#$! does that mean?

—Michael Bolton

Staring at a malfunctioning printer, uttering this line, Michael Bolton from the 1999 movie *Office Space* skewered the technology industry for its poor error messages. In fairness to HP, the old LaserJet printers' screens only had a limited number of display characters to work with. Today we have emerged from the Stone Age and have high-resolution screens to display more text. Think of all the helpful words you can fit!

Consumers are regularly confronted with diagnostic errors and warnings that they don't understand, and professionals waste hours acting on confusing messages instead of accomplishing their tasks. Users are often a "flight risk," meaning they might be turned off from our product at the slightest friction.

Yet, we engineers often treat errors and error messages as mere "edge cases" to be implemented as quickly as possible, rather than as a key element of our craft and a way to differentiate our products.

A fun error, more specific to programming, comes courtesy of the text markup system, LaTeX. LaTeX is a document typesetting language and system, useful for beautifully rendered mathematical and scientific papers.

In LaTeX, if you type this, wherein \\ tokens are newlines:

```
This is some text. \\
This is at the end of a block of text. \\

This is the start of a new paragraph
```

You'll receive this gem of a warning:

```
Underfull \hbox (badness 10000) in paragraph on line 2.
```

Want to try to puzzle this out? Turns out, LaTeX wants you to remove the redundant newline (\\) on line 2 before the blank line.

Inscrutable as this message is, it probably makes perfect "bottom-up" sense if we're looking at the code where the error message is thrown. It is probably also difficult to fix due to the organization of the code. I'll revisit this example once I've presented two skills:

- How can you bridge the gap between what makes sense to you, the implementer, and what makes sense to your user?
- How can you organize your code effectively to achieve this?

This matters: LaTeX is currently ranked only the 40th most popular programming language, but nonetheless, the most popular "underfull hbox" question on tex.stackexchange.com has been viewed more than 350,000 times. Guesstimating that each view comes with three minutes of the reader trying to figure out what's going on, we can estimate that the authors of LaTeX could have saved this slice of humanity about twenty thousand hours (and counting) with a better warning message—or simply allowing this extraneous newline without complaint.

Diagnostics can be delightful as well. Witness a classic: Google's "did you mean" feature in their search. Say a user searches for the misspelling, "compture." Google shows their search plus a convenient link at the top of the results:

> compture.
>
> Did you mean: *computer*?

This message accomplishes two crucial things.

- It shows users what they did—they searched for "compture."
- It suggests what to do by providing a convenient link to the most common spelling correction.

The first feature was trivial (but thoughtful) to build, catering to scenarios where users come back to a browser tab after a distraction. I imagine the latter feature has cost Google tens of millions of dollars to build and maintain, likely using massive databases and a possibly conscious artificial intelligence to determine what the user meant. They did all that for an edge case!

The Value of Diagnostics

Crafting well-structured diagnostics with useful messages is an incredibly valuable and high-leverage way to spend your time. For many applications and platforms with complex and open-ended inputs, diagnostics are the primary interface—the vast majority of the user's time will be spent dealing with errors and progressing to the next one.

Filling out electronic forms is all about being told about your missing or malformed input. My coding time is at least half dealing with errors and lint rules. Even writing in a word processor has become a constant process of looking at underlined text and being asked to proofread or rephrase.

And yet, as we design software, because errors often don't appear in screenshots, marketing materials, or API method listings, they can be out of sight and out of mind.

Autonomous agents shine a bright light on this problem. They are now regularly presented with error messages resulting from their actions and instructed to correct their mistakes based on them. If the message isn't sufficiently helpful, they fail at their task. The process of trying different things is slow and costly. Because agents are billed based on usage, the costs are directly measured.

> Diagnostics may be the most important interface of your product.

Scenarios for Diagnostics

When considering errors, warnings, and their associated messages, it is essential to think about a broad range of scenarios, starting with identifying edge cases, to understanding how developers can automate reactions, and how end users will understand and act upon them. Improve your ability to understand your users' knowledge, generate user stories, and simulate user interactions, and you'll improve your diagnostics. For users, we provide contextual and actionable errors. For developers, we carefully select our error types, codes, and metadata so that those who receive them can recover gracefully.

In the rest of this chapter, you'll learn how to craft refreshingly useful warnings and errors. We'll explore how to:

- Understand the scenario—the persona who will benefit from the error and their situation
- Provide enough context to our users for them to understand the error
- Provide actionable error messages that suggest what to do about the problem
- Choose error codes and types carefully to allow upstream developers to serve *their* users

- Raise errors at the API or UI layer so that messages can be written with full context about what the user's trying to do
- *Shift left*; that is, fire errors as early as possible to speed up your users, and before bad things happen

In Chapter 8, I'll address how to list out edge cases to figure out what errors to check for in the first place. For now, I'll focus on crafting errors once you already know what they are.

Categorizing Error Scenarios

When writing errors, you need to make a few main choices.

First, a user-facing choice:

- What is the error message?

There are also choices of concern to developers so that they can catch errors and automate responses:

- What is the error's class or code?
- What metadata is needed to pinpoint the problem?

Thus, when you craft errors in virtually any application or platform, you must think of two categories of user scenarios: the human one and the programmer one.

There are further divisions in the developer scenarios: are you communicating with members of your team who work on your codebase, or those from other teams or companies? This is especially important if you are building an API or service where upstream developers can catch your error and act upon it.

So, the first step is to pitch your message to the right person in the right circumstance. We've all seen errors that didn't seem to be meant for us, such as when websites show code listings to end users. To determine your audience, start by deciding your error's category. For our purposes, the five shown in Table 3-1 cover most cases.

Table 3-1. Categories of errors

Error type	Example scenarios
System error	The payments processor is down. Timeouts. Transient errors under load.
Assertion	This local variable should never be null.
Invalid Developer Argument	Received an integer when a string was expected.
Invalid User Argument	User typed in a bad credit card number.
Preconditions Not Met	User is unauthorized to access a given resource or hasn't logged in.

Start by mentally categorizing any error you write. This gives a huge clue as to who you're talking to—your own team, other developers, or users—and when the errors can be fixed—at runtime or during development. This will help you write with the right vocabulary and suggest helpful actions (see Table 3-2).

Table 3-2. The when and who of error scenario categories

Error type	Time of remediation	Common remediation
System	Runtime	End users should retry later.
User's Invalid Arg	Runtime	End users can try again after correcting input.
Preconditions Not Met	Runtime	End users can go fix some other issue.
Assertion	Your development time	Engineers on your team will be notified.
Dev's Invalid Arg	Their development time	Developers using our function will need to fix their code.

These five types of scenarios reveal drastically different strategies. For example, if an assertion triggers in production, it's usually catastrophic. If the code is in a state the authors didn't foresee, it will lead to unpredictable behavior—most likely in the form of a crash or a poor error message. Occasionally there are worse consequences, like data corruption. In some programming languages, assertions are stripped out in production to optimize their execution, meaning that you shouldn't rely on them for anything load bearing. In no case is the end user persona expected to interact with them successfully.

For some applications, all end users are not the same; in which case, messages should be tailored to each persona. A classic example is a Preconditions Not Met error caused by the user not having the necessary access. Is the user an administrator or an end user? This determines whether we will provide them with direct instructions or instruct them to contact an administrator.

Knowing your personas will help you speak to the user's ontology. (Ontology was defined in Chapter 2 as a structured graph of known concepts.) Consider "PC Load Letter," which tried to ask users to reload the printer's paper tray. It was actionable—it told the user to load the paper—but it failed because it was speaking to the wrong persona. "PC" stood for "paper cassette" and "Letter" referred to a size of paper—8.5"x11". Perhaps instead, they should have labeled the paper trays A, B, and C and said, "Reload tray B."

Categorizing Errors in Practice

Let's work an example to show how to use product thinking to categorize errors.

Which of the five categories does a divide-by-zero—in Python, a `ZeroDivisionError`—fall into?

Imagine you are writing a method to compute the average value of an online metric over a time window.

```
# metric_name: e.g. 'channelz.api_calls.count'
def recent_average_for_metric(metric_name: str, timespan: str = '1h'):
  metrics = MyMetrics.get_data(metric_name).withinLast(timespan)
  return sum(metrics)/len(metrics)
```

Look at the return statement. If this method threw a `ZeroDivisionError` when the metrics array was empty, callers would be quite confused—they'd need to know the innards of your function to understand.

> Users and developers should never have to understand your implementation to understand an error.

Thus, unless your code is literally a calculator, a divide-by-zero error is an Assertion, designed to be found at test time and telling your team that the code needs improvement. Avoid it—do some upfront validation before attempting the division.

So, we're going to validate, but what scenario category would *that* validation fall under? The circumstance that led to the `len(metrics)==0` condition could have been any of those listed in Table 3-3.

Table 3-3. Divide-by-zero error categories

Edge case	Category
Is `metric_name` valid?	Developer's Invalid Argument
Is the `MyMetrics` provider down?	System
Is there no recent data?	Preconditions Not Met
Is `timespan` too short?	Developer's Invalid Argument

As I'll discuss in the next section on messages, you'll want to suggest different actions in each of these cases and therefore will need distinguishing checks in the code. Further, you will need to perform these validations at a moment when you have the necessary context.

In this section, we categorized diagnostics as either interacting with developers or end users and distinguished between scenarios that were actionable at runtime and those that were actionable only during development. Next, we'll build on this to author awesome messages.

Warning and Error Messages

Writing diagnostic messages combines system thinking with user thinking. Know precisely what happened, but shoe-shift to your user's perspective. Explain what they need to know in terms they understand. Otherwise, warnings like "underfull hbox (badness 10000)" will result.

Users seeing a diagnostic will want to know two things:

- What precisely happened to cause the error, in terms from the product's ontology? This should help them know the impact of the failure and provide clues as to how to remediate it.
- What can they do about it, if anything? Actionable diagnostics will directly help them accomplish their task.

Let's tackle those two goals one at a time. But first, let me introduce an example that will thread through the next few sections.

Case Study Introduction

Channelz is a fictional software as a service (SaaS) company building a workplace communication tool like Slack, Microsoft Teams, or Discord.

Elise works on the API team, and her teammate Deng is the tech lead.

In Channelz, one can write direct messages to coworkers or send them to "channels," which are groups of employees organized around a specific topic; the API engineering team might have a channel called `#team-api-eng`. Elise's user handle is `@elisek` and Deng's is `@deng`.

Channelz is building out an API that can be used to send messages from bots, either directly to users or to channels. Their customers want to use it to send various notifications.

Before coding, Elise sketches a quick developer interface design and shows it to Deng. Channelz messages can go to a set of individuals or to a channel to alert employees when something has gone wrong or a job has been completed.

The method in the Python SDK they ship to customers will look like this:

```
class ChannelzBot:
    def __init__(self, bot_handle: str):
        # ...

    # One of channel, users is required
    def send_message(
        message: str, channel: Optional[str], users: Optional[List[str]])
```

She sketches some use cases for Deng:

```
bot = ChannelzBot('@bippity_bot')
# Example: Send to a channel
bot.send_message(channel='#some-channel', message="Hello world!")
# Example: send separate messages to a list of people with an emoji
bot.send_message(users=['@drew', '@gabriel'], message="Hello :world:!")
```

Deng looks at Elise's design and asks her to list failure scenarios as well. Elise has shown successful usages of the API, when callers already know what to do, but what about before then? If their users' coding session is a journey, Elise has shown only the end. It's as if somebody asked for directions with an online maps search, and she responded with only a pin on the destination.

Elise comes up with a few scenarios. (I will teach probing for edge cases in Chapter 7. For this chapter, I'll skip that step.) She raises one important scenario that we'll obsess over here: what if the user or channel passed into the API is invalid?

Provide Context

You might think users should know what they did to cause an error—they literally just did it! But very often, you would be wrong, so it's your job to reiterate the context and details.

Back to our example, consider:

```
bot.send_message(users=['@dneg', '@elise'], message="Hello :world:!")
```

Note: For brevity, I am leaving the *bot* part out for the rest of this section, as it is not relevant.

In a unit test, the message "user does not exist" is probably just useful enough—people can likely glance at their test code and see that `@deng` is misspelled.

To provide full context, we should:

- Echo back the relevant data
- Provide a detailed reason
- Remind the user what they did

Let's take these one by one.

Echo the relevant data

A real-world scenario is messier than a unit test. Here's a more realistic user story: passing in data from elsewhere:

```
bot.send_message(users=input.users, message=input.message)
```

If you thoughtlessly say only "user does not exist," the developer will not immediately know which person we're talking about or why their handle was wrong. Better to say: "user `@dneg` does not exist," and they will likely spot the misspelling. That may be enough for them to solve the problem.

> Echo the erroneous data back to the user, unless that information must be redacted for privacy or security reasons.

Deng points this out during code review, and Elise ships the better message.

Provide a detailed reason

The API team's design partner is a customer company named ChickenLittle, and Deng and Elise asked them to report any friction. They report seeing this error:

```
Error: User '@buckcluck' does not exist.
```

They are totally confused because Buck Cluck is an employee of ChickenLittle, right? They figure there is a bug in the Channelz API.

Elise asks them to double-check the company's directory and learns that, in fact, @buckcluck's account is inactive. Perhaps Buck just left the company.

Elise wants to avoid user confusion—and, selfishly, the ensuing support burden—in the future. She can clarify this in her API definition:

```
def on_missing_user(channelz_user: str):
    if is_inactive_employee(
        Employees.get_employee_from_channelz_user(channelz_user)):
        message = f"User {channelz_user} has been deactivated."
    else:
        message = f"User {channelz_user} does not exist."
    raise RuntimeError(message)

def send_message(users: Optional[List[str]], ...):
    for user in users:
        if not channelz_user_exists(user):
            on_missing_user(user)
    # ...
```

If the customer had read:

```
Error: User '@buckcluck' has been deactivated.
```

They would have had a big clue what to do.

Remind the user what they did

In unit tests it's often easy to tell what function call caused the problem. In reality, there are many cases in which the reporting of an error is separated from the action itself:

- Perhaps the error is going to show up as a one-liner in some logs, and it won't be clear what generated the error.
- Maybe the error is a delayed part of a long-running process such as an online order, and the user needs a reminder as to what they ordered.
- Your product, perhaps backed by an AI, interpreted the user's instructions in a certain way. You'd echo back your interpretation before giving an error.

For these scenarios and others, it's good practice to echo back not only what the bad input was, but what the operation was doing.

I'll return to Channelz. Say another month goes by, and Elise hears from the Observability team at ChickenLittle. They use the Channelz messaging API to alert employees to important but nonurgent production problems. (They use a pager service for very critical issues.)

They report to the Channelz API squad their experience that they were confused by some errors being logged from within their alerting service:

```
Error: User '@foxyloxy' has been deactivated.
```

At first, they didn't realize the message was important. They figured it probably wasn't, since `@foxyloxy` was gone.

But *then* they discovered that some important alerts had gone unseen, and an issue had persisted for two days before anybody figured it out.

The issue was that Foxy Loxy was currently on call, despite having left. They fixed the issue by removing Foxy from the on call rotation. (They also embraced the standard practice of having a fallback user to escalate to, for example if the original message can't be delivered.)

Elise had invited them to complain any time they got confused, and so they did. She takes the feedback and adds context to her error message.

She rewords the message to recap what happened:

```
Error: Cannot deliver a Channelz message to '[@foxyloxy, @buckcluck]'
because '@foxyloxy' has been deactivated.
```

Tell the user what they were trying to do.

With better technique and a little extra user empathy, Elise could have written this error message from the start, avoiding all the iteration.

This clearer communication also calls attention to an important fact: they didn't deliver *any* of the messages when *one* of the users didn't exist. Deng and Elise discuss whether or not that's "by design" and decide that no, it's a bug; since these messages might be important alerts, they'd better send as many as they can.

To recap this section, the context you add to your errors should usually answer three questions: what was being attempted, to whom or what was it happening, and why there was a failure. This will fill in anything the user might have needed to know.

Make Error and Warning Messages Actionable

Alas, in many circumstances knowing what happened is only half the battle. Users often need to be given suggestions or told what to do. And for read operations—and increasingly with AI—you can even correct the mistake for them, as with Google's "Showing results for: [correction]" feature, as well as coding or writing assistants automatically fixing your code or language.

We've all spent countless hours of our lives dealing with error messages, figuring out what to do, sometimes discovering after much investigation that the fix is simple.

In this section, you'll see how to routinely improve your diagnostics. To achieve this, you'll need to empathize with your audience, starting with the scenario categorization we did previously.

Returning to our Channelz example, suppose you called the API:

```
bot.send_message(message="The sky is falling!", channel="@barnyard-friends")
```

and got this error message:

```
Cannot deliver a Channelz message to channel '@barnyard-friends': chan
nel does not exist.
```

Can you tell what went wrong? It may take a bit to figure out, and if you're not super familiar with Channelz nomenclature, you may not realize that channels are prefixed with `#`, not `@`.

It would be better to give our users a couple of options for what to do:

```
Cannot deliver a Channelz message to channel '@barnyard-friends': it is prefixed with @. Did you mean to pass it into 'users'? Or did you mean '#barnyard-friends'?
```

Channelz could even query accounts to see if `#barnyard-friends` exists—and is public to the user—and show:

```
Channel @barnyard-friends is prefixed with @, but we found a channel, #barnyard-friends. Is that what you meant?
```

By eliminating chunks of "search space" for your users, suggesting actions can save hours or prevent them from giving up and churning out of your product. Even a simple "try again in a minute" after a System error can increase completions of workflows.

Sometimes, the advice gets complicated. You may need to introduce users to some concepts, like the concept of channels, or guide them through a number of decisions. Where appropriate, link out to documentation dedicated to resolving that error. For example, if this case were more complex, you might do:

```
See https://channelz.io/docs/errors/invalid_channel to learn how to resolve this error.
```

Raise Errors at the Interface

If it were straightforward to write good error messages, engineers would do it more often. One of the main reasons they don't is because it often takes diligent code organization to pull it off.

To write the best error messages, you need two pieces of information: What happened in the system? And, what was the user trying to do? The trouble is, in real life a different piece of code has each piece of information.

One place, near the API or UI boundary, knows who the user was and what they were trying to do. It is best placed to tell the user what to do without mentioning implementation details the user won't be aware of.

The other, deep in the bowels of your processing code, is where the problem happens.

This came up when we were categorizing errors. When we divided by zero, Python's division operation knew the exact law of mathematics being violated, but had no idea how the division was being used and therefore no hope of giving a good error.

The best place to raise errors is usually at the interface between the system and the user, where we can combine the bottom-up and top-down knowledge. (An alternative is to pass all the user context down, which I'll explore in a later section.)

Generally, people raise at the interface in two ways:

- They raise errors proactively, using upfront validations at the API boundary.
- They use error handlers to intercept a lower-level error and repackage it into an appropriate form.

To illustrate each, let's return to Channelz.

Upfront Validations

The Observability team at ChickenLittle has another problem.

The function powering their on call messages is `alert_team`:

```
def alert_team(bot: ChannelzBot, team: Team, message: str):
    team_metadata = get_team_metadata(team)
    bot.send_message(users=[team_metadata['on_call_user']], message=message)
```

`get_team_metadata` reads a database of on call rotations that people at ChickenLittle set in a user interface at *https://corp.chickenlittle.io/oncalls/*.

What happens if `team_metadata[`*`on_call_user`*`]` is invalid? Recall that `send_message` will raise this error:

`Error: Cannot deliver a Channelz message to '[@gooseyloosey]' because '@gooseyloosey' has been deactivated.`

This is accurate, but when Goosey Loosey left the company, users couldn't figure out how to fix the problem. So the Observability team added a validation upfront to tell folks what to do:

```
def alert_team(bot: ChannelzBot, team: Team, message: str):
    team_metadata = get_team_metadata(team)
    if not channelz_user_exists(team_metadata['on_call_user']):
        error_message =
            f"Cannot send alert '{message}' to team {team}'s on-call: " +
            f"On-call employee {team_metadata['on_call_user']} doesn't exist. " +
            f"Update the team's on-call rotation at {ON_CALL_BASE_URL}/{team}."
        raise ValueError(error_message)
    bot.send_message(users=[team_metadata['on_call_user']], message=message)
```

When a user is missing, this method is here to help:

`Cannot send a Channelz alert to team 'barnyard-friends'. On-call user '@gooseyloosey' doesn't exist. Update your on-call rotation at https://corp.chickenlittle.io/oncalls/barnyard-friends.`

This higher-level API `alert_team` captures the intent of the caller much more completely than `send_message`, which is a powerful basis for providing great errors.

> Throw errors from the outermost layer of your API or application code where you can capture the user's scenario.

The approach of upfront validation did the trick here, but it wasn't perfect. Can you spot any issues?

Let's look at an alternate technique of repackaging errors that your dependencies raise and see if it works any better.

Repackage Errors

There were two problems with the upfront validation. It's expensive—it uses an extra roundtrip with the Channelz API. More important for our purposes in this chapter, the validation would need to duplicate edge-case-checking code already being done inside the Channelz API, such as checking whether @gooseyloosey's account was deactivated. That info is still actionable—suppose the employee changed their Channelz handle because they changed their name. That would warrant a separate fix.

Since she's given such good support before, the Observability team complains to Elise. They would rather write something like this:

```
def alert_team(bot: ChannelzBot, team: Team, message: str):
    team_metadata = get_team_metadata(team)
    try:
        bot.send_message(users=team_metadata['on_call_users'], message=message)
    except ChannelzUserNotFoundError as error:
        error_message =
            f"Cannot send a Channelz alert to team {team}'s on-call: " +
            f"On-call employee {team_metadata['on_call_user']} doesn't exist. " +
            f"Update the team's on-call rotation at {ON_CALL_BASE_URL}/{team}."
        raise ValueError(error_message) from error
```

Notice the `from error` clause in the last line. This is Python's way of expressing "chained exceptions," which preserves the inner error. Many programming languages have similar mechanisms. This would be the output:

```
ChannelzUserNotFoundError: User @looseygoosey's account has been deactivated.

The above exception was the direct cause of the following exception:

ValueError: Cannot send a Channelz alert to team 'barnyard-friends'.
On-call employee '@looseygoosey' doesn't exist.
Update your on-call rotation at
https://corp.chickenlittle.io/on-calls/barnyard-friends.
```

This is a longer message, but it contains everything the user might want to know.

Observability asks Elise for specific errors in Channelz's SDK so that they can do this.

With all these employees leaving ChickenLittle, Elise hopes the sky is not falling over there for her favorite design partner. Then, she and Deng investigate making their exceptions more *programmable*.

Since we're diving into programmability, I'll end our discussion of actionability and raising diagnostics from the interface layer here, turning my attention to making errors actionable for developers and their users.

Raise Programmable Errors

Sometimes, there's a developer between your error and the end users. Those developers are following the same principle of handling errors at the interface layer, meaning they will need to intercept your error programmatically and take various actions.

None of this can happen unless the error is well designed. There are three main techniques you can use to make runtime errors—System, Preconditions Not Met, and User's Invalid Arguments errors—actionable for developers:

- Raising specific errors
- Grouping exceptions
- Adding metadata

Note that Assertions and Developer's Invalid Argument exceptions can all share a common exception type—they are actioned at development time, and people shouldn't be building runtime automations around them.

Raise Specific Errors

Generic error types, such as `ValueError` in Python, will leave your clients unable to tailor their automations or tell their users what to do.

When you're building an exception in any runtime error scenario category, you'll want to make specific errors, as Channelz did above when they created `ChannelzUserNotFoundError`.

While we're on the subject, it may have touched a nerve that the Observability team raised a `ValueError` when we just said to raise more specific errors.

```
if not channelz_user_exists(team_metadata['on_call_user']):
    error_message = # ...
    raise ValueError(error_message)
```

The Observability team isn't a platform team, but there could always be a user interface or middleware put around their component, so they should make a specific runtime error out of habit. They could call it `OncallNotFoundError`.

With a couple of tweaks to their handlers, Channelz made its APIs vastly more powerful and nestable than the naïve implementations.

> Design your runtime errors—System, Preconditions Not Met, and User's Invalid Arguments—for nesting, to allow code to be built on top.

Group Errors According to Scenario Category

A developer using your API might want to write a generic handler that handles errors from a given category. Maybe they want to display "Something went wrong. Try again later." to an end user any time there's a System error. In contrast, when emitting a User's Invalid Argument error, they might echo the message directly to the user and hope for the best.

In most languages, you can use inheritance hierarchies to group similar error messages. I like to have a separate base class for each scenario category.

You can use built-ins to some extent. Python, for example, represents (any) Invalid Argument errors with `ValueError`. `RuntimeError` is for system errors.

But the built-in types may not be expressive enough. `ValueError` doesn't distinguish between User's and Developer's Invalid Argument error categories, but the outcomes couldn't be more different. If the *programmer* screwed up, the user needs to, say, contact support rather than fixing their input. So I'll make a class for each, perhaps subclassing `ValueError`.

In a nonobject-oriented environment, you can provide error codes for categories and subcodes to identify specific failures. The standards aren't often great for this, so you may need to add your own. For example, the HTTP protocol categorizes errors as "client" errors by assigning them to the 400-level category. Like Python's `ValueError`, you can't express whether users or developers caused those client errors. However, there are helpful codes for certain Preconditions errors, such as authorization failures.

Keep Information Around for Diagnostics

To make good error messages, we need to keep around a lot of information, which takes diligence and well-organized code because the first developer who doesn't pass the information along breaks the chain. I'll show three examples of information chains.

Pass around high-level abstractions

Rather than passing lots of little bits of information around, pass around higher-level abstractions that group the information together. This will make it easier to provide rich diagnostics.

For example, rather than passing employee names, job titles, handles, and so forth around in case you need them for diagnostics, pass an `Employee` object that contains whatever you might need.

A callsite like this breaks the chain:

```
def foo(bot: ChannelzBot, employee: Employee):
    bot.send_message(users=[employee.channelz_handle])
```

Now, if a maintainer wants to improve `send_message`'s diagnostics, they must first refactor. They may just not bother.

This approach keeps the chain alive, giving more flexibility to the implementor:

```
def foo(bot: ChannelzBot, employee: Employee):
    bot.send_message(employees=[employee])
```

Of course, this trades off against flexibility for the caller—what if callers can't get an `Employee` object? Should we really limit access "just for diagnostics?"

Scenarios can help resolve these arguments. Is there really a need to send messages to nonemployees? Probably not. Are there legacy places in the codebase that don't have `Employees` objects? Maybe.

But in that case, someone can add a legacy version of `send_message` that takes raw user handles. This lets users who have `Employee` objects provide nice diagnostics, while providing an escape hatch for others until they get around to refactoring.

Keeping thicker information chains means you need little extra effort to author diagnostics, or for populating diagnostic metadata, discussed next.

Add structured metadata

You should also provide metadata as fields on your exceptions, which dramatically increases their programmability. Don't make people parse your error messages to extract data!

Always assume your caller might want to craft their own error message, so stick any data you used in the metadata as well. Maybe the Observability team would like to pull out the missing Channelz user, so Channelz will add a `user` property to their `ChannelzUserNotFoundError`.

Using this practice will keep your information chains unbroken.

Persist extra context

In phased data transformation architectures such as compilers, we may be several phases in before we recognize an error. Keeping around the original context is critical.

Recall the opening LaTeX example, wherein users were writing unnecessary \\ tokens, but the error is talking about `underfull hboxes`.

The lexer is the first pass of a compiler. It converts input tokens like \\ into abstract tokens that can be read by the next phase, which is called the parser. The parser doesn't need whitespace or line numbers and so the lexer can strip them out.

But it shouldn't.

I imagine the warning was probably thrown in some pass of the compiler after the lexer had read in the source code and spit out an `hbox` token, losing the original source context and hamstringing any attempts to write a useful message.

This was a frequent problem with older compilers. These days, lexers keep enough information in their output such that later compiler phases can provide a decidedly more modern experience:

```
This is at the end of a block of text. \\
                                       ^^
Unnecessary \\ to end a paragraph on line 2.
```

The key lesson that applies to passing around abstractions, adding structured metadata, and persisting extra context is:

> Keep your information chains robust. Hang onto useful information for diagnostics.

The best errors are possible when you maximize the amount of system and user scenario information at a single point in the code. This is achieved by making errors programmable.

Programmability is achieved by making a rigorous practice of keeping information chains alive and packing our errors with structured information.

There's one remaining topic I haven't addressed: timing. When we fire off diagnostics makes a massive difference to users.

Diagnose Early

Giving early diagnostics is often called *shifting left* and has numerous benefits for the system and for users.

> Shift left. Give diagnostics to your users as early as you can.

For the system, it reduces resource usage by cutting off useless code paths. This can be critical, for example to fend off denial-of-service attacks. It also protects that same code from processing unpredicted inputs, preventing bugs like data loss.

Users benefit even more. Erroring early saves them time—think about how much time you save getting an error in your IDE rather than when deploying to production. Also, users are more likely to remember what they did when they get quick feedback, and to be more certain of the right action.

Here are four common techniques for shifting left:

- Do static validations
- Validate upfront
- Let them test
- Request user confirmations

Engineers widely practice the first two, but unfortunately not the last two. I came here to evangelize them all.

Do Static Validations

When validating any input, static validations can be performed cheaply and without deep inspection or network calls, while dynamic validations require more work or context.

> Separate your cheap checks from your expensive ones and do the cheap ones early and often.

Many programmers are familiar with the pleasures of static typechecks and linters, but this comes up in products, too.

For example, when taking user input in application forms, look for cheap ways to tackle the users' most common mistakes early, and provide inline advice telling them what needs to be corrected. Postal codes can be verified to be of the right length for their countries. Credit card numbers, UPC codes, and ISBN numbers have built-in checksum digits that help protect against common errors like typos and transpositions. These techniques shift left and also provide more certainty to diagnoses. If the checksum fails on a number, we know it's not just missing from our database—it's just flat wrong.

Validate Upfront

When I talked about crafting errors at the surface of an application or API, upfront validations provided a tool for more actionable and understandable error messages. But validations are also a tool for shifting left.

Imagine you went to the laundromat to wash your clothes, and you washed them, only to discover that only one dryer was online and it was booked for hours. A sign on the door would have saved you from a lot of wet, moldy clothes!

Similarly, when moving money, it's essential to validate that the destination account is valid before withdrawing it from the source account.

Multistep workflows like laundry, money movement, and money laundering often benefit from upfront validation.

Let Them Test

If there's one set of user scenarios I see most often neglected by platform engineers, it's testing. They think of customers successfully using their production product without considering the trials their customers go through to get there.

If you're building a developer service, your customers will adore you—and you'll get adopted faster—if you build a *fake*. Fakes are high-fidelity versions of production systems that share as much code with the production path as possible, while taking certain shortcuts to avoid flaky runtime dependencies such as databases and online services that would make tests slower and less reliable.

Channelz should build a fake service for their messaging API. It would ideally:

- Run in-memory or in a lightweight local process so that it can be tested by its users in their test environments and locally on their development machines
- Allow users to input a bunch of users and channels so that they can then test various pieces of code that use the API
- Act just like the production service for as many scenarios as possible

For a real-world example, Stripe, a provider of payment and billing APIs and UIs, provides a popular "test mode" in which one can do realistic transactions without actually moving money around. For example, customers can pass in special credit card numbers to induce various Invalid User Argument and Precondition errors. The card number `4000 0000 0000 9995`, for example, simulates a `card_declined` error with an `insufficient_funds` subcode.

Stripe users spend far more time with test mode than with production, leveraging it when writing integration tests and testing user interfaces. For example, if a merchant wants to test their credit card input form, they can plug those magic numbers in manually and see how the site behaves.

Fakes are great ways to shift errors *far* to the left—to before developers even get properly authenticated or submit a production request.

Request User Confirmations

Confirmations are roadblocks in your app or platform that help users verify whether they have done the right thing. They are louder than warnings but not as intrusive as errors.

They frequently appear in user interfaces and developer tools when heuristics detect something odd about the user's input. They explain why it might be unexpected or dangerous, and provide the opportunity to correct it or confirm it.

Google's "Did you mean" is a fine example. When a user searched for "compture," maybe they really were referring to Compture, the band. So, Google can't just return an error, but they can report their suspicion to the user upfront rather than relying on them to figure it out after digging through search results.

Or instead, when you have just asked a user to fill out several pages of forms, show them a summary of what they're about to submit so they can check for errors.

Confirmations allow you to shift left at times when you can't be certain that the user is wrong without running the input through the whole system, but you can take your best guess.

One common method to allow upfront testing is with a "dry run" followed by a confirmation. In a stock-trading app, this is as simple as multiplying the number of shares someone plans to purchase by the current share price to show users how much they will spend.

Here's a more complex dry run at Channelz. Suppose Elise wants to add retry policies to her API, designed to be used like so:

```
ChannelzBot('@bippity_bot')
    .with_retry_policy(
            backoff_coefficient=2.0,
```

```
            initial_interval_seconds=10, max_interval_seconds=600)
    .send_message(...)
```

What happens if ChickenLittle authors a really spammy retry policy that retries once a second, forever? This could cause an accidental Denial-of-Service (DoS) style attack on Channelz, which would surely result in ChickenLittle's traffic being throttled.

```
# Too spammy!
.with_retry_policy(backoff_coefficient=1.0, initial_interval_seconds=1)
```

Elise could shift left with a heuristic-driven warning by simulating the retry policy and flagging bad behavior:

```
Your retry_policy (currently initial_interval_seconds=1, backoff_coeffi
cient=1.0, max_attempts=Infinite) will result in 601 attempts in 600 sec
onds. This exceeds our limit of 50. You may ignore this by
adding .ignore(Errors::RetryPolicySpamminess) to your policy.
```

Elise is not perfectly confident in her exact heuristic, but she can move fast and help her users out by providing this sort of confirmation that stops development temporarily. If her heuristic is off, users will complain, and she can adjust it upward.

In developer tools, `--force` flags override confirmations.

Confirmations aren't foolproof—users might blithely confirm or copy/paste a `--force` flag. So don't use them for inputs you really can't accept. That said, most developers I know are accustomed to absolutes—either the input is allowable, or it's not. You'll find that thinking about a middle case—the input is *probably* wrong—unlocks an incredible amount of richness and expressiveness in your interfaces.

In this section, we discussed the merits of shifting left and captured some of the many user scenarios that would benefit from the practice.

Since shifting left sometimes means we can't perform a full, perfect validation, I explored techniques such as service fakes, heuristic-based confirmations, and static validations like checksums to address the most common user mistakes as early as possible.

Chapter Summary

As you think about writing your next few diagnostics, start by shifting your focus to your users' experience and consider what they know, what they need to know, and what they should do. If you're writing an error, bucket it into its scenario category—System, User's Invalid Argument, Precondition, Developer's Invalid Argument, or Assertion. This will help you to reason about constructing the metadata and message.

In your messages:

- Give context. In most cases, echo back the operation being done and the bad data that was passed in.
- Use concepts from the product's user-facing ontology.
- Suggest actions, and be willing to suggest alternatives if there's not just one.

You'll be more likely to do a good job of all of this if you raise the error to show the user from the interface boundary. For developers, include enough context and structure with your error so that other developers can do their jobs. Organize your errors into hierarchies to provide developers with both generic and specific ways to serve their users.

Finally, find creative ways to shift left for common or important scenarios, such as via techniques like confirmations, static checks, and fakes.

Exercises

1. Search the web for "Windows Blue Screen of Death Evolution" and watch as a few decades of Windows teams struggle to improve their error messages. (a) Decide which personas its messages are tackling. (b) Later in the video, you'll see the Windows 11 screen. Analyze its message for the personas you picked.
2. For the next questions, pretend that you work on an e-commerce app. Users can fill their shopping cart and check out. The app finalizes orders via a `submit_order` API with the following fields: user ID, shopping cart ID, and credit card CVV code—the three- or four-digit code to verify a credit card. Your mobile client has the ability to do static verifications before sending up data to your API.

   What error scenario category are invalid user ID and invalid shopping cart ID?
3. What error scenario category is an invalid CVV code?
4. What about an empty CVV code?
5. Write an actionable end-user-facing error message for a missing CVV code.
6. Shopping carts can expire and are automatically deleted from the system after 24 hours. What scenario category of error is raised when the user tries to resume their session by adding to a deleted cart?
7. Can you think of a way to shift this expired shopping cart error left so that the user doesn't need to refind each item?

Answers

1. As of this writing, the Windows 11 message says: "Your device ran into a problem and needs to restart. We're just collecting some error info, and then we'll restart for you. For more information about this issue and possible fixes, visit *https://www.windows.com/stopcode*. If you call a support person, give them this info: Stop Code: SOME_ERROR_CODE."

   This message is targeted at end users and gives a clear action. Its use of a URL is a strong technique because that URL can be kept up-to-date and have nuanced instructions. At the end, it refers to the stop code, clearly framing it as relevant to IT professionals, which is a clue that there are two distinct audiences for this message. However, it's not trying very hard to help such people, perhaps reasoning that such folks are likely capable of searching online if they want to know how to, say, find crash dumps on their machines.

2. Invalid User IDs and Shopping Cart IDs are Developer's Invalid Argument errors. But, if the user is not logged in, resulting in an empty user ID, that's a precondition problem that the user can action.
3. An invalid CVV code is a User's Invalid Argument.
4. An empty CVV code is, on the face of it, a User's Invalid Argument. However, a well-built client should statically check for empty fields and prompt the user to fill them in before connecting to the server. Thus, the API might wish to treat this as a Developer problem. This would clearly spotlight missing fields as bugs, such as when the client forgets to pass up the code.
5. I imagine a red box highlighting a bad CVV value with a tooltip that explains: "Please enter your credit card's security code. For Visa, Mastercard, and Discover cards, this is a three-digit number that typically appears on the back. American Express cards have four-digit numbers that usually appear on the front."
6. An expired shopping cart is a precondition and is user-actionable. Thus, the implementation of expiring shopping carts should allow the API to distinguish between invalid IDs—a developer problem—and expired ones. For example, expired carts could be soft-deleted rather than completely removed from the database. (This practice is sometimes called tombstoning.)
7. You could email or push-notify the customer in advance of their shopping cart expiry, reminding them to finish the order.

PART II
Deliver

As a product-minded engineer, when you're headed toward delivering a major release, obsess over the question of how you're going to get users to validate that your product does what it should.

Popular social media firms are lucky in this regard. They have large, forgiving user bases and extremely powerful software distribution mechanisms—news feeds. They can rapidly ship experimental products and, whether they are polls, game invites, events, groups, videos, or stories, they can distribute them with their feed to a small percentage of users, get feedback and metrics, and perform A/B tests.

On the other end of the spectrum, self-driving car startups are unlucky. They must iterate for years before shipping anything to customers. They hire professionals to mind their cars while collecting data until they achieve beyond human levels of reliability—in other words, they must avoid fatal accidents on more than 99.999999% of the miles they drive.

These approaches have very little in common. The one shared aspect is that they are all validating their products.

> Validate your product with users.

Validating your product with users results in answering important open concerns about it and also discovering problems you didn't think of.

These next two chapters encompass some of the most cost-effective ways to iteratively delivery and refine software products based on user validation.

Before you ship, through the lessons in Chapter 4 you'll expose your product to early pressure as you and your coworkers try out your software, test it and provide friction logs, and thoughtfully document it.

Chapter 5 will focus after you've shipped, on hearing what real users have to say through feedback, experiments, and metrics.

CHAPTER 4

Experiencing Your Own Product

> *[T]he designer of a new system must not only be the implementor and the first large-scale user; the designer should also write the first user manual...If I had not participated fully in all these activities, literally hundreds of improvements would never have been made, because I would never have thought of them or perceived why they were important.*
>
> —Donald Knuth

Many of us struggle to track down and engage beta users.

Suppose you're preparing to launch a new version of your product, and you'd like to get it in front of users to test it out. Your product doesn't yet have significant scale and an avid set of beta users who can be counted on to exercise a pre-release product on short notice. Most users have other priorities to accomplish before trying out your release. Those that *do* try it may not use the riskiest parts of the design. You've got deadlines, so you are tempted to ship something unvalidated by users.

As it turns out, there *are* users that are easier to engage—yourself, your teammates, and others at your company. These people share in the success of your product and are pre-incentivized to help you out.

> Be your own first customer. This will validate your product early, cheaply, and harmlessly.

When team members use their own product, this is called *dogfooding*, a term popularized within Microsoft in the 1990s as it developed a culture of using the latest versions of its operating systems and compilers, coming from the phrase "eating your own dogfood" to show just how far folks would go to test their own product.

Dogfooding is ideal when you, or some of your coworkers, are within your target personas and can simulate real-world usage conditions. But even in nonideal circumstances, dogfooding can be surprisingly effective if your team knows their user base and can shoe-shift and pretend to be real users.

Find a way. If you're an agricultural technology company, you could buy your own farmland to test out your products. Or if that's not practical, simulate those conditions in a greenhouse, laboratory, or on a computer. Or you could hire a real farmer to allocate some of their land to your experiments.

Dogfooding has several key advantages:

- It can come earlier in the product lifecycle, before the release is ready for non-employees.
- It's cheaper to test things yourself or communicate with coworkers than it is with end users.
- It doesn't have adverse consequences on users or erode their trust.

Dogfooding takes a surprising number of forms. Here are four approaches I'll cover in this chapter:

- Write scenario tests that exercise the product, mirroring real-world usage.
- Lay out what it's like to use your product by writing usage guides. If you're attentive, this will give advance warning of problems.
- Write, or get teammates to write, "friction logs" which detail your experience as you dogfood. This will both motivate you to dogfood and produce more helpful feedback.
- Create samples (for appropriate products) and test them.

Documentation and automated testing are not traditionally thought of as dogfooding, but if done well, they have a heavy component of pretending to be users and putting useful pressure on your product.

Be creative and figure out the mix of these techniques that will cheaply validate your product every step of the way. You'll reduce risks and ensure that you won't waste users' time and trust.

Tests as Dogfooding

Writing tests is one of the best ways of experiencing your own product once you're ready to write code. According to Kent Beck, "Test-driven development (TDD) is meant to eliminate fear in application development." The best way to reduce fear is by writing tests that have high fidelity with production.

In TDD, one writes the tests before the implementation. But based on what? They can't be derived from the implementation—it doesn't exist yet! If it did exist, it would cause *implementation bias*—asserting what the code does rather than what it should do.

The main valid source of inspiration is therefore user scenarios. Rather than writing code and then writing the test to pass based on what you've written, write the tests before you're biased by what you did. This helps you stay closer to the user scenarios.

In this section, I want to show you how to apply tests as dogfooding opportunities. Using well-selected automated tests, we'll do the following:

- Verify correctness in key scenarios.
- Polish edge cases.
- Document the intended usage.
- Force ourselves to think about what we're building.
- Build something of enduring value that can be run time and time again.

But first let's survey various types of tests with an eye toward selecting the ones that will offer us the most value for our effort.

What Kinds of Tests Should You Write?

So that we can all get on the same page, I'm going to define several types of tests. These test types are a blend of system-oriented and product-oriented. System-oriented tests reduce system risks—the chance that the application will be buggy, unreliable, or won't scale. Product-oriented tests reduce product risks—the chance that users won't be able to complete tasks.

Your goal should be for your test suite to efficiently look for both system and product problems, so you will need a mix of tests. In my experience, many software teams under-use product-oriented tests. And engineers are not always aware of the breadth of test types available to them.

Let me first define a couple of basic testing terms:

Mocks
: Non-functional placeholders that verify that dependencies are called in certain ways.

Fakes
: Simplified replacements for complex functionality. For example, SQLite, a local filesystem-based version of SQL, can be used as a fake for a real SQL database.

The tests on this list are sorted in the order of the amount of "product pressure" they put on the codebase.

> Product pressure is validation informed by the sequences of actions users are likely to take, individually and collectively.

Unit tests
: Tests small bits of code, such as individual functions or classes. We write them early during feature development to probe edge cases and encode contracts. They should run quickly and be used for the innermost development loop. They often use mocks to keep focus on what they are testing. However, they are not very targeted at finding important system and product bugs.

Integration tests
: Test multiple components, recognizing that it's often the interactions between components that are the most fraught. They do not mock out as many dependencies to better sniff out system problems. They exercise mostly real production code, calling fakes where necessary. While more likely to find product issues than unit tests, they don't emphasize product scenarios like the tests below.

Functional tests
: Focuses on the product behavior of individual features. They may use fakes to simulate dependencies, such as other services and databases. Some tests use mocks if fakes are unavailable, but this is a "bad smell" because it makes it harder to trust the test.

Scenario tests
: Like functional tests, except they exercise common user scenarios rather than specific features. They often hit multiple features or exercise a given feature with the most common sets of inputs. They ensure entire user tasks can be completed.

Load simulations
: Stresses the product with lots of synthetic requests. Those requests should ideally simulate real-world conditions, as I discuss these in depth in Chapter 9.

End-to-end (e2e) tests
: The most comprehensive automated tests of user-facing behavior, and they can also find unforeseen system integration problems. They are essentially scenario tests that don't stub out anything and usually include the user interface.

User acceptance testing
: Real users manually put your product through its paces and reporting problems. I'll discuss this further when I introduce friction logging.

Figure 4-1 roughly plots the relative strengths and weaknesses of the test types.

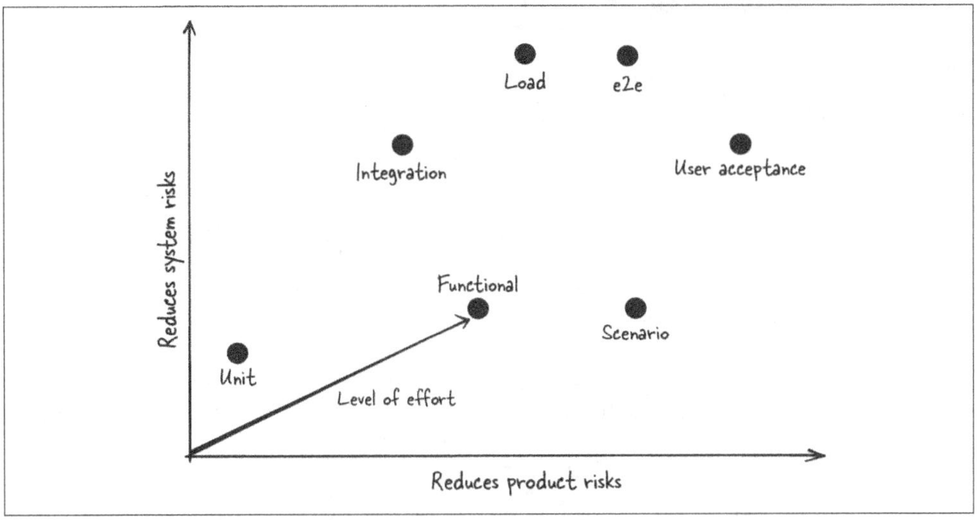

Figure 4-1. Test types, plotted by the amount of system and user risks that they uncover

Choosing test types

My typical goals when crafting a testing strategy are the following:

- Minimizing the most important system and product risks that could cause the product not to work
- Making sure the key scenarios we came up with during Discovery are tested
- Avoiding repeated user acceptance tests by automating testing
- Making tests highly valuable, given the effort of writing them
- Having high signal-to-noise tests whose failures are likely to matter
- Covering important edge cases via functional tests

Features with a lot of system risk should include tests like load simulations and integration tests. Features with a lot of product risk should focus disproportionately on functional, scenario, and user acceptance tests. End-to-end tests are good for both. Think about what's the most novel about your product and therefore the most likely to break. Perhaps you're dropping in a new infrastructure component that will improve on an older one, but you're keeping the same semantics that have been used for years. Then you might want to focus on system tests and rely more on existing tests to test product behavior. Then again, if you're building a novel product using hardened infrastructure and best practices or "paved roads" at a mature tech company, you can focus more on product risks. Both types of risk are important, and most tests should incorporate elements of both. But since this is a book on product thinking, I'm going to focus on scenario, functional, e2e, and user acceptance tests. I'll revisit load simulations in Chapter 9.

Test only what users care about

Above, we talked about covering our system and product risks. But with a limited time budget, how do we prioritize the most critical tests, and within those, the most critical assertions?

The overriding goal should be to have tests assert behaviors that matter directly to users.

Here are some classic examples of tests to avoid:

- Unit tests that hinge on too many implementation details and mocked dependencies often end up needing frequent maintenance as the codebase evolves. I even sometimes delete unit tests that I wrote during implementation once I have functional tests in place that cover them.
- Fussy e2e tests that make overly specific assertions break frequently as the product surface changes.
- Load simulations that provide unrealistic traffic patterns can lead you to scaling and hardening in ways that will never come up.

To show test selection in practice, I'll use Netflix, a popular service that streams movies and television shows. Users can access Netflix via web browsers, so let's suppose we are on the web team, and our main job is to make the home screen display options for the user to watch. The page shows a grid of shows that users can click on to play. Each row has a separate theme like "Critically Acclaimed TV Shows" and "My List", and one can scroll down to reveal more rows like "Classic Science Fiction and Fantasy" or whatever their algorithm thinks the user will be interested in.

Scenario Tests

Scenario tests capture real-world product use cases. They are quite likely to catch important bugs simply because they represent what users will do. In fact, we can directly translate the scenarios we come up with during Discovery into scenario tests —a process discussed in Chapter 7.

Scenario tests encourage us to think outside of individual features and think about the product from the user's perspective. They can't tackle the entire test matrix alone, but if chosen well, they help ensure that any bugs we ship will be relatively minor.

These tests tend to combine at least two elements that go together. For example, they would:

- Combine two or more features that often appear together in a user flow. Interactions between components are often the flakiest parts of software. Scenario tests exercise these.
- Run features on the most common types of data in quantities that match real-world circumstances.

Scenario tests should be as end-to-end as is practical, and we use high-fidelity fakes for the rest. If we're on the backend team, it may be convenient or economical not to run a browser, but instead to use a simulated DOM environment. (The DOM is a data representation of the objects that comprise the structure and content of a web page.) And using Netflix's real distributed database would be prohibitively expensive in a test. Figure 4-2 shows a system diagram for a backend test of the Netflix library with a fake on each side.

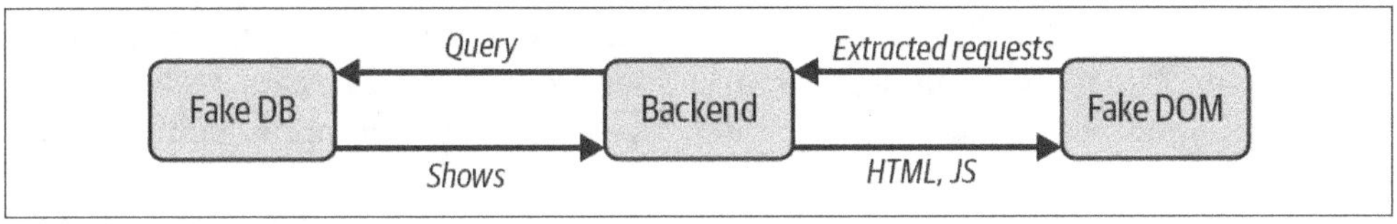

Figure 4-2. A typical backend scenario test setup

Here's an example backend scenario test using that setup: A logged-in user wants to watch a movie and navigates to netflix.com. They click one of the movie's thumbnails, which loads the movie and starts playing it.

Here's pseudocode:

```
# A logged in user wants to watch a movie, so they load the home page
def watch_movie_from_homepage():
  set_up_fake_movies() # Don't want to download and play movies in our tests.

  # User sees the home page.  It should have thumbnails of movies.
  home_page_source  = get_source("netflix.com")
  home_page_dom = get_dom(home_page_source)
  movie_listing = find_one("movie_thumbnail", home_page_dom)
  assert(movie_listing)

  # User clicks one of the movies.
  watch_movie_page_request = movie_listing.click_target()
  watch_movie_source = get_source(watch_movie_page_request)
  watch_movie_dom = get_dom(watch_movie_source)

  # Movie page loads successfully and starts playing automatically
  assert_autoplay_on(watch_movie_source)
```

Notice how the test chains each action to the next one. We don't hardcode the `watch_movie_page_request`, we extract it from the HTML and JavaScript. It won't find all UI-layer issues, like if the widget is hidden on the screen, but it will make sure the movie page link returned from the home page is correct.

The test also tells the story of the user scenario in comments and names. Self-documenting scenario tests are particularly important because they are essentially our product requirements made permanent. When a new team member ramps up on your team, the scenario tests are one of the first things you should show them.

Here are a few more test ideas:

- Scrolling down to reveal the second page. Render the home page, then simulate a user scrolling down, which results in loading more rows of shows. Assert that the initial page was rendered with a URL that can be called to retrieve additional data. Call the action that hits that URL and make sure new content is loaded.
- New user experience. Create a brand-new Netflix test user account. Since you don't know anything about the user, the home page should show the most popular stuff. The show database is populated with some synthetic data, with a certain list of shows being the most popular. Make sure that the most popular show appears.
- A user wants to resume a show they are currently watching. Render the library and make sure that an element to resume that show from where they left off is rendered somewhere on the page.

Functional Tests

Not everything needs to be a scenario test. Use functional tests to test individual features more thoroughly by exercising lists of cases within the broader test matrix, especially edge cases.

In our Netflix example, we might write these functional tests:

- Rendering a themed row, such as "My List" and "Critically Acclaimed TV Shows"
- Edge cases, such as rendering "My List" when the user hasn't added anything to their list
- Clicking on various elements in a movie listing, such as play, the thumbs up button, or more info, and making sure the appropriate page renders

End-to-End Tests

End-to-end tests are like scenario tests except they are more all-encompassing of system and product behaviors. Set them up for some of the most mission-critical scenario tests.

Continuing our Netflix example, these tests might use a "headless" browser—a browser missing its graphical user interface—to simulate actual user clicks on buttons, rather than only testing the underlying functionality. They may also operate on a database in a pre-production or QA environment rather than a fake database, as shown in Figure 4-3.

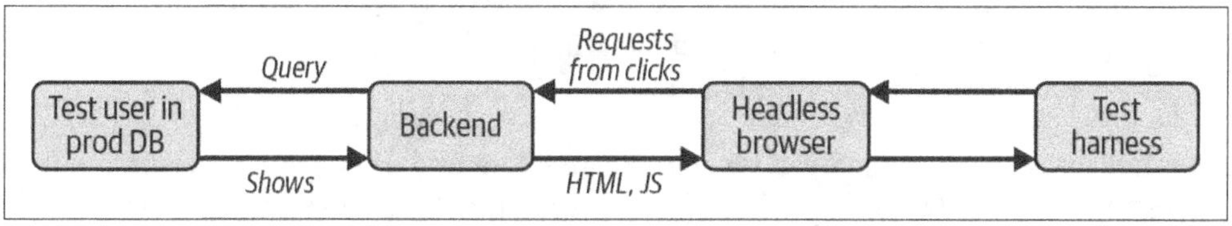

Figure 4-3. A typical e2e test setup

Since they are running on real production show data, they'll have to be resilient to content changes. Take the "new user experience" scenario test. As an e2e test, rather than hardcoding the most popular movies, we would separately query within the test to find out the most popular show. If it's the latest season of *Squid Game*, we'd expect that to show up on the home page.

This test will find bugs in a variety of places that the scenario tests might have missed. Perhaps the nightly job that populates the popular movie database didn't run. Maybe the new user account creation is about to regress. Maybe a user interface element was inadvertently hidden from the screen.

It could also spot latency regressions. While the speed of an individual run might vary too much to make a reliable test, you could average the speeds of a few runs of each of your e2e test to see if any flows regressed.

Teams don't tend to author as many e2e tests, but they occupy a critical niche. They may run less frequently than other tests, as long as they block important releases.

End-to-end tests will punish you hard if you have assertions and assumptions that don't reflect user value. That short sleep you hardcoded will time out in a busy test environment—use callbacks or polling to wait for the test instead. The third element of the page you're testing will change when a designer reorders things—use persistent semantic tags on your UI elements so that they can be searched for via automation. For example, we should be able to search for buttons on our Netflix page via `play_video` or `more_info` tags.

User Acceptance Testing

In user acceptance testing, you give some employees or volunteers some test scenarios to run through in pre-production environments, requiring those tests to pass before shipping. Here are a few scenarios where it comes up:

- Internationalization and localization, where speakers of different languages in different locales verify product behavior across a variety of circumstances that would be too dizzying for engineers to test themselves.
- Testing that's required for compliance standards.
- People validating the output of Large Language Models (LLMs). In particular, *red teaming* is when users adopt an adversarial mindset and try to get the AIs to perform actions they are not designed to.

Leaning on actual humans for testing can be slow and expensive, but since you're obsessing over validation, you should be ready and willing to set these up if automated tests aren't ready or viable.

More often, I see people mining user feedback in other ways, which I'll explore in Chapter 5.

All told, automated tests are a "dual threat," valuable both early because they provide critical dogfooding, and later because they persist and continuously deliver value as the product evolves.

Documentation is another dual threat for the same reasons.

Documentation-Driven Development

Have you ever heard the proverb, "The best way to learn something is to teach it?" That's true of teaching products, and writing documentation is an awesome way to learn about your product—and how to improve it—while teaching.

Engineers are often called upon to write or review documentation for technical products, and I endorse getting deeply involved in this process. If you aren't comfortable writing, partner with another coworker and/or an AI assistant. Provide the technical content and the editorial insight of someone who's been immersed in building the product and learning about their users.

But, for dogfooding, sketching documentation earlier in the product cycle can protect you from later mistakes when they are costly to fix.

You'll notice problems and improve the product. To the extent that the last section was about Test-Driven Development, this one will be about a topic I've found to be nearly as useful: Documentation-Driven Development. Drafts of documentation can be written earlier and more cheaply than tests, even before the code is written.

Before I talk about using docs as dogfooding, I'll provide general advice on structuring documentation to answer the right questions at the right times.

In this section, I'll present four topics:

- Caveats about the limits of documentation
- Building different documentation for different user scenarios: discovery, understanding, and usage
- Helping users find your docs and transition between scenarios
- Writing docs as a dogfooding exercise

Documentation Shouldn't Be Load Bearing

Users would prefer not to read your documentation. Any time spent finding the content and reading it, they could be spending accomplishing their tasks. Users who do consult your content will read it selectively, not cover-to-cover.

Per Chapter 2, be careful when relying on documentation to provide an edge for your product discovery map. Remember that there are three tiers of user knowledge: knowns, known unknowns, and unknown unknowns.

Known unknowns are often features and behaviors they know to expect based on their experience with other similar products, even if they haven't experienced them directly in your product. Here are common unknown unknowns:

- Unexpected dangerous behaviors
- New features
- Nonstandard features that differentiate you from your competitors

Find signifiers (Chapter 2) such as notifications and pop-ups to alert users to new features and non-standard features that differentiate you from your competitors. To prevent users from harmful behaviors, limit affordances (Chapter 8) and provide confirmations (Chapter 3).

With that caveat established, for more complex products, documentation is inevitable and useful. Even in the unlikely event that users never look directly at it, AI assistants will read everything you write and teach it to users.

Scenarios for Documentation Readers

Many software engineers I've worked with, including my past self, either don't document at all, or when they do, it's reference documentation. It's natural to take what we've built, go feature by feature, and explain those features.

But let's shoe-shift: how often do you use reference guides? Of those instances, how many times did you try other types of documentation before you fell back on them? I'll break it down.

In Chapter 2, I introduced the user journey in which users proceed through the discovery, understanding, and usage phases. Each of those activities could need documentation.

Discovery
: A user, often a new one, knows what their goal is, but not which product or feature to use to do it.

Understanding
: A user has gotten stuck somewhere and needs to deepen their knowledge of your product, learning reusable concepts to make them more effective. They are likely intending to become a sticky user, if they aren't already.

Usage
: The user knows which product or feature to use, but not how to use it correctly. They may be a new user or an experienced one tackling an advanced feature.

Here's an example that I'm also shamelessly using to make myself feel better about my early struggles to learn C++.

I took my first university programming course in C++. The textbook was Bjarne Stroustrup's *The C++ Programming Language*, and in the 3rd edition the book was a comprehensive overview of the language. I was just trying to stay afloat, discovering the right tools to solve my algorithms assignments and learning the basics, and instead I got chapter after chapter of the author showing off all these cool and esoteric features of the language—advanced usage documentation.

Maybe it was a good book. As a seasoned engineer with years of C++ experience I might have gotten more out of it, but it was not useful back then. I wish my professor had selected a persona-appropriate text. One of the reviewers of this book confides that they dropped out of computer science because of poorly targeted learning materials, only to return to the field later and become a senior staff engineer and professional computer science teacher. A product as complicated as C++ begs for a careful introduction.

The book was a reference guide when I needed a getting-started guide. That is, it optimized for usage when I needed help with discovery and understanding.

Each of these scenarios requires different types of docs, as summarized in Table 4-1, starting from the outset of the user journey.

Table 4-1. Categories of documentation

Documentation type	Scenario
Persona menu	Discovery
Scenario menu	Discovery
Getting started guide	Understanding
Conceptual guide	Understanding
Usage guide	Usage
Operational guide	Usage
Reference guide	Usage

In this segment, I'll consider documentation for Docker, a popular platform for developing, shipping, and running applications. Its most famous abstraction is the "container," which is an executable program that bundles its dependencies so that it can be distributed and executed across a variety of computing environments.

Discovery

When users are discovering your product, they want to map their scenario onto it.

First, they want to know if they are the target persona. Is your product or feature "for them?" This offers them assurance that, as they work through its details, your design choices will work for them.

One of the most common and effective ways to do this for brand-new users is to provide a *persona menu* on your app or website. Today, when I go to lyft.com, a ride-hailing site, I see headings for "Rider," "Driver," and "Business." I'm told that I'm welcome if I fall into one of these personas, and I can click to learn more.

> Make it clear which personas you are targeting and tailor documentation to each persona.

With a persona match established, now prospective users want to see if it handles their scenarios.

Docker doesn't currently have a persona menu on its website, but it does have a *scenario menu*. It lists three scenarios:

- Fast, consistent delivery of your applications
- Responsive deployment and scaling
- Running more workloads on the same hardware

Users come away with a better idea of whether Docker solves their problems.

Notice how none of these headings has the word "container," the concept for which Docker is best known. This is because users who are unfamiliar with containers won't search for "container," but they may search for the terms in the messages above.

> Meet users where they are; distinguish between what users come in thinking about and what they will need to learn.

Beyond the top-level product discovery, there will be numerous smaller discoveries as users use your product and uncover its features. You'll guide them from one part of your docs to another, or from the product surface to the docs, as illustrated by the product discovery maps we sketched in Chapter 2.

Understanding

Getting started guides propel users to a point where they can start to explore and use the product. That is, they help users transition from discovery to understanding and usage scenarios, while also teaching users via a "learn by doing" approach.

In Chapter 1, I wrote that users want to allocate as little brain space as possible to learning your product. It's easier to follow instructions in a getting-started guide than to memorize concepts.

But for complex products, you may need a *conceptual guide*, which teaches users the product's ontology—a term for a structured product vocabulary introduced in Chapter 2.

> Use conceptual guides to teach primitives or concepts that users will reuse throughout your product.

Conceptual guides are for when users need to take a step back and actually learn things. Once, I was attempting to package up a program into a Docker container. I was flailing, and Docker's usage guides weren't helping. I realized I needed to understand Docker better to make further progress, without knowing exactly what I was missing. So I read through a *conceptual guide* that presented important Docker primitives. I learned something very valuable for my use case—that Docker containers could *nest* within one another. The solution to my problem became simple.

I, like most readers, was a reluctant student, hoping I could skate by on usage guides alone so I could complete my task and move on.

As with all documentation, you need to be able to tell a story of how users will discover your conceptual guide. Link to it liberally from other types of docs. Perhaps Docker could have saved me a lot of time by pointing me to this concept of nesting from its usage guides. I wouldn't have had to read an entire guide.

A key discovery trick is to use synonyms for your concepts to help search-optimize your content, in case people are coming in with a different ontology.

Usage

Once documentation readers are working on a specific task, they become users. For Docker, once I understood nested containers, I needed to know how to create them.

Three common types of usage docs are usage guides, operator's guides, and reference guides, catering to slightly different needs.

Usage guides, or how-to guides, look a lot like getting started guides, in that they provide a step-by-step flow to accomplish a task, but rather than just introducing users to the product, they help them accomplish a specific goal. If your product needs documentation, write usage guides for all your most important scenarios, such as your north star scenarios from various projects. If your product doesn't need docs, you can sketch them to do purposeful dogfooding.

How will users find these docs? It depends on their scenario:

- If they know what they want to do, but not what feature to use, the doc should be named after, or searchable by, that task. Docker's website has guides called "Configure CI/CD," "Deploy to Kubernetes," and so forth.
- If they already know what feature they need, they can find it by the name of the feature. Docker guides include "Building Compose objects," "Containerize your app," and so forth which mention the feature name.
- They may find the desired doc from your product itself, such as via an error message, or via docs for other related tasks or concepts.

Make sure you're embedding ways to find your usage guides from various angles. Docker has an interesting tagging system for their docs. You can click a tag like "DevOps" or "Deployment" and find matching guides.

Operator's guides are a special type of usage guide, often called troubleshooting guides or runbooks. Users in those docs have likely never encountered this failure mode before and are on unfamiliar ground.

Because users need them when something goes wrong, they should be discoverable from error messages, as discussed in Chapter 3. Make them deep linkable (e.g., *docs.docker.com/dhi/troubleshoot/#no-shell, … /#no-package-manager*) for specific problems so that support personnel, error messages, and automated bot responses can link to remediations for specific problems. And keep those links stable and up-to-date!

The final type of usage documentation is a *reference guide*. These are specific to individual features and often cover those surfaces in more detail.

In the same way that scenario tests don't cover every feature in detail like functional tests do, usage guides won't cover all the details either. Usage guides can link out to reference guides which cover the product feature by feature or concept by concept. Reference guides can talk details, corner cases, and advanced usage.

In fact, these guide types correspond to kinds of tests:

- A scenario or e2e test could cover the same ground as a usage guide or operator's guide entry.
- A set of functional tests for a certain feature will be testing everything mentioned in a reference guide.

It's not a bad idea to look over your scenario tests and see if there are any corresponding missing usage guides, and vice versa.

The web of documentation

> *Learning should take place when it is needed, when the learner is interested.*
>
> —Don Norman, author of *The Design of Everyday Things*

Users don't always proceed from discovery to understanding to usage in a straight line. Instead, they seamlessly glide between these scenarios as they do their work. Discovery becomes understanding once they settle on a product, and usage becomes discovery if it opens a new can of worms. Users are thrown into operator's guides as soon as something goes wrong. They switch from usage to understanding as soon as they can't figure out what to do.

Therefore, it's important that docs are heavily interlinked with one another and from your product. Build "trails of breadcrumbs" that help users escalate from usage or troubleshooting scenarios to learning modes, and from problems they are facing to solutions. Usage guides should link to conceptual guides when referring to important concepts. Conceptual guides should link to illustrative examples. And so forth.

Build a web of interlinked documentation.

Writing Documentation as Dogfooding

Imagine you're writing an open source developer tool and you're authoring a getting started guide telling people how to install your software package.

To shoe-shift, you've set up a fresh environment and are installing it from scratch on your machine so that your environment matches that of new users.

You keep running into errors and begin to realize all the tools and environment variables you've set over the weeks as you've developed your project. When you look back at your guide, it's gotten long!

Dissatisfied, you decide to ship a container that folds all the dependencies in so that users don't have to install them. Now you delete all those annoying steps from the guide and replace them with much shorter instructions to run the container.

Measure the quality of a feature's interface by how short the usage guide would be.

Or imagine that you are on call for your SaaS service and have just supported some users whose processes ran out of memory and were struggling to debug what happened. As you create a runbook entry to document what they should do, you realize you could have avoided the problem entirely by letting them set certain resource limits for themselves. You ship the runbook entry, but then you set about demolishing the need for it by adding the configurations.

The process of writing documentation forces us to shoe-shift and consider the user's journey. We get annoyed when what we're writing feels tedious or like it's hard to explain.

If you write thoughtfully, you can channel this pain into improving the product. The main trick is to do it early when it's still cheap to make adjustments. Here are a few examples of incorporating docs writing into your development process:

- Write persona and scenario menus before you start designing. Amazon famously writes fake press releases at the beginning of projects that predict how they'll communicate publicly once the product is launched. These explain to users the value proposition of the product just like a normal press release would. Adopting this "marketing-first" practice will help you understand your target persona and evaluate your product's value to them.
- Write usage guides early while using early versions of your feature. Note unneeded steps or tricky decisions to catch usability problems when it's still cheap to fix them.
- Write conceptual guides to align with the team on precise descriptions of key abstractions. If it's a struggle, consider renaming or reframing. If the concept doesn't seem like something the user should care about, maybe you need to present something higher-level.
- Force yourself to explain to users how to troubleshoot problems that your feature allows to happen. It may even be cheaper to fix safety issues than it is to document, communicate, and support customers who run into them.

Another way to effectively use documentation is to imagine the ideal product experience. Before you've written any code, explain the product experience to your future users and share it with teammates. Your project should then do all the features necessary to make the document true.

This kind of Documentation-Driven Development can be integrated early and deeply into your development process.

Overall, for certain products, documentation aids in discovery, understanding, and usage scenarios, both for humans and AIs. Even for products that don't ship documentation, you may find writing fake docs focuses you on these same scenarios while making dogfooding more engaging.

Testing and documentation are great, but we also need outside perspectives. Since outsiders don't have all day, we need a lightweight option for them to help out. Enter friction logging.

Friction Logging

We've written scenario tests and authored guides, often while using early versions of our product to ensure accuracy. But even the best product thinkers will be frequently surprised by what other humans get up to. So it's time to engage users. But let's start with more forgiving ones.

When dogfooding, we use software built by our company, and *friction logging* is a great way to go about it.

A friction log is an informal document that you write as you use a product. You report any confusion or roadblocks you experience. When you've finished, you hand it off to the engineers or PMs responsible for the product.

Friction logging directs your dogfooding energy toward productive use. Having a short document to deliver helps motivate you to keep going.

In the next two subsections, I'll explain how to write a friction log and then recommend how you can enlist others to log friction for your product.

I learned about friction logging when I was at Stripe, where it was part of the culture. Notably, David Singleton, then the Chief Technology Officer, spent a couple of weeks a year writing friction logs from using various corners of the product and the internal infrastructure.

The week he dogfooded the internal Workflow Engine I was building was very exciting for me and the team. He even went "undercover," asking questions in our support channel via other engineers so he could understand the support experience without us being biased by knowing that the CTO was asking. His friction log was positive and constructive.

David improved our product, inspired us, and helped maintain a culture of cordial friction logging across engineering, while helping him stay up-to-date with the product and infrastructure.

Writing Friction Logs

A friction log is a journal of a scenario with emphasis on the friction. Your goal is simply to report your experience with the product, which the product team will use as they see fit.

Use scenarios to guide your information flow:

- Start by introducing the persona you represent—are you new to the product? What priors do you have that might color your experience?
- Express your intent for using the product.
- The bulk of the document will outline the most important parts of what you experienced.

Here's a friction log for editing and posting a video to Instagram, a social media application:

Example Friction Log

I'm Drewbie (Drew + Newbie), a new user of Instagram, but I've used TikTok before. I want to upload a video but with the sound turned off.

I start a post on my iPhone, and, because I haven't given Instagram permission to my entire photos and videos library, I click into the "manage privacy" and select a video to give permission to. Then I select it again to choose it for a post. I know some recent apps now have a more streamlined flow for this and wonder why Instagram doesn't use it.

I see a row of icons including a microphone. I click the microphone, hoping that will mute the video, but instead I see a "scrubber" pop up with a play button and a "tap to add audio" button. Not what I expected.

I don't see an icon that looks helpful, but then as I play around, I happen to swipe right and notice that there are more icons that were off the screen to choose from. Now I see a "loudspeaker" icon, which allows me to mute. This part was super straightforward, and I noticed the cool "voice boost" feature which I think I can use in the future.

See how I described my experience rather than giving prescriptive advice? It's likely that the Instagram team will have a better idea of what's possible or advisable. For example, if they want to deal with the undiscoverable loudspeaker icon, they could put the icons into two rows, or they could show one of the icons halfway off of the screen to clue that scrolling is a possibility.

My job as friction logger is just to call attention to the problem. If I just said "you should put the icons into two rows," they might feel like I'm trying to do their job for them, decide on their roadmap for them, or they might reject that specific idea and not brainstorm other options. The less I know the people I'm friction logging for, the more important it is to tread carefully.

I glossed over some of the flows that worked well, but I did sprinkle in some praise when the product experience suited me. This makes the friction stand out and lets the product team know where they're on the right track.

When you're done, hand it over to the team, expecting that they'll sift through the feedback and triage any action items.

Receiving Friction Logs

It's very useful to receive friction logs. Knowing the ground truth of how a user experienced your product is gold.

But how do you get other people to engage with your product? Even though friction logging can be fun, people are busy, and they won't do it for nothing in return. Here are some people to consider:

Yourself
: Put on your newbie hat.

Early adopters
: Ask them to write friction logs.

New teammates
: Invite them to log friction as a way to ramp up on the details of the product.

Developers, designers, data scientists, etc.
: Gather folks for social product usage, such as for "bug bashes" or hackathons.

And when you get the feedback, don't be defensive—treat it as a gift:

- As mentioned above, don't ask people to open tickets or follow any kind of process. This puts up hoops that make people hesitant to spend the time. It also sends a signal that their feedback isn't worth your time.
- Close the loop. If somebody's friction log results in an improvement, let them know, ideally in a way that their manager can also take note of. My company has a "kudos" system for this sort of thing.
- If you or your team are feeling overwhelmed, don't shoot the messenger. Deal with the time crunch when triaging the product improvements implied by the feedback.

Friction Logging Culture

Friction logging should be a safe space in which you are free to comment and nitpick on others' products, and in which the receiving team feels comfortable choosing whether or when to prioritize what's been found. If each side knows their role, the interactions are generally awesome.

It helps if it's a cultural norm. Without specific norms, providing feedback to a team out of the blue can feel aggressive or critical, and it can be unclear about whether you're expecting them to drop what they're doing and fix your problem. If you nitpick, you may worry that others will find you pedantic. Unclear expectations heighten worries about offending people.

If it's not already a norm, you might leverage the fact that it's a predefined practice that you can find on the internet. When I introduced it to folks at my current company, I referred to existing blogs to explain what I was doing, and it was well-received. Soon after, I noticed others starting to do friction logs.

Friction logging is a fun and productive way to engage in dogfooding, and it's something you should solicit as part of your product process.

I wanted to cap off this chapter by talking about samples, which are reference examples showing common applications of your product. Samples, done right, beautifully combine testing, documentation, and friction logging.

Samples

Not all products can use samples, but applications for productivity, creativity, and product development often benefit. By way of example, suppose your product is a spreadsheet program like Microsoft Excel or Google Sheets.

Like tests and docs, samples come in multiple varieties:

- Feature samples, like functional tests, focus on demonstrating a single feature like sorting or filtering.
- Scenario samples, like scenario tests and usage guides, demonstrate a combination of features that aid a key user scenario. For example, an office supply budget shows off general budgeting best practices while also being directly useful for folks doing supply budgets.

I'll use this latter example to work through a few pieces of sample-writing advice:

- Subject your samples to automated tests to keep them working and to double as scenario or e2e tests. Make sure your budget spreadsheet template loads without errors. Your test could plug in some numbers and check the remaining cash on hand.
- Be specific, using concrete scenarios and language. Prefill your data with a software company like "iniTECH" with plausible purchases like red staplers and roach killer. Users have a much easier time extrapolating from concrete things than they do disambiguating abstract terms like "item 1" or "foo."
- Teach users why you made certain choices in your samples, as you would with code comments. If your budgeting sample is targeted at spreadsheet beginners, perhaps you would make little descriptive headings and link to documentation on the use of relative versus absolute cell references.
- Think about the discovery scenario—how will users find the right sample given a problem they are facing? For feature samples, what if they don't know the feature that solves their problem? You could list your template in a template catalog, and if you have a lot of templates, use a tagging system and file it under "accounting" or "finance."

- Friction log as you author the sample and use your experience to feed back into the product. If another team is responsible for writing the samples, welcome them to report friction.

Chapter Summary

Throughout product design and development, seek ways to use your product and put product pressure on it, ensuring it will stand up to real-world usage.

Testing, documenting, and sharing friction logs are all effective ways to do this.

Not all tests are created equal—some are better suited for product testing, others for system testing. Scenario and end-to-end tests reliably document your product and ensure it continues to function, while functional tests round out your test coverage.

Similarly, not all documentation serves the same purpose. You may need a few types of documentation for different scenarios in your users' journeys. Usage guides and getting started guides are great structured ways to try out your product, and writing early conceptual guides helps you and your team refine your ideas and your product communication strategy.

Finally, friction logging is an excellent way to get actionable and candid experiential feedback from your coworkers.

Exercises

1. Choose a Wikipedia page you're interested in, and a line from that page. Find the original author of that line and record your experience with a friction log.
2. Read the friction log I wrote in answer to the first question. Suppose you were new to the Wikipedia development team and tasked with processing that feedback and polishing the UI. What information would you gather, and what improvements would you investigate?
3. You're on the WikiBlame feature crew and shoring up test coverage. (You can go to WikiBlame by picking an interesting Wikipedia page, clicking "View History", and then selecting "Find addition/removal"). Make a test plan with at least two of the most important scenario tests. Assume your test framework allows you to simulate UI interactions.
4. Microsoft PowerPoint has a feature called "Animation" that allows presenters to make a series of clicks to reveal content on a slide progressively. Their usage guide has a section called "Animate or make words appear one line at a time." In terms of the three major user scenarios for documentation, why did they choose that phrasing?

Finally, here's some homework. Document something you're working on. If you haven't built it yet, document an important user scenario based on how you imagine it will be. If it already exists, go through a recommended flow yourself and write docs to match your experience.

Answers

1. Here's my friction log for trying to attribute a line of Wikipedia to an author. Make sure yours records a bit about your persona and intent, and that it reports your experience without being too overt about suggesting concrete improvements.

   I'm Drewbie, a software engineer, and I've mainly used Wikipedia as a reader, with very few edits to my name, so I'm new to the power-user tools. In reading the page listing past Microsoft Puzzle Hunts, I noticed that one listing had a broken link, and I wasn't sure what the appropriate link was, so I'd like to contact the original editor.

   I'm a software engineer used to *git blame* for attributing lines of source code to authors, so I'm hoping for something similar. I first clicked "View history", but it wasn't in a usable format, and there was no "blame" button. I thought maybe "View source" would do the trick, and looked for "blame" and similar, but that didn't work either.

   I went back to the revision history and looked more carefully. "Find edits by user" didn't work because I didn't know the username. At this stage, I consulted Google, which told me to click "Find addition/removal."

   On that page, entitled WikiBlame—ooh, "blame"—I found a search box for a term, so I picked a phrase from the line of text I was interested in and searched for that. I found a list of entries like so:

   ```
   Comparing differences in 02:48, 31 August 2005 between 210 and 211
   while coming from 196:OO Comparing differences in 04:34, 11 August
   2005 between 217 and 218 while coming from 210:XX
   ```

   I didn't understand much of this, especially the numbers and the XX and OO, but at the bottom of the list, I found:

   ```
   Insertion found between 02:37, 31 August 2005 and 02:41, 31 August
   2005: here
   ```

   Insertion sounded like the origin of the line, so I clicked the *here* link. I couldn't find a user name anywhere! After a minute of searching, I found an IP address, and I realized that an anonymous user had posted the edit from that IP. (It would have been clearer if it were labeled.)

If I gave this to the Wikipedia team, they would sift through my friction log. They might ignore my feedback that there was no "blame," reasoning that most editors aren't software engineers. On the other hand, my confusion that the IP address was standing in for a username seems generally valid, and it might prompt them to put a label there, such as *Author*.

2. If I were on the app team, I would tend to ignore the feedback about *blame* because only a software engineer persona would resonate with that terminology unless it's more common among Wikipedia editors than I think. I'd be more inclined to clean up the "Comparing differences" text, which seems esoteric. And labeling the IP address/username field as an author seems like a straightforward usability win, especially if anonymous editors are common.

3. Here are the two tests I chose. Are the ones you picked as, or more, common?

   I assume most people arrive at WikiBlame via the View History page, so I want to test that flow. I'd create a simple test page with a couple of edits, then render the corresponding View History page. I'd search the page for "Find addition/removal" and pull out the corresponding link to WikiBlame. Now I want to make sure a simple search will work, especially given all those pre-populated boxes. So, I would plug in a search term into the Search box and simulate a click of Start. I'd do a very light verification of the results, as I likely have functional tests that check the results list more thoroughly.

   I imagine the most popular pages are also very popular for people to use WikiBlame, so I want to test scalability. I'd look at how many edits there were to a page like Taylor Swift and programmatically generate a test page with a similarly long edit history and edits scattered throughout the document. Then I'd initiate a search query on that page and make sure it completes within the timeout. I'd also check the results and make sure the correct number of edits for that term were returned.

4. "Make words appear one line at a time" is an attempt to help people who don't know the "Animate" term find this documentation and caters to the discovery scenario. "Animate" is for users who already know the feature they need, and helps users in the understanding or usage scenarios.

CHAPTER 5

Keeping Up with Users

> *In [the] Diffusion of Innovations, it is not people who change, but the innovations themselves...The success of an innovation depends on how well it evolves to meet the needs of more and more demanding and risk-averse individuals in a population.*
>
> —"The Innovation-Adoption Curve" by High Tech Strategies

My two-plus decades in the software industry have given me a front row seat to the rise of incremental shipping. I have felt the benefits deeply, and it leads me to push my teams to ship more frequently.

My first ship, and therefore my first shipped bug, was Microsoft Visual C++ compiler in 2005, and it was a doozy. Customers received the compiler on CD, installed it on their computer, ran it and, if they happened to be using Simplified Chinese, the compiler simply crashed. Always!

There was no way to distribute a patch, and the next release was years out, so instead, we put an article in the knowledge base with the workaround—to delete a certain file from the app's directory before attempting to compile code.

That was my worst bug ever. This says more about the improving software industry than my improving skill.

Later, I worked on Windows 7 which took three years to build and ship, still in boxes of CDs for some customers. We had no unit tests or feature tests—we still relied heavily on test engineers to test our code. But at least Windows could be patched for critical fixes.

In 2009, I moved on to Facebook, where deploys happened every week! I was so happy. We'd cut the build on Sunday night and stabilize it before a Tuesday release. Releases were a paranoid and nerve-wracking experience, but they were weekly.

I joined a platform team that ran an API service to power developers' social applications. A few weeks into my tenure, my team held a testing hackathon. Someone had built a rudimentary test framework, and our job was to test our existing APIs. To my knowledge, we were the first team at Facebook, now five years into the company's life, to write automated tests.

The company evolved. As teams tested more of their code, deploys needed less manual testing, and rollouts went to five days a week, and then finally to continuous deploys multiple times a day. Feature flags and A/B tests peppered the codebase, ensuring safe and controlled feature rollouts.

By the time I joined Stripe in 2018, there was already a good testing culture along with multiple deploys a day, but they were managed by a human being who shepherded the deploys. But soon they switched to automatic continuous deployment of most services. I stopped paying much attention to most deployments, trusting in my tests and the existing test coverage to spot regressions.

The software industry has changed for the better. More software has moved to the cloud. Even venerable client software like Visual C++ gets far more patches than it did twenty years ago.

I imagine the change has been even more wrenching in the auto industry, where 8 of the top 10 manufacturers now receive over-the-air (OTA) updates. Even Mars rovers can!

One result is that users get more value faster. Even if it didn't improve the overall product trajectory, Figure 5-1 demonstrates that at any point in time, users are getting more value.

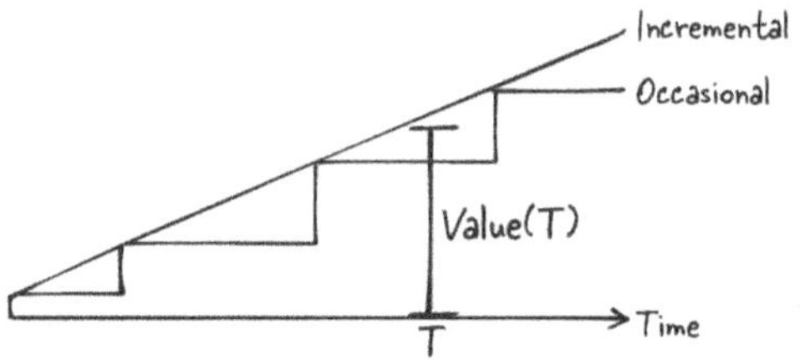

Figure 5-1. The value of a product delivered to a user over time

Even better, these days it's so much easier to listen and respond to users. No more permanent bugs.

And because we've automated so many change processes, we end up moving faster, even though we spend more time testing.

In this chapter, we'll discuss how to capture qualitative and quantitative data, making good use of it to define and refine a product continuously.

I'll start by noting that our engineering job description is not just developing a product but is also creating the means of that product's improvement over time—a set of artifacts I'll call a digital twin.

But first, and most fundamentally, we must architect the code so that we can iterate quickly. So I'll lay the groundwork of "designing for change"—the software engineering principles that make our codebases and products more malleable and allow us to change them with more confidence.

Then, I'll talk about qualitative data—getting user feedback throughout the product cycle. I'll dwell on support interactions, creating a virtuous cycle of providing users with responsive support, which leads to more great feedback.

Finally, I'll turn to quantitative data. You'll learn to choose and collect product metrics that help your team make great decisions.

By the end, hopefully you'll know everything you want to know about your product's performance.

A New Job Description—Digital Twin Caretaker

None of this revolution was free. The amount of work the industry underwent to achieve these faster cadences was borderline heroic and amounted to nothing less than a near-complete revision of our job descriptions.

Famously, in 2014 Microsoft merged the Test and Engineer disciplines into one role to achieve faster cadences—handing off your code to a tester is just too slow—and to encourage software engineers to own their own quality outcomes.

As a rule:

- We write tests ourselves.
- We create metrics and monitor our product.
- We emit data into data pipelines and assist with product analytics.
- We're exposed to feedback channels to have direct connections to our customers.
- We stage rollouts and perform A/B tests.

The combination of technologies designed to capture and simulate what happens in the real world is called a *digital twin*.

> A digital twin is a virtual representation and set of simulations of a production system and the hardware substrate it runs on.

You might have heard of digital twins in the context of technologies like self-driving cars, where the R&D department has a high-fidelity digital representation of the car, its sensors, and a simulated world for it to operate in. It knows about human driver behavior and passenger safety constraints, and can test and refine the driver software in simulations.

What would the equivalent be in a typical software product?

The digital twin is a combination of automated tests and test environments, metrics and alerting, beta tiers, production instrumentation, analytics, and traces. It also contains feedback from feedback forums, customer support chat logs, repro cases, and transcriptions of customer discovery interviews. It's got anything that helps paint a quantitative or qualitative picture of how our product is performing in the real world.

Our modern role is to complete that picture—to build out our products' digital twins alongside the product itself, and then to learn from it when monitoring rollouts, comparing performance in A/B tests, and feeding feedback into our roadmap. Several parts of the digital twin are covered in other chapters:

- We craft the tests discussed in Chapter 4 based on what we're seeing in production or think we'll see in production.
- We load simulations (Chapter 9) that are fed with captured real-world requests or reasonable facsimiles to stress test our digital twin.
- We document friction logs, also Chapter 4, which capture what it's like to use our product.

I survey the rest here.

Designing for Change

In *Diffusion of Innovations*, Everett Rogers points out that technological innovation and the spread of technology happen in a loop. This cycle is anchored by feedback and iteration. To spread, a product must adapt itself to appeal to increasingly risk-averse and poorly connected demographics. If we want our technology to spread quickly, we must therefore build in rapid feedback cycles so that we can find out what's blocking each new wave of new users.

To this end, the engineer has three roles. Each feature we build should:

- Fulfill the product requirements, of course.
- Establish trust that it does so and will continue to as more changes come in, so that we can automate our delivery mechanisms.
- Make itself easy to evolve as new requirements come in so that we don't get stuck.

Without these three ingredients, you will find your team more distant from your customers, subject to too many constraints that prevent you from serving them. But doing all these things at once is, to me, the fun challenge of software engineering.

Here's a case study that will show how a team built more trust and evolvability into their codebase and was therefore able to reconnect with the users and their most urgent needs.

Case Study Introduction

Iterating decisively requires a combination of culture and technology, as I learned firsthand in 2015, when I moved from Facebook to join its recent acquisition, Oculus VR, a virtual reality company.

In the 2010s, Facebook was obsessed with rapid iteration, infamously adopting a "move fast and break things" approach before getting enough blowback that it refined the tagline in 2014 to a more mature, if less catchy, "move fast with stable infra."

This approach was new to the Oculus team, who had been struggling with slipped deadlines and a hard-to-evolve codebase.

From my perspective, the most important part of this approach was that Facebook built a lot of great developer tools—tools that Oculus could use if only their product were built on Facebook's stack.

Developer productivity engineering

In the 2000s, Google pioneered the concept of a centralized team whose mission was to make development for the company's engineers iterative, safe, and fast. Today, this is often called the Developer Productivity team. As of 2025, teams geared toward engineering productivity now tend to comprise about 15–20% of engineering headcount at medium to large tech companies.

Before I joined Oculus, I worked on Facebook's developer productivity team. Here are some examples of what they built by the time of the Oculus acquisition in 2015:

- A type system, Hack, that they had layered on top of PHP to allow for safer code changes and refactorings.
- An easy-to-use feature flags system for experimentation and safe rollouts.
- A fast, flexible production observability platform in which one did not need to specify the indices being queried in advance. This allowed us to query whatever we were curious about without making changes to the data pipeline.
- A database abstraction layer, `EntSchema`, that made model development easy and powerful. I'll present this one in more detail in Chapter 8.

Some of the first tasks for a new "dev prod" team are often geared toward building and making use of digital twins—think, continuous integration solutions that exercise all of our tests.

Analysis paralysis

When I was assigned to help Oculus replatform their app store and login system on top of Facebook's infrastructure, with the goal being to speed up the team's progress, I wanted to make the goodies I was used to available to my new teammates.

As we drew up plans to rewrite their codebase, I noticed that the engineers on this team tended to try to predict the future two years out and imagine features they might want to build one day. This made for marathon design sessions and over-engineered solutions.

Over time I gained more empathy for this approach. Their attitude was appropriate, given their tooling situation. Iteration wasn't easy on their existing technology stack. The team lacked a good digital twin and was missing proper abstraction layers—their REST API was mapped one-to-one to their database, so the database was tightly coupled to their clients. They felt like they would be stuck with their decisions for a long time.

Our job as cultural and technology ambassadors was to sell them on the tech and practices of their new corporate parent. To show what designing for change looks like in practice, I'll report how it went.

The Technological Underpinnings of Change

What are the components of an iterative software stack that will allow teams to keep up with changing product requirements and increased user demands?

Before I present the list, I want to acknowledge that some teams have far more constraints than others, such as the need to maintain backward compatibility, and with varying ability to collect usage data. Thus, there may be items on this list that may not apply to your current team. Others will seem daunting but doable, and I'm here to give you an extra nudge. There should be something here for everyone.

Here are my top technology recommendations for adaptive teams. If you have or want a Developer Productivity team, this is a solid TO-DO list.

First, the basics of quality:

- Always write automated tests (Chapter 4), directing particular effort toward exercising the most important scenarios. Solid test coverage, with the most important scenarios tested, breeds confidence that changes won't break the most important user interactions with the product.

- Use *continuous integration* (CI) tests, which must pass before new code is committed to your source repository, so that you quickly find bugs when they are introduced.
- Leverage *feature flags*, which are toggles that allow you to turn features on or off, independently from deploying code. Feature flags enable careful and yet near-instant change. And they should allow you to gradually ramp up the introduction of new code, creating a sense of confidence in safely trying new things.
- Code review to ensure that each code change meets customer needs and is maintainable and well-tested.
- Instrument your product with *operational metrics*, which track factors like error rates, flow completion rates, performance, and capacity in real time. Monitor them and alert when they go awry, and especially make sure that they are calibrated to catch errors early during a bad release.
- Adopt resilience primitives such as queues, retries, and rate limits, which limit the "blast radius" or damage that one faulty system can do to other systems in the event of a problem.

What's the common theme of those items? Well, if we are going to build a system that delivers for users, say, 99.9% of the time, even as we constantly update it, we must be able to trust our change management systems to prevent the worst problems.

> Build into each component the mechanisms for trusting it. That is, each change should come with validation that it works and fulfills the product requirements and will continue to do so.

At Oculus, one of my key contributions was to establish a culture of testing. We were able to leverage Facebook's test frameworks, combining them with some Oculus-specific test helpers that made testing a breeze. That, along with a couple of months of asking for more tests in code review, successfully established a new culture. This ultimately led to more shipping and better quality.

Beyond trust, we also want to make changes themselves easier and more effective:

- Track *product metrics* that are tied to business outcomes, customer adoption, and customer success, to help you make good decisions about what to change.
- Obsess over tools and processes to overcome backward compatibility constraints that build up over time. For example, build database migration tools or the ability to make new versions of your API that will help users who upgrade without breaking existing users.

- Use abstractions such as modules, type systems, and protocols designed for versioned backward compatibility, to help teams coordinate using well-abstracted interfaces. These help teams make independent progress by separating concerns.

> Build into each component the mechanisms for its evolution. Components should be extensible, maintainable, and instrumented for key decision-making.

I remember showing EntSchema, a modeling framework (discussed in Chapter 8) that made it trivial to safely codegen new fields and do database backfills, to an Oculus engineer. I argued that we could remove unnecessarily speculative fields from their PRs because we could always add more later.

Okay, so if we establish trust and make change easy, what comes next? Here are some more advanced techniques:

- Deploy as frequently as possible so that you can ship critical patches and new features frequently. If you're running an online service, prefer continuous deployment (CD) and use blue/green or rainbow deployments so that you can roll out new versions gradually and instantly roll back if there are issues.
- Run a beta program or early adopters program so that your most avid customers can help you test and refine new features and can flag upcoming releases that might break them. This can sometimes be enabled using feature flags.
- Have gradual rollouts, given to a random, unbiased selection of people before ramping to 100%. Make sure it's not the same cohort each time so you're not always subjecting the same users unwittingly to unstable versions.
- Have a flexible analytics platform that allows you to easily change the queries you're performing as you become curious about new dynamics or need to narrow down unforeseen problems.
- Experiment using an A/B testing framework to compare the performance of different versions of features.

In fact, a flexible analytics platform called Scuba was the key selling point about Facebook's infrastructure that convinced the Oculus team to migrate. The fact that they could do real-time slicing and dicing of product data without having to manually build an index for every query they might want to do was a huge draw.

Find the time to improve

How much trust in code is built into your current codebase? How easy is it to evolve the code? Which of the above techniques and technologies might help?

It's a big TO-DO list, but there are reasons for optimism. The developer technology ecosystem is becoming increasingly sophisticated, allowing you to integrate brilliant off-the-shelf technologies. Meanwhile, coding assistants and agents are increasing our collective productivity—we can use some of the extra time to level up as software organizations.

While product requests are coming in from all sides, it feels like there's never time to invest in my stack. How to find the time and motivation? Above, I mentioned that companies spend 15–20% of their headcount on developer efficiency, and I think that's often a good number for individual teams as well. See if your team will carve out time on the roadmap for the highest priority productivity improvements, being aware that these tend to pay off over longer time horizons. They are critical but may never seem urgent.

Oculus certainly had specific needs relative to the rest of Facebook—our user accounts were not Facebook accounts, we supported high-performance, graphically intensive games, and so forth. We needed special libraries and infrastructure while also sharing as much common infrastructure as we could.

Technology shapes culture

Technology has a profound effect on team culture, which means that often the solution to problems with process or practices is technological, not cultural. That's good news because engineers can be part of the solution.

After a few months of rewriting their product on the new infrastructure, the Oculus team were full converts. With a better digital twin—well-tested code to guard against regressions, powerful production observability, and infra designed for rapid change to help them correct design mistakes—they wouldn't have to be so risk-averse and painstaking in their thinking and could focus on delivering awesome stuff. Someone even distributed a fun T-shirt celebrating the new tech stack that I still wear sometimes.

It was easy to see the downstream effects of the rewrite. Over the next couple of years, the team was able to design and build a lot of new features rapidly on the new stack. In Chapters 7 and 8, I show how teams can take advantage of an iterative approach to improve focus during design and prioritization, resulting in higher-quality products.

You don't need to do a big rewrite to lower the fear in your team. I remember a famous series of posters that were pinned up on the walls of Facebook's headquarters, asking us, in all caps:

> WHAT WOULD YOU DO IF YOU WEREN'T AFRAID?
>
> —Facebook Analog Research Laboratory

I believe that the posters were intended to foster a spirit of creativity and boldness, whether by investigating an unproven high-impact idea or by giving a coworker some tough, but needed, constructive feedback.

But fear is often valid and rational. So my extension of this question would be: "What would it take not to be afraid?" What sorts of problems with process and practices could be addressed by technology?

- Do you feel that your teammates consistently under-test their code? Consider an improvement to your test frameworks that makes it easier and more fun to write tests. Or craft a fake library to make it easier to test a service that your team depends on.
- Does it take weeks of careful testing to stage and roll out a new version? Perhaps feature flags that can ramp traffic will make the deployments run more smoothly. Continuous integration testing can reduce the need for dogfooding or manual testing.
- Do you argue for hours over prioritization decisions? Maybe you lack data. Maybe collect more product metrics, and if they are difficult to add, look for a better product analytics solution.

One of the primary benefits of a trustworthy and adaptable tech stack is that it's ready to spring into action the next time you get that unexpected user feedback that makes you realize you need a new feature.

Getting User Feedback

When users give us feedback, their stories go into our digital twin alongside the tests. We learn how the outside world perceives our product, and how they interact with it.

In Chapter 4, we gave ourselves feedback through dogfooding and friction logging for early in the product lifecycle.

Now, it's time to learn from external users. We can rely on techniques like: Beta versions, feedback widgets, champions programs, surveys, and user support.

Beta Versions Lower the Blast Radius of Failures

Whether your early adopters are friends and family, consumer enthusiasts, or enterprises who want to test your software before deploying it widely, testing with users who've opted into a less solid experience can get you feedback without losing the trust of the masses. They help you move a little faster and lower the blast radius of bugs.

I've seen this work well in two ways: early release programs and beta tiers.

Early release programs give consenting users updates before everybody else. Even these people will have limited patience, so you should still maintain enough quality to keep them as happy customers.

Beta tiers are versions of your internet service that customers can point to in some of their environments to run tests before those changes hit their main production traffic. This lets them run the tests that matter to them and let you know before their users are impacted.

Feedback Widgets Help People Raise Their Voices

Embedded forms that make it extremely convenient for customers to give you feedback will hint to users that you care while directing their insights at you, rather than venting their frustrations using one-star app store ratings or rants on social media.

It's best if feedback is *contextual*, meaning that they can give feedback with all the context you need without being particularly thoughtful. For example:

- In documentation, allow inline comments about what's confusing or out-of-date.
- Pop-up a feedback request when you notice users have been using a new feature you want responses about.
- In a mobile app, collecting context like screenshots, app routes, app version, phone model, and OS version, along with their comments.
- Inline widgets in the offensive content they want to flag.
- Prompt them to provide the specific types of additional context that you care about.

Champions Programs Offer Depth

Sometimes you need deeper contributions from your community—in-depth feedback, evangelism and brand ambassadorship, or open source contributions. Champions programs, such as Microsoft's Most Valuable Professional program, can offer incentives to such people to help them feel appreciated for their desire to help and motivated to keep doing so.

Example perks range from free software or services, early access, networking opportunities, conference tickets, and reputational benefits.

Surveys Offer Breadth

Designing scientific, repeatable user surveys is outside the scope of this book, but I wanted to highlight two uses of surveys I've seen be useful for product-minded engineers.

First, free-form answers are often a goldmine of user empathy. For example, if your organization sends Net Promoter Score (NPS) sentiment surveys, ask to see the answers to the free-form questions.

Another type of survey is a *feature survey*. In these, you point to individual pain points you think users have and ask users to rate or rank how much they would like you to fix them.

During product planning, such surveys help validate assumptions about what users actually want versus what teams think they want. And with free-form responses, they can also reveal surprises.

The User Support Flywheel

Let's dwell on user support, because for many teams, it's the most powerful source of product feedback. Engineers are also commonly heavily involved. In many organizations, engineers have opportunities to provide support, whether directly with users or indirectly when support personnel escalate requests.

Every support interaction is product feedback in disguise. That is, you should always be thinking about two things: directly unblocking the asker as well as gaining their feedback to improve your product. Thought of this way, support is not a burden but a win-win proposition.

Even better, this becomes self-sustaining because, if support is good, users will come back for more, providing the critical qualitative feedback and user insight that your product needs. Meanwhile, the team becomes more practiced and efficient at providing support. These "flywheel effects" are powerful, once they get going.

In this section, I'll show how to spin up a great support practice without overburdening the engineers on your team.

> Strive to spin up a feedback flywheel in which users keep coming back to get great support while helping you improve your product.

Providing quality support has a few simple components:

- Be responsive and eliminate barriers to entry.
- Be gracious.
- Explore the user's scenario.
- Unblock them.
- Ask how your product could have served the user better.
- Scale your support, making it more efficient as the user base grows.

To illustrate these aspects, here's a case study.

At Stripe, I was the tech lead for an internal framework for engineers called the Workflow Engine. It orchestrates other engineers' stateful or long-running processes. Built on popular open source technology, it is scalable, fault-tolerant, and helps developers avoid common problems of distributed systems.

It's a big framework, and developers from hundreds of teams stress it in various ways, so there are many questions. In surveys on Blind, an anonymous professional community, our team was repeatedly voted best for internal support by the engineers across the company. This reputation reportedly persisted after I left the team.

How did we do it while still building new stuff?

Eliminate barriers to entry

Feedback is a gift, and if you disincentivize your users, they won't give it.

The Workflow Engine team was committed to responding to questions within 30–60 minutes during business hours. We called this our "support SLA."

Many product and infrastructure teams avoid engaging directly with their customers. They create barriers, such as requiring users to open support tickets and wait days for assistance. Even if the initial response is quick, delays often occur during the follow-up. This reaction is a natural response to the pressure and distraction that a flood of customer inquiries can cause, but it harms both users and the product.

In contrast, Workflow Engine offers direct support in Slack, the corporate messaging app, allowing better responsiveness and enabling others to jump in easily to answer questions.

Welcoming users also means being gracious during your interactions.

Be gracious

They may feel like it's their fault that they have to ask for support, and you can embarrass them with the wrong words. Users have much less knowledge of your product than you do, so it's easy to assume they're asking silly questions or doing silly things. Don't fall into this trap. Practice empathy, and you'll find it's much easier not to get frustrated.

Always make it clear that constructive feedback is allowed and welcome. It's not them, it's the product. (If they made a mistake, there's no need to point it out; they will figure that out on their own, and if they don't, it's not your job to correct that.)

Little empathetic notes like, "that sounds frustrating," or explicit goal alignment, like, "Let's get this fixed," can show the user that you're in their corner.

Also, lead with curiosity, not contempt or impatience. Your goal is to improve your product and your users' experience with it, not to improve *them*.

For example, it can seem like users think you can read their minds. You'll need to get used to that. Patiently ask for the relevant information that they've left out.

Explore the user's scenario

By exploring the timeline of the users' interactions, you can gain more insight into their goals, what went wrong, and how to unblock them.

A *root cause analysis* (RCA) pinpoints what went wrong. Perhaps the user did something unusual, the user is confused, the product has a bug or feature gap, or some combination of these. I don't mean that you should immediately be trying to identify the exact line of code that caused a bug—that can come later. But you should be figuring out whether it's a bug and roughly where it is, enough so that you can show the user how to work around it.

Let's see how the timeline can help us both find a root cause and unblock the user.

Configuration
: Knowing facts about their setup, such as their application version, will help perform an RCA and inform remediations like "please upgrade your app."

Intent
: Were the actions they took the right ones given that goal? What are the workarounds? Is their scenario even supported?

Prior actions
: These will inform the RCA, because often the thing that went wrong was before the incident itself. You might rewind a user back to an earlier action and have them try it again or take a different approach.

Incident
: Understand the details of what happened and what its impact was, to aid in RCA and in prioritization.

Further attempts
: What did they try afterwards? Asking whether they are still blocked will help you prioritize a resolution or choose which advice to give them.

Which of these is most useful depends on the situation, so treat them as a menu to choose from. The Workflow Engine was a complex, flexible platform, meaning people didn't always know the best design patterns to reach their goals. Therefore, we often had to trace back to their original intent to see if they were on the right track. Stripe even had a Slack emoji, "WAYRTTD?" standing for "What are you really trying to do?" It was a quick, lightly humorous way to ask.

Start by unblocking the user

What's best for the user isn't always answering the question they asked. Often, it's the answer to a question they didn't know to ask.

For example, one common issue for Workflow Engine users was nonidempotent operations.

Idempotency is a property of a function that allows it to be called multiple times without producing different effects after the initial call. For example, if our customer were transferring money, we wouldn't want the operation to move the money a second time if the first attempt timed out. (If there's one rule for using distributed systems effectively, it's to make your operations idempotent!) In performing an RCA, I would notice that users in sticky situations had nonidempotent operations. I was always tempted to suggest hardening their operations to prevent future issues. But that wouldn't help them unwind their immediate problem—the damage was already done.

Which advice should I give? Should I offer an immediate solution or revisit their earlier design decisions?

I've made a lot of users happy by giving both answers, leaving it up to them to navigate their constraints. I usually provide the immediate unblock first, to unwind any tension they may be feeling, and then follow with the advice.

Ask: how could your product have served the user better?

The platonic ideal of a product is dazzlingly perfect. It requires no support. It's safe to use; the documentation answers people's questions; and all user needs are automated. It sings. It dances.

So whenever I receive a support request, I also perform an RCA on the product. How did it allow the user to reach this point? The user may not be trying to give feedback —they are often more focused on getting unblocked—but that doesn't mean I shouldn't pay attention to the clues.

The same user scenario timeline that helped unblock the user helps me pinpoint product feedback. I retrace the user's decisions, wondering "how could my product have helped here?" Perhaps a better error message or better documentation would have created a better timeline.

On the Workflow Engine, after a few customers got themselves into trouble with nonidempotent operations, I had a brainwave—we could easily add testing!

Stripe developers used our integration test framework to test their Workflows. So I made an improvement. If the dev marked their operation as retryable, our test framework would run the operation twice and compare the results between the two runs. If they mismatched, it would raise an error.

This found lots of issues. It improved our users' products better and reduced our support burden. And the idea arose, not from product feedback, but from support.

You're busy—what if you don't immediately have the time or knowledge to isolate the product feedback?

Now that you've collected the user scenario, just log a TO-DO to come back to. Later, you can open a ticket or consult with your team. Keeping an organized task list that recalls the original context is a great way to make sure you don't forget the important details or the strategic questions they imply. Writing things down also reduces stress and gives you space to focus on customers during support.

Next, let's talk about how to scale support. First, we'll try to keep a direct connection to our users for as long as is reasonable. Then, when that strategy has run its course, I'll address the engineer's role when there are go-betweens such as AI assistants and support personnel.

Scaling support while keeping your direct connection to users

The Workflow Engine team managed to scale support to hundreds of other engineering teams while not de-focusing the team entirely from feature work. We used a few tricks:

- We had a support "rotation."
- We carefully codified the role of the support person.
- We set up a culture of continuous improvement of the product and the documentation.

First, we created a support rotation. Every week, the rotation designated a "runner" whose main job was to provide support during business hours. The rest of the team focused on their work in depth, and were encouraged not to jump in on support unless the runner hadn't responded within a reasonable timeframe.

When, a few months later, the load became exhausting, we needed to lower the runner's burden without disrupting the whole team. Here's what we developed over time:

- The runner's role was like an (American football) quarterback—they always got the ball first, but sometimes they would hand it off or pass it to another team member if they had too much to do or were not the right expert.
- The runner should not complete normal work during their support week. Project schedules treated run weeks like vacations. This lowered stress and increased support quality over time.
- Leave it better than you found it. The runner should make at least one improvement that would make support more efficient over time, be it a bug fix, an automation, a product usability win, or extra documentation. At the end of each week, they'd report their improvement in the team meeting.

In other words, during run weeks, support was the job.

This worked well! Here are a couple of notable improvements that came out of our culture of continuous improvement:

Early on, we noticed there were too many back-and-forths with users, so we added an automated bot that asked users to provide their configuration, such as their programming language, to be available when a human arrived.

We also made many improvements to the docs to more efficiently answer users' questions.

We adopted the practice of "answering with docs." That is, if a user's asking a question that isn't clearly answered by documentation but should be, we'd update the docs and link the user to the answer. Because we needed to be more thoughtful when writing docs, the user has to wait a bit longer for an answer, but now the content is available for future users and AI support bots.

If you can't show the user the updated docs, for example, because they need to be reviewed before going out, you could author a draft change and then copy that for the user, then get the update reviewed and checked in later on.

Just as codebases should be adaptable, so docs should be. Make it very easy for team members to edit the docs, or they will rot.

Overall, scaling support required continued creativity and investment, but at no point did we need to undertake some massive project to make it work.

That said, there are limits. We were an internal framework. If your product has hundreds of millions of users, what I outlined won't scale.

Providing support when there are added layers

Your company may have layers in between engineering and customers, such as AI chat assistants, support personnel, community moderators, or solutions architects, depending on the nature of your product. Or, it may simply charge for engineering support. You may only be given support problems that the first line cannot figure out, which is a separate set of problems from the ones that will give you the most useful product feedback. If this is your situation, find ways to stay connected to users. For example, if you've never done a rotation with a support team, I highly recommend it! Be sure you've set up channels where those extra layers are giving you the feedback you need. Welcome their feedback just as you would an end user's.

Recently at my current company, I've been reading many interactions between users and our support bot. I search for terms related to the features I'm working on to see what confuses users. I've noticed that when the bot is wrong, it's often because something was under-documented. I then address those gaps, and the bot learns from it during the next training.

The power of user support

Here are the takeaways:

- Provide users great support to create a flywheel effect.
- Lean into the customers' scenarios, giving you more insight into fixing their problems and improving your product.
- Pre-allocate a certain amount of your team's time to support, but do it in a way that doesn't randomize every team member.
- Focus explicitly on scaling support so that you can support more users with the same amount of effort.
- Make it easy to do both code and documentation improvements.

I spent a lot of pages on support because it is a compelling and interactive way for engineers to get feedback. It happens at a time when users want something from you. The other feedback channels I presented, whether surveys, feedback widgets, champions programs, or beta testing, all lack this dynamic, meaning they are less reliable and need to be juiced with additional incentives. Let's transition from qualitative feedback to quantitative metrics. User reports can be your sole source of feedback only to a certain scale, at which point you need to start counting.

Product Metrics

Any good digital twin is informed by sensors that track the real-world environment. Just as a digital replica of an airplane is going to be fed with flight data from millions of flights, your digital twin should sense what's going on with your users, the network, hardware, and so forth.

In Chapter 9, we will think about metrics for nonfunctional requirements. We'll instrument user flows in addition to individual operations, mapping our metrics more closely to user outcomes.

Here, we'll talk about high-level metrics that directly account for user engagement and business success. These counters and percentages should motivate us to build a more useful product, facilitate decision-making, and help grow the business.

It's important to pick the right mix of metrics to incentivize your team or company. But on what basis?

Before even starting the project, you'll want to make sure your project fits with your organization's product strategy. There are many ways to serve users, but not all of them fit with your mission. One way is to show which of the company's or organization's key performance indicators (KPIs) you would expect to be improved by the project.

Second, and most importantly—you'll no doubt be shocked to hear me say this—focus on serving your users. Having *value metrics* as goals holds your team accountable for having a purpose.

But you can't deliver value to users unless they know about your feature and use it. And sometimes it takes time to identify user value. So you'll also want to track *adoption metrics.*

> Product Metrics come in three distinct flavors: Key Performance Indicators (KPIs), Value Metrics, and Adoption Metrics. Think about all three when instrumenting your digital twin.

The broader organization tracks KPIs, but the latter two may be specific to your product or feature.

Picking the right metrics in each category requires care. I'll start by introducing a case study that reveals wisdom in each of those three types of metrics.

Case Study Introduction

I currently work at Temporal Technologies. In a nutshell, Temporal provides a framework for the reliable execution of workflows. Its users are developers who write code using an open source framework.

One of my product areas is called Safe Deploys, and our goal is to help users upgrade their Workflows without errors.

Our users' workflow code sits in a variety of environments and is deployed and upgraded like any other code. The odd thing about Workflows is that they can run for minutes, hours, or even weeks, and can go dormant. They can, and often do, resume in a different process from where they started. What happens if one wakes up and runs on a newer version of code than it started on? Without getting into details, this may sound tricky, and it is.

We recommended that developers "patch" their workflows with something akin to a feature flag. Here's some pseudocode:

```
def my_workflow():
  do_stuff()
  # It would be dangerous to run new code in an unsuspecting old workflow.
  if (originally_started_on_new_version()):
    do_new_stuff()
  else:
    do_old_stuff()
```

This "patching" works fine if done right, but there's a discoverability problem—developers don't always realize they need to do it; and a usability problem—it's easy to get wrong with more complex changes.

Without proper patching, workflows would get stuck with what I'll call *workflow upgrade errors*. (If counting these errors looks suspiciously like a product metric, stay tuned!)

Our key challenge was to help our users deploy their code without breaking it, and there are several high-level product approaches possible. You don't need to remember the details, but I want to give you a flavor. We could:

- Develop a system to help users keep workflows pinned to individual code versions, sidestepping the upgrade problem.
- Provide testing hooks to help them test in advance whether their workflows are going to hit workflow upgrade errors.
- Let users gradually ramp up traffic to new deployments, limiting the blast radius when there are problems.

To simplify, let's just say we're building a feature called Managed Deployments that helps users with these things. We don't know which solutions will work best, or whether users will adopt our solutions, so we need metrics to hold ourselves accountable.

I'm going to list a series of metrics, starting from very tactical metrics and moving toward strategic ones. I'll complain about each metric in turn and try to fix it with the next idea.

I've broken up the list of metrics into the three categories.

Then, in the following sections, I'll select three metrics from the list: one adoption metric, one value metric, and one strategic KPI. I'll choose metrics that incentivize productive behavior for our team, aiming at good user outcomes and aligning us with the company's mission.

> Aligning team incentives is the key consideration when deciding on metrics.

Adoption Metrics

One of the key problems with Managed Deployments is that they primarily benefit application developers by simplifying change management. But they required changes in deployment systems, which at many companies are often managed by a different persona we call platform engineers. This meant the app developers might have to convince the platform folks to make changes, which is a political issue that could hamper our adoption.

We can't wait around for months, wondering if anybody is using it. We'll have no idea whether to keep investing in improvements, improve our marketing, or try out other approaches.

But what makes a good adoption metric to goal on? The key question is to understand how it incentivizes our team.

Here's an ordered list of items, starting from the quickest thing to measure. Each item in this list carries a complaint about itself, which the next item will solve. Then I'll choose something as far down the list as I can—as certain as I can be that users are adopting while also having a practical, measurable metric we can influence.

Let's dive in:

1. *Views of the documentation or press release*
   Captures user interest, but we don't know whether they adopt the feature.
2. *Managed Deployments ever created*
   The problem is, we count users who may have tried the feature out in the past and churned out when they didn't like it. In general, be skeptical any time

somebody markets a metric that looks like "lifetime users," as it could include many dormant accounts.

3. *Active Managed Deployments*
   This is better because active deployments are more likely to stay active if users like them. But we're counting empty deployments the same as deployments with lots of workflows, which means we're not incentivizing adoption by the most important deployments.

4. *Workflows on active Managed Deployments*
   Weights the above metric by the number of workflows running. Is this better? I'll discuss the trade-offs below.

Those first two are often called "vanity metrics." They look impressive on the surface, but don't provide meaningful insights into business performance, user behavior, or product success. They are all too tempting because they are easy to track—just count the size of whatever database.

Avoid vanity metrics.

In contrast, the "Active Managed Deployments" measurement looks juicy. This leading indicator measures potential user value. And because it gets decremented when a user stops using the feature, it hints at real user value as well.

The choice between the final two metrics is more interesting and reflects common trade-offs. The last one weights Active Managed Deployments by workflow count, meaning an individual customer with a thousand workflows would count 1000 rather than 1. How would using this as a goal change our incentives?

- It's harder for us to control. If our biggest customers adopt it, the metric could explode. If not, it won't. That's an element of luck that will make teammates uncomfortable.
- The productivity of our developers doesn't depend much on whether they had a thousand or a million workflows fail due to an error. Either way, they've got to go remediate the incident.
- It would incentivize us to focus on our customers with the highest volume, which is usually big companies. Perhaps we would build extra features to make it friendly for large enterprises. Or we would reach out to app developers at big companies and enlist them to pester their platform engineers to add it.

The right answer depends partly on our strategy. If our KPIs focus on enterprise adoption, maybe we should goal on the workflow-weighted metric, even if it will swing more wildly. But if we're focused on developer productivity and positive word-of-mouth, Active Managed Deployments, unweighted by size, will do nicely.

In the event, we chose Active Managed Deployments.

Still, we don't know whether it's truly helping. Users could be using managed deployments simply because it's the default or because the docs instructed them to do so. Let's address that problem with value metrics.

Value Metrics

> *Suppose we have an AI whose only goal is to make as many paper clips as possible. The AI will realize quickly that it would be much better if there were no humans because humans might decide to switch it off. Because if humans do so, there would be fewer paper clips. Also, human bodies contain a lot of atoms that could be made into paper clips. The future that the AI would be trying to gear towards would be one in which there were a lot of paper clips but no humans.*
>
> —Nick Bostrom

This famous "paperclip maximizer" thought experiment illustrates what can happen when you give beings weird incentives.

That's extreme, but if you think that only AIs fall prey to weird incentives, consider the case of Wells Fargo.

In 2016, it was revealed that Wells Fargo employees had opened millions of unauthorized accounts for their customers solely to meet sales goals. This caused a massive customer uproar and much legal trouble.

How did this happen? One key mistake was to use an adoption metric—the number of accounts—to set goals for employees, when a value metric would have been more appropriate. Customers ended up with products they didn't need. A value metric would have, for example, counted the amount of money under management.

Our instinct is often to choose metrics we can easily control in the short term, but this backfired for Wells Fargo. Excessive control made it vulnerable to manipulation, costing the company over $3 billion in legal settlements.

> Choose value metrics that challenge you. Some level of discomfort about your ability to influence the metric will motivate the team to deliver something great.

With this in mind, let's continue with Managed Deployment metric candidates, complaining about each in turn:

1. *Managed deployments per day*
   We reason that if developers deploy more, they must be having more confidence and success with their deployments. But this feels like it could be influenced by many other factors we don't care about, and if those deployments still result in upgrade errors, we haven't done our jobs.

2. *Workflow upgrade errors*
   If we watch this metric go down for users with Managed Deployments, we'll clearly see that users have gotten value. However, if the overall number of running workflows is increasing, this number could go up despite our best efforts.

3. *Workflow upgrade errors percentage*
   If we see users with Managed Deployments having a lower percentage of their workflows getting errors, we've done our jobs. And this metric better controls for the number of workflows in the system. But this doesn't measure how many running Workflows were saved from production problems, so it doesn't reward adoption. (Though we already have an adoption metric, so this might be okay.)

4. *Workflow upgrade errors averted*
   This usage-weighted metric addresses complaints from the previous two. We can guess how many extra errors would have occurred if we'd never shipped safe deployment features.

For none of these metrics do we understand if Managed Deploys increases their usage of our product or gets them to recommend it to others. KPIs will plug this gap in the next section.

The "Workflow upgrade errors percentage" metric looks pretty good to me, combined with our adoption metric of Active Managed Deployments. Showing management that we've reduced errors for users will be super compelling, if we can pull it off, and if not, we can interview users whose metrics didn't improve to find out why.

Even better, if we get good numbers, we can use those to market the product to holdouts who haven't adopted it: "Reduce your deployment errors by an average of N% by adopting Managed Deployments!"

The main downside is that developers may not encounter deployment issues for weeks or months at a time, so it may take time to show up when we only have a few early adopters. Our adoption metric will tide us over until that time.

The last metric, which tracks the total "errors averted," is weighted by workflows just as the adoption metric "Workflows on active Managed Deployments" was. The tradeoffs here are similar.

If you're building a substantial feature, as you think through the value metric, you may find yourself unable to come up with a good one. If you can't, be concerned! There are two main reasons this might happen:

- It might be useless or even exploitative, making money in the short term but probably turning off users in the long run.
- Your digital twin may be underpowered. You may want to add instrumentation to your product.

Key Performance Indicators

Let's rewind back to the beginning of the Managed Deployments project. Before we even begin, we should consider KPIs and figure out how our product idea aligns with the broader company goals. Many products can be valuable, but not something we should be doing at this particular company. We need to stay somewhat focused so we can continue to build and maintain the best products in our areas of specialty.

You can tie your project to KPIs in your product thesis (Chapter 6) or product brief (Chapter 7) when you're trying to sell your project to management.

KPIs are totally unopinionated as to *how* you improve them. They cast a wide net and invite creativity to figure out the best way to move them.

What KPI works for Managed Deployments? Let's audition a few:

1. Net Promoter Score (NPS)
: Gauges customer loyalty and satisfaction. It measures the willingness of customers to recommend a company's products or services on a scale of 0–10.

  This metric could compare whether users of Managed Deployments are more likely to recommend Temporal than those who don't use them. Tracking actual referrals would be more reliable, but we're fairly confident that if this number increases, it indicates users value the improved safety we've provided.

2. Net Revenue Retention (NRR)
: A ratio of revenue from a customer now versus an earlier period. It can benefit from increased usage, but doesn't account for growth.

  If developers who use Managed Deployments increase their usage of workflows over time more than those who don't, we've conclusively nailed down the business value. Perhaps they write more workflows because developers like and feel safe using the product, or they can achieve higher scales by focusing on other things that grow their business. But what if Managed Deploys is expensive to operate; is it worth the extra revenue?

3. *Gross margin*

   Gross margin subtracts out costs such as running our servers and databases, making sure any extra resources we deploy are well-spent. We could compare how much profit margin we make from users who use Managed Deploys versus ones who don't. But this doesn't reward us for gaining new customers based on positive word of mouth.

4. *Operating profit*

   The company's bottom line. Rewards us for growing the customer base, not just improving performance within a customer. Accounts for everything, but very challenging to measure how our product contributes.

Not all projects will be able to move these metrics in a scientific experiment, especially smaller projects or at smaller companies.

That's why we consider KPIs at the beginning to motivate the workstream. For example, if in the NPS surveys, we noticed somebody doesn't recommend Temporal, we can ask why. If they report trouble deploying new code, we have our smoking gun.

Likewise, if we notice somebody churns out of using Temporal—as we'd discover while tracking NRR—we could ask why and discover the critical feedback.

When trying to sell our project idea to management, those customer testimonials tied to NPS or NRR will go a long way to convincing them to fund the project. And we'll mention gross margin if costs are a concern.

Tactical and Strategic Metrics

The combination of KPIs, value metrics, and adoption metrics keeps our team honest and engaged.

You can think of the metrics list above as a spectrum that ranges from tactical to strategic. The most tactical possible metric might be counting views of your brand ad campaign. Simply make an ad, spend some money, and watch the number go up.

Value metrics are more strategic but usually take longer to conclusively measure. For that reason, value metrics are sometimes called *trailing metrics*.

Operating profit is *extremely* strategic. Unless we are an exploitative monopoly, it clearly shows that users value the unique benefits of the product while also indicating business sustainability.

Alas, it's very common for the metrics that are most aligned with user value to be more challenging to measure quickly and precisely pinpoint what feature created the value. This core tension is what makes the art of picking the right metric so much fun!

Table 5-1 neatly summarizes the trade-offs in different metrics:

Table 5-1. A table comparing tendencies of tactical to strategic metrics

Tactical metric	Strategic metric
Is a leading indicator	Is a trailing indicator
Focus will move it	Creativity will move it
Is easily gameable	Is hard to control
Measures potential user value	Measures actual user value
Is easy to measure precisely	Is hard to attribute to your feature

There's rarely one metric that nails all of our goals, so we track KPIs, Value, and Adoption metrics.

With only tactical metrics, you could become a paperclip maximizer, forgetting your original strategy.

Then again, if you only have company-level metrics like profit, you'll have little insight into how to drive it. You need more specific metrics to focus individual teams.

Chapter Summary

In this chapter, we covered three huge topics. It's difficult to oversell how important it is to stay in touch with your users and be responsive to their needs. These should be core competencies of any software team.

First, I demonstrated how you can structure your product to build trust and adaptability into each feature. You'll be prepared to move quickly and iterate with frequent, automated releases.

With such a software stack, you can respond easily to users. At scale, neither qualitative nor quantitative metrics alone reliably help us make decisions, so we embrace a combination of both.

Our qualitative feedback is anchored by user support. When users knock on our doors, they give us a golden opportunity to learn their stories.

Each substantial project should be founded based on KPIs and tracked with a mixture of adoption and value metrics that demonstrate user impact.

I chose the framing of digital twin for all of this to bring these concepts together and concretize something that otherwise seems so diffuse. A software team should nurture its digital twin with simulations, tests, data, and feedback. If you don't have the ability to measure and understand your product's real-world behavior, you've got no leg to stand on.

How do we use all that feedback and data? Well, I'm about to hop back to the beginning of the product cycle. Product discovery and definition make up the last four chapters of this book. In the two upcoming chapters on discovery, you'll use a combination of user research and, if you've already shipped versions of your product, data from your digital twin to generate ideas, plan, and prioritize.

Exercises

1. Think of an action that your team could take that would make their code easier to evolve. Consider tools, frameworks, abstractions, or refactoring.
2. Think of your team's deployment or release process. What's something you could do to give customers new value more frequently? Consider test coverage, automation, feature flags, and so forth.
3. If you were to train an AI Assistant to provide user support for your product, what context would you collect into your digital twin to feed it?
4. How could your team eliminate a barrier to getting quantitative user feedback?
5. You work at a social network that has comments and a single upvote button, and you're experimenting with giving users more types of reactions, similar to Facebook (care, haha, angry, etc.) and LinkedIn (support, insightful, etc.). Your company strategy is to get people posting a lot of engaging content, and you think reactions will help readers give a wider range of feedback to posters, which will, in turn, help posters feel comfortable sharing more. Name at least one good adoption tactical metric and one trailing value metric. I'll name two of each.
6. What would be a KPI that you think this reactions feature would influence?

Answers

1. One tool that came in handy at Facebook was a scalable "codemod tool." It could detect code patterns and transform them across a massive repository. This allowed much faster changes and deprecations to widely used libraries, which in turn let engineers dream bigger about making impactful changes.
2. For high-availability services, I recommend blue-green or rainbow deployments. Traditional "rolling deployments" replace code in-place on a fixed set of machines. But if something goes wrong, you've already replaced the old version of the code, and it's slower to roll back.

   Blue-green and rainbow deploys, in contrast, keep multiple versions of your code —thought of as colors, thus the names—deployed simultaneously. When you roll out a new version, you can gradually ramp traffic to it and instantly shift traffic back if something goes wrong.
3. For my technical product, I would feed it documentation, conversations in our community message board, and tickets opened with our support agents.

4. We could use an ad hoc analytics platform to enable custom querying. For example, we could use this to correlate Workflow Upgrade Errors from the case study with various features users have adopted.

5. Adoption metric: I would run an A/B test and measure the total number of reactions, including the old upvote button and the new ones; this will help me discover if engagement is increasing. I'd also watch the impact on comments since one concern would be to decrease meaningful comments. (One could argue that decreasing simple comments like "Congratulations!" is okay, but lowering more nuanced comments would not be desirable.)

   Value metric: Another A/B test. Hold out some people from even seeing the new reactions on others' posts. Do people who've received the new reactions on their posts, or witnessed others receiving such reactions, increase their posting in the future? This could tell whether they feel more comfortable sharing. A second idea is to perform sentiment analysis of the posts to see if there's a larger diversity of post tones.

6. Most social networks track a KPI called "time spent." I would guess that reactions would improve it for both those who post and those who read more engaging posts.

PART III
Discover

Let's hop back to the beginning of the product cycle, either starting fresh or building a new iteration based on feedback during the most recent delivery phase.

As there are two components to scenarios—personas and simulations—this part is divided into two chapters. In the first, we'll interview customers and flesh out descriptions of the personas we'll be serving. In the second, we'll develop full stories around what users want to do, translating those stories into prioritized requirements.

CHAPTER 6
Understanding Your Target Audience

> *We can't simply ask customers what they need or want. Cognitive biases interfere with our customers' ability to answer these questions reliably. Instead, we want to listen for needs, pain points, and desires in the context of specific stories.*
>
> —Teresa Torres, author of *Continuous Discovery Habits*

The key perspective switch of the product-minded engineer is to build for someone specific. Knowing our customers, we can select complementary feature sets (which we'll design in detail in Chapter 8) and prioritize the truly needed efforts on requirements such as latency, scalability, and security (Chapter 9).

> Build for someone.

It sounds simple, but in practice doing so requires frequent, active effort, given all the other demands on our attention. Like sea otters, we dive for our food but also come up for breath.

In this chapter, you'll meet your target audience. For now, I'll focus on your initial interactions as you interview prospective customers, learn about them, and decide which ones are in your target audience. (In contrast, in Chapter 5, we were iterating on later versions of our product, and we consulted existing users.)

You'll use that info to build personas (and nonpersonas) that will guide the work of your whole team. These techniques should help you develop a strong vision and get the big decisions right.

Real Users, Not Straw Men

As I mentioned in Chapter 1, real humans have certain universal characteristics—for example, they are forgetful, give limited brain capacity over to our product, and are busy. Those rules of thumb will serve you well, but they—like every rule of thumb—aren't always right, and they aren't nearly specific enough. Lacking a complete character profile of your users to ground your decisions, it's easy to accidentally start building for yourself or the personas you were serving on your *previous* product.

Just as you can look for plot holes in your simulations, you can detect implausible characters. Ask yourself, "What kind of person would use our product at this stage?" Sometimes, if you're being honest, the characters sound like these:

The Irrational Actor
: Takes actions that contradict their motivations. This cash-strapped thrifter springs for an $8 latte. Or he's an influencer who makes thousands a month being on social platforms with a critical mass, but will try out your empty social network because you offer $10 Amazon gift cards.

The Manic Pixie Dream User
: Loves your product for no particular reason. She's willing to post on social media to tell all their friends about it, and her infectious enthusiasm will get them to try. She will instantly adopt every feature you release, posting screengrabs and videos of her usage.

The Stoic Monk
: Sits around in a monastery all day using your product. They are willing to learn whatever you throw at them even when it's hard, use features even if they are time-consuming to use, and if there's excessive product churn and flakiness, they'll meditate on it with Zen-like poise and try again.

Your Clone
: Knows just as much about the system as you do and therefore needs no discovery mechanisms. Their knowledge of the internals means they have an unusually high tolerance for unintuitive behaviors. The Clone highlights the trap of the "Curse of Knowledge" presented in Chapter 2.

Mom or Dad
: Real, but alas, you've only got one or two of those, tops.

I think of these as "straw man users," along the lines of what we discussed in Chapter 1 when criticizing poorly motivated scenarios.

People often picture straw man users due to other biases that they may not even be aware of.

Biases Are Dangerous

I recently consulted with an owner of a social card gaming startup whose pitch for his company was that the incumbent product was complacent and extractive. But when I asked what would motivate users to switch to his product, his argument was, effectively, "people will come to my site because we have video chat," even though it meant needing to convince their friends to leave the familiar interface of the established site.

Would they? The argument wasn't ridiculous.

In fact, my friend had inherited the video chat feature from the previous owner. He'd spent money on this company. His engineering team had limited resources, and therefore, he *needed* video chat to be a killer feature because it was what he had. Was it really one of the top two or three features that these card gamers wanted? Was it so important as to justify an exodus from the previous site? Nobody really knew.

Another friend is in the same space, competing with the same incumbent company. He developed an innovative and engaging tournament format and got a few famous experts to compete in the tournament and stream branded videos on YouTube. These videos attracted new users who wanted to challenge the experts. Crucially, it was a single-player mode of the game, meaning it could gain traction before everyone's friends were already on the site. This single-player product became self-sustaining and introduced users to the multi-player game modes, which he hoped would grow over time.

The first company folded after much toil and wasted capital. The second is, so far, still alive and kicking. At least his strategy is based on a coherent set of user motivations. I think he has a fighting chance.

We must constantly steer clear of biases that cloud our judgment. A clear and honest statement of our users, documented and shared with the whole team, acts like a GPS for a ship's captain. It consistently guides us toward our goal, even as the winds of bias, expediency, politics, flights of fancy, logical fallacies, and egos try to blow us off course.

In this chapter, I'll first introduce the scientific mindset we'll bring to assessing whether our product will work.

Second, I'll help you build a picture of what users want using user interviews such as customer discovery interviews and sales calls.

Then, I'll talk about developing personas and writing them down to share with the team and get everybody aligned.

Next, I'll put you in touch with prioritizing among possible personas to develop a target audience for your product.

Finally, I'll touch on the surprisingly frequent topic of multisided marketplaces, that is, communities with multiple personas who interact with each other, such as ride-hailing drivers interacting with riders.

To kick it off, I'll introduce a case study that will provide this chapter's through line.

Case Study Introduction

In the early 2010s, I worked at Facebook on the design and launch of its App Center, which was a portal that users could use to discover social apps—mostly games. It was similar in concept to any modern app store, with featured apps and ranked lists. This experience was foundational on my journey to becoming a product-minded engineer.

I chose to showcase this project because it highlights an interesting combination of user and developer personas that drove our strategic decision-making. This product made an impact because the engineers, PMs, and designers on the team understood our target audiences, boosting both gaming on Facebook and the bottom lines of our developers. The success lasted for a couple of years, until the juggernaut of mobile gaming arrived and took everything over.

Stand Back, Wield Science

A *product thesis* defines the user problem you're addressing, who you're helping, and your compelling idea for how to address it.

Our starting high-level product thesis for the App Center was something like this:

> The App Center will help social gamers discover great games being played by their friends, and incentivize app developers to compete for placement in the App Center by building quality apps. This will in turn grow the Facebook gaming ecosystem.

I like the term "thesis" because it sounds like science. You may be excited, bright-eyed and bushy-tailed, and eager to build, but you should push your pet idea aside in favor of a curious, scientific mindset. An experiment such as a clinical drug trial is an apt analogy because, like drug trials, most products will fail.

There are two aspects of the scientific method for performing experiments that we'll embrace: the null hypothesis and avoiding confounders.

The "null hypothesis" claims that the intervention will have no effect. An experimental result can "disprove" the null hypothesis.

Let's call it the *product antithesis*, which says that the customer will not need, want, benefit from, or be able to use your product or feature.

You can flesh out the antithesis with reasons it might be true. For example, "social gamers already get game invitations from their friends using much more viral mechanisms like notifications and the news feed. The App Center won't drive enough traffic to matter."

We'll refine this antithesis as we dive into more specific scenarios.

Thinking about the antithesis will keep you skeptical. If you spend all of your brain cells trying to prove your product thesis, you'll keep finding reasons for your product to work. With the antithesis, you'll listen more closely when customers say what you don't want to hear.

We will carry this scientific mindset through our customer interviews and surveys, explored next.

Customer Discovery

Before you can build a product or feature, learn what might motivate users to use it or to turn away from it. When enough users share similar incentives and means, these combine into a persona. Personas are crucial early to figure out who you should talk to, and later to test many different product and feature ideas.

The goal of customer discovery is to develop and refine your product thesis. To do this, you'll figure out what problems people are facing, who is facing them, and why.

You may start with a concrete product idea, but don't grow too attached to it, as you may need to be willing to change plans.

You're exploring the problem space more than the solution space. You want to inhabit the interviewees' minds and learn as much as you can.

You can conduct customer discovery in several ways: interviews, sales calls, and surveys are common.

I'll cover each of those, and then conclude by pointing out how any of these can help us grow a valuable network to lean on as the product cycle progresses.

But first, how do you even get interviews in the first place?

Getting Interviews

Interviews are one of the most accessible opportunities for engineers and are helpful at all phases of the product cycle, but particularly during discovery. And yet, for many engineers, just getting an interview with a prospective customer is the most daunting part.

Here are a few techniques that may help:

- Lean on a more customer-facing role, such as a User Experience researcher or Product Manager. Or look into your sales organization and hook up with an Account Manager, Customer Success rep, Marketer, or Solution Architect. Ask them if you can tag along with an existing meeting and take a few minutes to ask questions at the end.
- Network with more customer-facing folks, and you'll be able to ask for more dedicated interview slots—they may even bring some to you. Offer to provide technical support or to present your upcoming roadmap. Customers often feel special when an engineer takes the time to talk to them.
- Ask users during the types of support interactions that I covered in Chapter 5 if they're up for being interviewed. If you've been helpful, they're likely to say yes!
- Lean on people who know what lots of other people want. For the App Center interviews, we can ask folks at game studios, who in turn should know what *their* customers want or can point us at individuals we should talk to.
- Circulate a survey and use it to see who will volunteer for follow-up interviews. We'll cover such surveys after covering interviews themselves.

Customer Discovery Interviews

Customer discovery interviews (CDIs) are structured conversations with current or prospective customers.

In a full-length CDI, you have three basic goals:

1. Understand the user's root motivations and circumstances. This unlocks your creativity to come up with different solutions to users' problems in case your initial ideas weren't right. Knowing the user's complete set of problems helps you design a holistic solution.
2. Tease out the strength of their motivations. Many products fail, not because users didn't want them at all, but because they only *kinda* wanted them.
3. If you already have a concrete product idea, invite the interviewee's creativity in giving feedback on your product idea, mock, or prototype. This will help you find answers to the questions you didn't realize you needed to ask.

That's a lot of ground to cover even in sixty minutes, and there are a lot of ways you can get off track. My best advice is (a) to adopt a curious, scientific mindset, and (b) to slowly transition the interview from talking about the interviewee to talking about your product.

Both of those will take a bit of explanation, so let's put them under a microscope. Then I'll apply these insights to the App Center example.

The customer interview funnel

Think of a CDI as a funnel. At the beginning, you're in the user's world, talking about their stories, problems, and desires. You're nailing down their persona. As the interview progresses, you start bringing them more into your product's world, asking them increasingly pointed questions about it, as manifested in Figure 6-1.

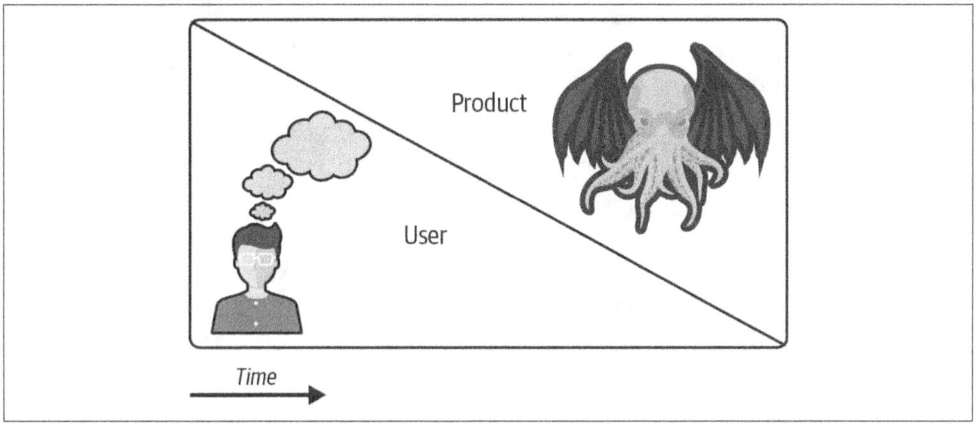

Figure 6-1. The Customer Discovery Interview funnel

Yes—I like to pretend like my product ideas are the eldritch entity Cthulhu, and if I'm not careful, I will show the users things they can't unsee, polluting their minds forever. I may not drive them mad, but I could bias their responses. The final moments before I introduce my product or feature idea are therefore precious.

In this section, I'll partition this funnel into early, middle, and final phases to describe how interviews proceed.

Start the interview by helping the interviewee feel comfortable sharing, because you're going to be asking a lot about their experiences.

In the early phase especially, try to avoid questions that would lead them toward specific answers.

> The less you prompt your interviewee, the more you can trust their answer.

If they enter the interview asking for your feature unprompted, that's a much stronger signal than if you present the feature idea and they say they like it.

You aren't the only one who can influence the user—they may also lack self-awareness or the ability to predict their own actions. You could ask them directly about their needs, but a better approach is to ask them for recent stories relevant to your product thesis.

Asking for stories has numerous advantages:

- Users will dwell in the concrete, telling you what they *actually* did rather than inadvertently constructing a skewed narrative of what they think they want or what they aspire to do.
- Going through a concrete story helps you build scenarios to guide your later design work, which I'll discuss more in Chapter 7.
- Stories jog users' memories, highlighting important details about their experience.

In this early phase of the interview, they may bring up problems they care about that you hadn't considered. Be willing to chase those, as it may mean you aren't yet solving the right problems and should modify your product thesis.

For Facebook Games, you could open with, "Do you have any feedback about your recent experiences playing or discovering Games on Facebook?"

Once the user has gotten whatever is top-of-mind off of their chest, you could ask them questions aimed at discovering their persona. "What are some games you like?" This could help you determine whether they like puzzle games, social games, etc.

In the middle phase, stay in their space, but narrow in on the topics you had planned, asking about the specific problems you set out to solve. They may not have those problems, which is a useful signal that feeds into the product antithesis. Perhaps they are not part of your target audience, or maybe they are, but you're not solving the right problems.

More specific prompts like "Talk about your typical gaming session" or "How do you decide whether to try a game?" will help us understand the problems users face and what motivates them. These will deepen our personas and add detail to use case simulations.

During this middle phase, many people naturally tend to be agreeable and helpful. Make sure to ask neutral questions that are phrased so it doesn't seem like you're expecting a positive or negative response.

At this point, you have the ingredients you'll need to create a customer persona based on their responses.

Then, in the optional final phase, if the interviewee seems like someone who would benefit from your product idea, describe it and ask for their reaction. Visuals can help make things more concrete, so if you have mockups or sketches, show those.

This segment helps users determine whether your product idea is for them. You could convey your intent by describing a scenario in which it might be used, then ask if it sounds like it solves their needs.

Most importantly, create a welcoming space for them to express opinions and confusion.

This section has a funnel as well.

We want to figure out which information to present for each game, and whether there are any privacy concerns related to sharing game-playing information.

First, we could show them a list of features (for example, genre, star rating, friends who play, description, popularity) and ask them to select which ones matter most to them.

Then we'd get more concrete, saying, "Here's a rough concept we've been playing with. What do you think of this?"

Let's suppose we are worried that gamers don't want friends seeing their game playing as shown in Figure 6-2.

Figure 6-2. An App Center prototype

We don't just ask it. "Do you care about privacy?" is a leading question if there ever was one. But if a user says, "Um. Does this mean my friends would see what *I'm* playing?" that's a strong signal. We can create a user persona who is "privacy-conscious" if enough people flag this.

Barring that, we could ask them to bring up Facebook and load the list of games they've recently played, asking "which of these games would you want to endorse for your friends or to bring them into?"

How would their responses translate to product changes?

- Maybe users don't want to be seen to endorse games that they only picked up and played for five minutes before abandoning, in which case we'd require them to play a certain amount before sharing.
- Perhaps they find certain games "guilty pleasures," in which case we'd allow them to opt out of sharing on a game-by-game basis.
- Others might not want people knowing they "waste time" playing games at all. We could let them default to not sharing *any* game activity.

Given that open-ended questions can take time, and that the funnel phases must be carefully orchestrated, we need effective time management. Let's talk about preparing for efficient interviews.

Scripting your questions

A little structure will help you manage your time more effectively. Prepare an *interview guide* that you can consult as you proceed through the interview.

It might feel natural to go into interviews with a full list of a dozen questions you want to ask in order. But that won't leave you time to probe users more deeply when they tell you something interesting. And you'll end up sounding robotic. If you find yourself wanting to cover a lot of ground and get consistent answers from every customer you interview—that's a survey.

Probe deeper when the customer tells you something interesting, while not wasting time on topics that turn out not to be relevant to the user. Don't fall into the trap of asking, "Well, if you did want <cool feature>, how would you want it to work?"

Your interview guide might have one or two starter questions for the user segment, one or two for the middle user and product segment, and something to showcase for the product segment. Or, if you prefer to be thoroughly prepared, create a list of possible questions depending on where the conversation goes. Many of them will be conditional, so don't plan to get to all of them.

Don't sweat it if you let a couple of interviews get away from you. You'll get a feel for how and when to move interviews along as you do more of them, and anyway, the content at the beginning often provides the highest signal.

Response analysis

Afterward, we will summarize our takeaways from each interview. We should determine how much signal we got for the customers' answers so we can assess the relative importance of different factors.

For the App Center, if we wanted to figure out if star ratings would be valuable, users might tell us in various ways, each with a different signal strength shown in Table 6-1:

Table 6-1. Star ratings feedback

Prompt	Customer response	Signal strength
How do you decide whether to try a game?	I wish there were star ratings.	High
Talk about your typical gaming session.	The last couple of games I tried sucked.	Medium
Any feedback about gaming on Facebook?	It's hard to tell which games are good.	Medium
Tell me about a time when you wished you could see star ratings on apps.	Definitely. Just the other day, I...	Medium
Rank these in importance to you: genre, star rating, friends who play, description, or popularity	Star rating ranks third.	Low
Do you think star ratings on apps would be helpful?	Yeah, sure.	Low

Since the signal strength decreases with each prompt, we delay those later questions until we've had a chance to get the high signals.

The motivations from earlier in the funnel will contextualize their suggestions here as well. If the user isn't that interested in new games, we don't care as much about their opinion on star ratings as if the user is an avid seeker of new games.

Let's turn our attention to another customer opportunity—sales calls.

Sales Calls

Engineers are sometimes asked to tag along on sales calls to provide the customer with technical answers, impress them, present a roadmap, or assess the feasibility of addressing the customer's special needs. You can use sales calls for customer discovery because the salesperson will want much of the same information about the user's persona that you want.

However, the salesperson's goals are different than yours. Whereas your goal is to figure out your target audience and product roadmap, they are trying to sell a tangible product. Whereas you might be planning for releases that come out in a year, the salesperson likely wants a deal in the next quarter or two.

Be sure you align on the goals of the interview beforehand and ask the salesperson for advice on what to say or not to say. Aligning in advance will help them feel more comfortable adding you to these valuable conversations. For your part, make it clear what you are and are not willing to commit to in your roadmap.

Once you're in the meeting, the sales rep will want you to help build trust with their customers, and you achieve that when you empathize with and advocate for their needs. Customers can usually detect when they're being manipulated or given a "sales pitch."

In short, within guardrails set by the sales representative, bring your same scientific approach to sales calls. Be willing for the product antithesis to be true: perhaps your product won't solve the customer's problems. Maybe it needs work before it's ready for this customer. Better to clear that up now than after a painful integration and negotiation period.

At Facebook, we wanted to attract established, high-quality game studios to our platform, and we felt like the App Center would be an enticing place to feature their games. But what if what the game developers really crave is a stable API and better support for in-app purchases? Funnel-style, we should listen first before revealing our product ideas.

We'd also want to be frank about disqualifications. For example, we didn't want developers of graphics-intensive games that can't run in web browsers on most machines. Establishing those boundaries up front makes sure nobody's wasting anybody's time.

Customer Discovery Surveys

Customer discovery surveys determine users' needs more broadly than you can cover in interviews, although they cannot be as adaptive or as in-depth. Crucially, they can be used to find people to interview.

These surveys are basically condensed versions of interviews, which means many of the same suggestions apply: start open-ended, try to determine personas, ask about specific behaviors and scenarios rather than opinions, and try to determine priority.

A good questionnaire should also excite customers to fill it out. Depending on your audience, you might offer an incentive or simply tell them that you are listening and that they have the opportunity to influence your product direction.

Finally, it should screen for people interested in follow-up conversations to chat more. As I mentioned above, they are a great way to generate leads for interviews.

A survey for the App Center might look like this:

The Facebook Games team wants to hear from you! We're trying to make sure you can discover great games and, to guide our feature roadmap, we want to hear more about what you like and don't like.

- Have you tried gaming on Facebook?
- Do you have any feedback from your recent experiences discovering or playing games on Facebook?
- How important was this to your enjoyment?
- Name some games you really enjoy or have played a lot.

- Think of some recent games you've noticed. How do you decide whether to try one out?
- Think of the most recent games you tried out. How did you discover them, and what did you think of them?

Would you be interested in chatting with a member of the team and sharing more?

This last call-to-action isn't the only time we'll try to grow our networks. We can also do it at the end of CDIs and sales calls.

Networking with Interviewees

Customer interviews are important networking opportunities.

In Chapter 5, we talked about how to iterate on your product with users guiding you. One of the key enablers of a user-interactive mindset is to have a set of trusted people that it's easy to reach out to for feedback.

Keep an eye out for interview subjects who give insightful feedback, perfectly embody a persona, or are likely to be early adopters when you've built your product. See if they're willing to keep in touch.

They may even become a *reference customer*, who is an actual person or company who stands in for a broader persona. They can act as design partners, guiding you through requests and feedback. Later, your marketing can refer to them to show others that "customers like them" use your product.

Next, I'll recap this section with some rules of thumb to consider when crafting your prompts.

Customer Interviews Rules of Thumb

Whether you're creating the interview guide for your Customer Discovery Interview, or creating your Customer Discovery Survey, keep some things in mind:

- Interviewees should feel welcome to express opinions, feedback, and confusion.
- The less you lead them, the more you can trust their responses. Make this a top priority early in the interview.
- Ask neutral questions stripped of any desires you might have.
- Ask for concrete situations rather than abstract opinions and speculation. "Tell me about a time when" is often a good start.

After the interview or survey, write up takeaways. These should be informed by the strength of the signal you got from the interview so you remember how urgent the problems are.

Finally, leverage the introductions to some of your interviewees for follow-ups.

In the next section, we'll focus on creating a target audience from the results of our interviews and other research.

Crafting and Communicating a Target Audience

With some interviews behind us, along with other data like market research, we can brainstorm different product concepts and match them up with target audiences. As necessary, we'll refine our product thesis with these personas in mind.

First, we'll need to make compelling and practical choices as to whom we're targeting.

And then we'll need to communicate those choices out to the team to get everyone to buy in.

Choosing a Target Audience

In Chapter 1, I presented the elements of a scenario's character:

- A persona, which is a combination of demographic and a set of means.
- A motive for using your product.

The target audience is a generalized version of a persona. These prospective users should:

- Be based on a real-world demographic.
- Have a substantial motivation to use the product, especially relative to competitors' products.
- Possess the means to purchase and use it.
- Not have compelling motivations *not* to use it.

If your product is brand-new, you'll generally need your near-term target audience to be small. That's because it's difficult to motivate everybody everywhere all at once. You generally need to find a core audience not being well-served by existing products and focus. You can expand later, as shown by the stories of many of the products I've worked on:

- Facebook started as a network for American college students, then high schoolers, then all English speakers, before expanding internationally.
- Stripe enticed startup developers and technical founders with "7 lines of code" before later growing into enterprise usage and developing no-code solutions for nondevelopers and vibe coders.

- Temporal focused on infrastructure engineers at large tech companies who wrote in Go before expanding to serve financial and product engineers with other programming languages, then later adding enterprise and AI features.

Luckily for us, people's wants and needs are not random. They often come in mutually reinforcing groups. To home in on a smaller cohort, look for correlated sets of motives from your interviews.

At Facebook, after a bunch of interviews and audience analysis, we could see that gamers divided into two groups—casual social gamers and so-called "mid-core" gamers. Mid-core gamers are drawn to the complex tactical or strategy games that hard-core gamers play, but aren't willing to invest the same kind of time and money.

Social gamers tend to want social context, the ability to show off, and to have a lot of their friends playing.

Mid-core gamers tended to be privacy-conscious, enjoy competition, and seek well-reviewed, quality content.

We'll leverage these groupings to select a feature set later in the chapter. For now, let's turn these audiences into something we can communicate.

Gaining Alignment with Personas

If everyone on the team is thinking of the same types of users with the same needs, they can each make good decisions, or at least ones that all point in the same direction. The more complex the product, the more crucial it is for everyone to use personas to stay on the same wavelength.

When you write out a target audience, you collect their needs in one place. You can then use those to align everybody on what success looks like. If you've only fulfilled two of the audience's three table-stakes needs, you're not done yet. It's not time to ship.

Also, say whom you're *not* targeting. These are called *nonpersonas*.

Nonpersonas will help you avoid adding more work that will slow development down without serving your immediate goals, often called scope creep.

To communicate your personas and nonpersonas, in a shared document, perhaps a slide deck, write memorable personas and then accompany them with character sketches to flesh out their motivations for using the product. Link out to your interview transcripts in case people question how you came up with them or whether they really represent reality.

One way to make personas memorable is to give them catchy and evocative names.

The Mort, Elvis, and Einstein Controversy

I was first introduced to personas when I was in Microsoft's Developer Division ("DevDiv") in 2005. Those personas leaked out into the public and became controversial memes, but in fact they were quite effective, and I still hold them up as a great example of persona use for the way they communicated and aligned a large division of engineers and product managers. DevDiv was responsible for Visual Studio, and in particular, the compilers, runtimes, and IDEs for Visual Basic, C#, and C++. Their personas were something like this:

- Mort is an opportunistic developer who likes to create quick-working solutions for immediate problems and focuses on productivity and learn as needed. They may code to supplement another job such as accounting.
- Elvis is a pragmatic and busy application programmer who creates specific, long-lasting solutions addressing the problem domain. They learn while working on the solution so that they can quickly move on to the next problem.
- Einstein is a paranoid system programmer who needs to create general and efficient solutions. They often learn in advance before working on the solution.

Different teams were instructed to target different personas as they built out their libraries and experiences. Visual Basic's target audience was Mort, C#'s was Elvis, and C++'s was Einstein.

When the personas became known publicly, there was a backlash. Developers didn't think they should or could be pigeonholed into these simplistic categories. Nobody wanted to be called Mort, which in English literature is often a bumbling character.

In understanding personas and their purpose for product development, it makes much more sense:

- While the joking disdain for Morts was jarring, the overall approach of making catchy names was sound and helped align DevDiv.
- Mort was chosen as a name, not to be derogatory, but to drill the Visual Basic team with the idea to keep simplifying their abstractions.
- People may have one or more personas based on circumstances. Someone may be a Mort when building little productivity scripts and an Einstein when checking into the codebase for their firmware.
- Personas are not stereotypes. They use concrete, memorable language to inspire and inform designs. Users are much more diverse, and product designers should remain aware of that. The Einstein persona should not be used as an excuse to make C++ unnecessarily challenging.
- Focusing the different languages on different personas made these products holistic yet distinct.

Let's bring everything together into writing some character sketches for the App Center.

Audiences for the App Center

Above, I mentioned social gamers and mid-core gamers, who are both represented below. I've also added a third persona of a "whale," which is a term from the free-to-play gaming industry for a gamer who spends substantial money. That industry makes most of its money from a small percentage of gamers, so we need to capture this persona because the business models of the games we support depended on such users.

Penny Pincher
: A social network user who values keeping up with her friends. She finds games a fun way to pass the time and hang out with her friends, though she's not particularly competitive and doesn't consider herself a "gamer." Therefore, she tends to prefer light games that either mirror aspects of real life or enact realistic fantasies of a more relaxed life. She will only play free games and is okay to look at the occasional ad, but isn't going to spring for in-game add-ons.

Moby (the whale)
: An avid social gamer who dives fully into whatever he undertakes. He likes playing games with friends and achieving high statuses, either competitively or via cooperation. He is willing to pay for in-game upgrades that he can show off to his friends, or time-savers that speed up his game progress.

Patton (named after the World War II U.S. General)
: A committed gamer who already plays PC games but balks at the high prices. He wants a meaty game with some strategy in it, but doesn't want to pay $1000 upfront for a gaming rig and a AAA hardcore game that he might not enjoy. He values cheaper "mid-core" games. He cares more about game quality and immersion, he likes gaming with his gamer buddies or solo. He's willing to pay for it as long as he gets to try before he buys, and he's willing to try games with a good reputation.

These characters stand in for common types of folks. They also demonstrate the value the players get out of games and what they're willing to exchange for it, which helps us determine the business case for investing in the personas, which I'll talk about in the next section.

I used concrete, opinionated language, including specific genders and amounts of money, in order to evoke strong images. When communicating our audiences, being concrete helps in the same way that fictional characters are more memorable than dry listings of their attributes.

If we don't recognize that users are more diverse in reality, we risk turning personas into stereotypes. The character descriptions are intended to spark fruitful discussions rather than be narrow, prescriptive lists of attributes.

How would these audiences affect our strategy?

Patton was the most speculative persona and the one that we were most hoping to bring into the App Center. We knew there were fewer Pattons than Pennies, but luckily, we had a reference customer. A game on the platform, War Commander, that served Pattons and was making good money on a per-user basis. It was successful enough that we hoped we could replicate its success by attracting and highlighting more strong games.

Of course, being a marketplace, there was another side to the coin: we needed personas for our games' developers as well. The makers of War Commander, Kixeye, exemplified a persona of mid-core game developers, and they would have distinct needs from casual game studios like Zynga (who developed Farmville and Cityville).

Kixeye was a reference customer. By talking to them and understanding their needs, we could better learn about similar game studios. And by pointing to their success, we could entice other game studios to come make games with us.

Personas also offer a holistic view of users' needs. Separating Patton out from Moby and Penny also shows us that we have work to do. Patton cares about immersion, quality, and different genres of games from Penny. We need to think holistically about it when we design the App Center if we want to build a complete solution.

Suppose instead that we simply took some individual feature requests from mid-core gamers or game studios without treating them as a separate persona. We would build half-solutions and never reach critical mass.

Armed with a reference customer and a bunch of customer discovery that highlighted the Patton persona, we can now be more opinionated and specific in our product thesis:

> The App Center will help social gamers, in particular Pattons, discover great games being played by their friends, and incentivize game studios to compete for placement in the App Center within more diverse genres by building quality apps. This will in turn grow the Facebook gaming ecosystem to new demographics.

Later, we'll select coherent feature sets for the App Center based on this new thesis. But before then, I want to show why it helps to be clear about who we are not targeting.

Nonpersonas

The App Center team needed a clear nonaudience: hard-core gamers. They have less interest in casual gaming because they're willing to invest more time and money into premium experiences, which were also not available in browsers. This doesn't say that no hard-core gamers will ever play games on Facebook, it just means the team won't put special effort into attracting them. When somebody proposes a feature that seems like it's for hard-core developers, we will deprioritize it and be able to explain why.

Nonpersonas could have helped me on the Games team. I'm a competitive bridge player, so I regularly play in-person and online tournaments with strangers. I was also a strong Words with Friends player and had trouble finding available friends who were competitive.

My pet project idea for after the App Center was to build a skill-based matchmaking service, so gamers could play competitive games against evenly matched strangers. I spent a decent amount of time with a proposal, but I was never able to convince management, and they were not really able to explain why—other than that it wasn't high enough priority.

The hard-core gamer nonpersona would have brought me clarity and saved a bunch of time. Such folks love games so much that they are willing to play with strangers, whereas Patton is more interested in playing with friends. Matchmaking wouldn't appeal, so investing in matchmaking was a dubious proposition.

Let's now turn our attention to feature selection. As we imagine features, we may have to revisit some of our audience choice as we learn how feasible they are to build.

Selecting Features Based on a Target Audience

I'll work an example of feature selection and how it interplays with the product thesis and target audience.

Let's suppose the App Center will list apps as follows:

- Feature new games, like ones our editors think are good.
- Give a personalized ranking of games for each user, based on a combination of quality, their friends' activity, and whether it's like other games they play.

To a first approximation, all three of our personas would probably appreciate those attributes. Everybody's playing with friends and everyone prefers good games to some extent.

The product thesis for building this might be "a place for Facebook users to discover great games relevant to them. Developers will be incentivized to create awesome games, which will increase engagement, which will bring revenue to Facebook via in-game purchases and advertising."

Let's test this against each persona by writing an antithesis for each one:

- Penny, the low-intention casual gamer, may not be proactive enough to come to the App Center. She's more likely to respond to direct invites from friends.
- Moby is more likely than Penny to come, but he's not really an explorer. He might just stick to his existing favorite game that he's invested so much into.
- Patton may not find enough games that appeal to him and judge the App Center harshly before it has a chance to get going.

To me, the Penny and Moby antitheses are the more convincing. I think some of them will use the App Center, but it doesn't sound like a big hit. But the Patton antithesis seems fixable.

Let's look back at Patton's needs— immersion, affordability, friends, quality; and means—willingness to spend for something he enjoys.

Maybe we add scope to help Patton discover games:

- Allow users to filter games by genre so that, for example, Patton can filter out Farmville and focus on strategy games.
- Commission a few new launch games for the App Center so Patton can hit the ground running.

Keeping Your Focus

If you want to win a customer, you should solve a complete problem for them. Half-catering to two different personas is like designing a 2XL shirt with size S sleeves—technically, the small persona could wear it, but they wouldn't want to.

Here's an example from Facebook Games of what wouldn't be complementary: building a store that allows games to charge users upfront, and friend game invitations, i.e., inviting your friends to come help on your simulated farm. These are both fine features in their own right, but invitations to games with paywalls are unlikely to have very high conversion rates. They also address separate personas, which is fine over time, but not sufficiently focused for an initial release.

Building complementary features may sound like straightforward strategic advice, but it is hard to keep focus in practice:

- Those three features are not likely the lowest-hanging fruit. Others will be tempting.
- Game studios who make casual games are likely clamoring for new features, and if we pause developing to focus on the mid-core market, they may get impatient.
- Users may also be requesting features.

That's why communicating broadly and getting everybody aligned on target audience is so important. I'll cover more about prioritization in Chapter 7.

Multipersona Products

Most successful products eventually target multiple personas.

One of the more common dichotomies is between power users and regular users. I explore how to build products that please both cohorts in Chapter 8. Moby is an example of a power user, in contrast to Penny, but he and she are in the same category of social gamers.

Other times, personas represent different categories. Patton and Moby are both avid gamers, but they differ in the details. Serving diverse personas is one of the main ways products reach scale, just as spreadsheets are now for marketers, accountants, scientists, and many other groups. Spreadsheets are both extensible, allowing different professions to optimize them for solving complete problems, yet generic.

Each persona needs the special attention in each part of the product cycle, from interviewing, prioritization, and testing, to marketing, samples, and documentation.

In this section, I'll cover:

- What happens when personas have conflicting motivations with one another.
- Assessing the value different cohorts bring to your ecosystem.
- How to therefore decide which personas to spend more effort on.

When Personas Are in Conflict

Sometimes, the personas have potentially conflicting needs, and those needs need to be brought into alignment for the product to work.

Ride-hailing drivers and riders
: Drivers want to make more money, and users want a safe, cheap, timely ride.

Blog platform writers and readers
: Writers want large audiences and ways to reach them, whereas users want great reads and spam-free inboxes.

Facebook game developers and players
: Game devs want access to users' data, for example their lists of friends so they can make the games go viral. Users want to keep their privacy.

Navigating differing incentives of contrasting personas are some of the toughest and most valuable product problems to solve.

Multiapping

Here's a frustrating example of incentives misalignment. In the United States, Lyft and Uber are the most popular ride-hailing mobile applications.

I was recently trying to hail a ride from Lyft. To my surprise, as I watched the dot on the map to see when my driver would arrive, I noticed it move away from me—the driver was driving away! This persisted for minutes before I finally canceled the ride. The app popped a dialog asking me why I was giving up. To my surprise, there was an option for "The driver is driving away."

That piqued my interest. Why would drivers do that? And why was this oddity a common enough driver behavior that there was a dedicated option?

Later that day, I summoned another Lyft. The car arrived and I hopped in. Curiously, the driver had two phones attached to his dashboard. Later, a couple of minutes before he dropped me off, he switched on his *other* ride hailing app. I watched as Uber connected him with a rider before he dropped me off.

It all started to make sense—the drivers were "multiapping." I imagined this rider staring at their own phone, bewildered as their driver went the wrong direction to drop me off.

This was a classic case of mismatched incentives. Drivers want to work for Uber and Lyft simultaneously to make more money, whereas I want a reliable and timely ride.

How could Uber and Lyft solve this thorny problem? I imagine Lyft's asking me if the driver was driving away was part of their attempt to crack down on it. According to my research, Lyft and Uber will warn, suspend, or deactivate drivers when they detect violations, thereby bringing incentives back into alignment.

Here's an example at Facebook Games that I'm proud of. When we introduced star ratings for the App Center, we didn't want Game developers to game the systems. Game developers should want to build great games so that more users will want to play them. Star ratings hold studios accountable to those goals.

However, studios also want to make money, which means they might try different shady tactics to try to inflate their rankings. How could we combat this?

We didn't want developers to have control over when users would rate their games, or who would rate them, as this would leave them subject to manipulation. Therefore, we controlled the timing and sampling by displaying them to users in their news feeds and side bars on Facebook.com. This unbiased, random sampling technique resulted in ratings both from users who did and did not like the games, resulting in games with a wide range of star ratings, usually from around 3 to 4.5. The ratings seemed meaningful.

Apple, when faced with a similar design challenge, got this wrong. Developers can prompt users to rate their applications. I'm betting you've seen an "Are you enjoying this app?" pop-up just after you performed the most gratifying action in the app. Of course, you're asked to rate the app only if you said "yes."

Whereas there used to be famous apps with low ratings in the App Store, now, unless there's a political controversy or a major flub, they are invariably rated 4.5 stars or above. The ratings are nearly useless.

Any software ecosystem needs not only aligned incentives but a healthy mix of personas. To understand what's healthy, we'll need detailed understanding what value each persona brings to our community. Let's explore that further.

Understanding the Value of a Customer

Each customer brings value to an ecosystem. Perhaps they write content, send bug reports, provide goods and services, or pay money to the company which can be used to fund product improvements. Understand this value and then work to nurture the users you need more contributions from.

Wikipedia editors may be small in number compared to overall readers, but they are mighty in their impact because without them, the site would collapse.

Somewhat less obvious: At Facebook Games, Penny contributed no revenue, but that doesn't mean she didn't bring value to the ecosystem. She helped games gain critical mass which would attract other personas like Moby who were willing to contribute financially. This logic may seem clear today, yet it was surprising to the world when free-to-play games started making lots of revenue. Likely, some product-minded person thought this through and was able to pitch this business model.

Value can even be dynamic based on market factors. In ride-hailing, the value of a driver is higher when drivers are scarce. Increasing their payments will put more driver butts in seats to make more money.

Prioritizing Among Competing Personas

If your product supports a multisided marketplace, you'll need to prioritize feature work among the sides. This is a special case of selecting your target audience as discussed above.

If your platform has content creators and readers, you'll need to constantly grow both sides, but there will be times when one or the other needs more immediate attention.

Products that get this wrong are in trouble. Take a current example, stackoverflow.com, a software question-and-answer site. Historically, they obsessed over their "answerer" persona with incentives like feedback, a reputation system, special message boards, and achievements. It felt good to get upvotes and feel you were being helpful.

However, with the rise of AI assistants, readers stopped coming and answerers got fewer kudos. Their contributions were still equally, if not more, important because AIs were reading and using those answers. But, how would you know if an AI used your answer? If contributions dry up, AI answers could suffer, too, due to a growing backlog of unanswered questions.

The software engineering community needs to figure out how to rebalance these incentives, show question-answerers some love, while also getting their answers to where users are asking for them.

Chapter Summary

Software teams should have a list of personas that they are targeting. Those personas should have details about the background and motivations of those users, and should speak to the value they bring to the community.

If you use a list of personas to align with your team, you'll find strategic decision-making much easier.

- You'll find that design discussions will be easier because everyone will share a conception of the target user.
- You'll solve complete problems for people because the details in the persona will inspire you to notice gaps.
- You'll be able to select a target audience from candidate personas. That is, you'll prioritize different personas which in turn will make it much easier to prioritize features.

To determine these personas, you'll often need to talk to users to determine what they want. Customer discovery interviews are a good way to do this, but keep in mind that many users will have trouble predicting and communicating what they really want and will use in practice. To ensure you get the best signal, eliminate biases from your questions and try to tease out the strength of a user's conviction.

Exercises

In these exercises, you'll be working on a map app akin to Google, Apple, or Bing Maps called Applebingoo Maps.

You want to build directions for mixed-mode travel, namely trips with bike+transit or car+transit. You have two product theses:

- First, you have usage data showing that multimodal trips are somewhat common. You think that people who already have mixed-mode trips would switch to Applebingoo Maps due to the extra convenience of getting holistic directions.
- Second, people would use public transit a lot more if multimodal trips were more convenient and discoverable. You imagine the best way to make it more convenient is to provide routes that get them to the train or bus station and then to their destination.

You're going to interview a few dozen people in urban areas with access to high-quality transit.

As you complete these exercises, check the answers for each question before moving on to the next one.

1. First, you need to select your interviewees. Start with some questions for a screening survey. These will be designed to make sure you interview a few different groups of people in reasonable numbers. What will you ask, and whom will you select?
2. In your interviews' first phase, understand the motivations and knowledge of your interviewees. Come up with a few questions to discuss.
3. You're interviewing an occasional or rare transit rider, and you want to find out whether your second product thesis, that you could increase transit ridership, is true. What do you ask, and what are the types of responses you think could indicate whether or not your idea is good?
4. Write a persona paragraph that would represent yourself, as a user of Applebingoo Maps, and your stances toward modes of local transport in a generalized way. Imagine you'd been interviewed and a few other people gave similar responses to you. Make sure to give your persona a fun name.
5. Finally, in the last phase of the interview, how will you get feedback on your specific product idea?

Answers

1. For starters, find out if transit is a possibility for trips they take. Ask a similar question for car and bike. For each of the three modes, ask how often they use it. You'll want to stick to people with transit access who have a bike and/or a car. For the first product thesis, select people who frequently or occasionally use transit. For the second, select people who rarely or never use transit (but could).
2. I'd start with getting more detail about their transport patterns. I'd divide my questions between their commute and chores/personal trips, since it seems like

those would have different dynamics. Here are my questions relative to commuting, but the questions for personal trips would be similar:

- "Talk me through a typical recent commute at a high level." I'm asking this in a neutral way, not: Why don't you use transit more? And I'm asking for a simulation of their commute, which may reveal unexpected insights or explain their later answers.
- "How satisfied with your commute are you, and why?" They may already have complained, but if not, I want to make sure to give them a shot. I'm curious if they complain of factors like parking, traffic, concern about their climate impact, or trip length. Or maybe they give answers I didn't expect, like their apartment has a car lift that often breaks down, or they have trouble finding parking spots where they can charge their car at work.

3. I'd prompt: "Talk about the prospect of using transit (for your commute/chores)." I don't want to "lead the witness" by asking about mixed-mode directions yet, nor do I want to make them feel bad for not using transit. I'd expect answers like "too slow" and "service too infrequent or unreliable." More interesting for my product thesis would be answers that show a lack of awareness of their transit options, which I think Maps could highlight. I'm also interested in responses like "I'm too far from the station" where cars and bikes could bridge the gap. I might also learn that paying for transit is a pain. Or maybe it's unfamiliar, and they haven't gotten around to setting it up. If I hear that a lot, maybe my team should be focused on payment integrations with transit providers rather than our initial idea.
4. Here's my transport persona for a suburban railfan, "Suburban Rail Stan": "Rail Stan is a car owner in the suburbs of a city with some nearby trains. He's an occasional transit user because trains don't work for most of his trips. However, when he goes into the city, he will drive to the park-and-ride and take a train in. He likes that this avoids stress of driving and parking in the city, or because it decreases his carbon footprint. He may read or work from the train, not minding if the trips take him a bit longer because he doesn't see it as lost time. It annoys him that maps apps don't support his use case." If I'd written, "he channels his frustrations into exercises in his software engineering book," that might have been a bit too specific.
5. My goal would be to help them simulate their real-world circumstances as closely as possible to maximize the fidelity of their feedback. If I had a prototype—perhaps an AI-generated one—I'd ask people to use it with locations they normally commute to. Ultimately, I want both feedback on the product concept as well as a sense of whether it would change their commute patterns. Thus, I'd want to place the mixed-mode directions side-by-side with whatever mode they might have used traditionally and ask them to compare.

CHAPTER 7

Discovering Your Product Through Simulation

> *You've got to start with the customer experience and work backwards to the technology. You can't start with the technology and try to figure out where you're going to try to sell it.*
>
> —Steve Jobs

In Chapter 6 we discovered our customers. We wanted to learn who our customers were and what their problems were. In doing so, we refined a product thesis, our high-level claim of what an awesome product would be for those folks.

But we held off on thinking too much about solutions.

In this chapter, we'll open the floodgates and turn our attention to *product discovery*.

That is, considering the character and the simulation that make up a user scenario, we only have the character so far. Now it's time to write simulations.

But this product or feature you want to build—it doesn't exist. No story has ever been told about it. If we have any hope of getting it right the first time, we must tell miniature science fiction stories that predict how users will navigate the new superpowers we're giving them.

Thus begins the great journey from product land to system land.

From Vision to Requirements

One of the bugbears of software development is late-breaking product requirements that we didn't notice up front. Sometimes we get them from user feedback and sometimes we just notice more things as we design and implement. This delays roadmaps and increases scope. A huge reason for such unwelcome surprises is insufficient discovery work.

To minimize surprises, here's an itinerary I've found effective for medium- to large-scale projects. Every team works differently, so rather than prescribing a specific process or document template, I'll highlight the key points I think you should focus on.

- Finish your product vision with user scenarios, called *north star scenarios.*
- Slice and dice those north star scenarios into requirements in the form of a *use case compendium.*
- Create a roadmap, focusing on a first milestone that will encompass the most important requirements.
- Propose what you will build for the first milestone. Flesh out detailed stories, called *user flows* or *storyboards* if they show user interfaces.
- Add in detailed system requirements for each use case you chose, feeding back into the original requirements as necessary.
- Create a list of *jobs to be done* based on your user flows and system requirements.

At this point, you've transitioned from discovery to definition, which typically involves more detailed design, and will be covered in the following chapters.

No process can make you all-seeing, and it's only natural that you will learn surprising things late in the cycle. But the size of those surprises should be much smaller and hopefully not existential to your product.

Figure 7-1 shows a workflow illustrating what a process built around product discovery could look like by dividing it into three documents:

Product brief
: A vision document that gets everybody aligned on the goals. This is sometimes called a "problem brief" or a "one-pager." It includes, at a minimum, a product thesis/antithesis and target audience (Chapter 6), goals or product metrics to track (Chapter 5), plus *north star scenarios* which are defined later. In Double Diamond process model terms, the goal is to unblock discovery.

Product requirements document
: Fleshes out the attributes that such a product should have, not only in the long term but also proposing a first deliverable or milestone, while keeping prescriptiveness to a minimum. The goal is to unblock definition.

Product specification
: Shows how that product should be designed. Aim to unblock development.

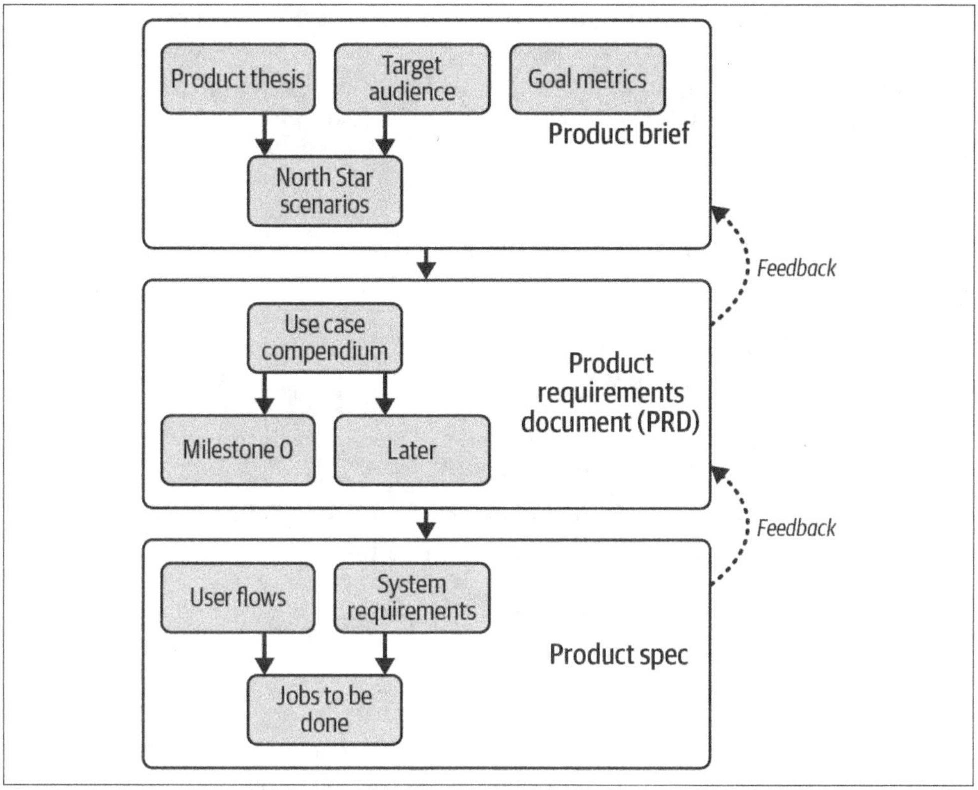

Figure 7-1. An example product discovery process

I'm not here to sell you a specific process, and most teams I've run into don't formalize all three of these steps. But I'll use this process for this chapter to illustrate how to systematically go from vision to a workable design, and I hope it's valuable even if you only use it in your personal workflow.

However your team works, here are three key attributes to aim for.

First, formally or informally divide up the work into multiple phases: why, what, and how, all from a user's perspective. Loosely speaking, phase 1 focuses on *why* users want us to take action, phase 2 on *what* users are demanding, and phase 3 on *how* users will accomplish their goals. At each stage beware of ratholing on details that you don't need to think about until later.

Second, use scenario simulations in each phase to make sure the team is aligned and solving complete problems—a practice called *scenario-driven discovery*. I'll dive into this further later.

Finally, allow for feedback to earlier phases. The engineers and designers working on the product spec need to be working closely with the engineers and PMs who worked on the product brief so that the team can learn. Without this feedback, you have the "waterfall" approach, which has fallen out of favor given the messiness of software development. Waterfall approaches tend to lead to overthinking the early phases due to the difficulty of making changes later, while also not adapting to changing information.

In this chapter, I'll cover this whole product discovery process step-by-step.

Along the way, I'll highlight important concepts related to discovery and prioritization:

- How to keep your use cases organized
- The transition from product thinking to system thinking
- How to think critically about the value your product will provide to users, including the four "brutal truths"
- Holistic assessment of the level of effort required to build and maintain software
- Using user flows to figure out your jobs to be done

To kick things off, I'll start with a case study in building AI agents.

Case Study Introduction

As I write this, it's 2025, the so-called "year of the agent," so I would be remiss if I didn't include a case study on AI assistants or agents. This case study is fictional, but it combines aspects of products that real companies are experimenting with—nobody is quite sure what will happen. Readers of the future: let me know how this all turned out.

Let's pretend we're on the support engineering team at Kabletown, an internet and cable provider. Our team charter is to make support run smoothly. There's a legacy automated system that chats with customers to try to help them before a human gets involved, but it's using pre-Large Language Model (LLM) technology, and it's too inflexible for the diverse needs of customers. Customers say they hate Kabletown's support and feel trapped. Meanwhile, human support agents are overwhelmed, with users waiting days for email and chat replies.

We've noticed that the top seven types of account actions account for 65% of support volume, but our current solution has only effectively automated about 15%.

First, here are some definitions related to AI you need to know.

Assistant
: An AI that can answer people's questions, perform analysis, and execute tasks within a single interaction with a user.

Agent
: Can also plan and act autonomously toward a goal.

Tool
: A function with a description that tells an assistant or agent how to use it.

Because Kabletown is not sure whether it needs an agent or an assistant, I will sometimes use the terms interchangeably when precision isn't needed.

Let's fill out a few sections of our product brief.

AI Assistant Product Brief

Our automated support agent, Helpy McHelpface, will revolutionize technical and account support at Kabletown.

Product thesis

We make two basic claims:

Reduced user frustration
: Users are frustrated with our current assistant, who does a poor job on most requests and does not even understand when to delegate to a human agent, getting this wrong 80% of the time. Helpy McHelpface will handle direct communication with customers better than the old technology because it understands users' intent better, lowering user frustration.

Lowered support toil
: Today's assistant must bring in a human whenever it wants to make a change. By giving Helpy tools to make changes to accounts, create appointments, or order shipped packages, we can automate up to more than half of the remaining unautomated support volume. By speeding up these routine-but-toilsome actions, we can dramatically improve wait times and user happiness while easing the backlog for our support representatives.

Antitheses/risks

What might cause this not to work as we expect?

- Helpy will take actions that it shouldn't, causing users to be unpleasantly surprised.
- We won't be able to achieve this with an assistant as opposed to an autonomous planning agent, increasing costs to build and run.
- Our knowledge base isn't good enough to provide the context that Helpy needs.

Target audience

We have two target personas, though we may start with one or the other:

Account support user
: Tinker Tia is a longtime Kabletown internet and cable TV customer who wants to make changes to her account, such as upgrading or downgrading her service or adding or upgrading hardware.

Technical support user
: Sad Lisa is a newly joined Kabletown internet customer who has something not working and wants to get it fixed.

Product goals

Our primary goals are to increase user happiness and improve our support backlog without hiring a bunch more people. We think we can do both at the same time. We're not aiming to improve profitability in the short term.

Adoption metric
: Increase the number of fully automated support interactions from 15% to 65%.

Value metric
: Improve customer satisfaction ratings after assistant and human support interactions from 2.1 to 3.5 (out of 5).

KPI
: Profit-neutral. While we hope to reduce expenses on human support over time, we may also lower revenue by, for example, making it easier to downgrade users' plans. We will track downgrades to understand revenue impact.

North star scenarios

We'll circle back to this section later.

Finish Your Product Vision with North Star Scenarios

Before I write north star scenarios, let me explain scenario-driven discovery, and then I'll talk about brainstorming, selecting, and refining scenarios for the product brief.

Scenario-Driven Discovery

Scenario-driven discovery (SDD) is the practice of using scenarios throughout your discovery process. I'm inventing this term, but not the practice—in the industry, the most related concept is "scenario-based design," but it's not super well-known, and I wanted a term that specifically spoke to the way we use scenarios to hunt for requirements and jobs-to-be-done.

You can lean on scenarios to ensure that you deliver a complete and useful product to your users. This is because:

- By highlighting the needs of characters, it makes the *why* clear, ensuring alignment between requirements and original intent.
- It illuminates comprehensive stories, meaning we're more likely to discover important features or edge cases.
- Stories are harder to misinterpret than lists of abstract requirements. A shared set of stories makes it easier to get aligned with the team.
- It's easier to find plot holes in scenarios than it is to debug lists of requirements.

The scenarios in the product brief are often referred to as *north star scenarios*.

> North star scenarios are the set of highlighted stories that you'll carry with you throughout the product lifecycle. You'll explain them to people when they ask what you're up to. They will justify and feed into product requirements, and later, you'll check them to see if you've missed building something. You'll make demos out of them. Depending on your product, they will likely result in marketing materials, getting started guides, or samples.

In the product requirements document, scenarios are sliced into fine-grained "requirements," or in agile methodologies, "stories."

In the product spec, scenarios are called user flows or storyboards.

In this section, I'll go through the preparation of north star scenarios with an eye toward finishing the product brief for Helpy McHelpface.

Brainstorm Scenarios as a Team

Not every engineer likes writing full user stories. Some find it daunting because it's unfamiliar, and others are wired to critique stories rather than author them from scratch. One way to overcome these gaps is to pair or team up. Collaborative story creation is really fun. For a given scenario, one teammate might write the kernel of it, and then someone else could add steps. Everyone exits with a sense of shared ownership and craftsmanship.

As with any brainstorming, collaboratively dreaming up user stories requires being receptive to everybody's ideas and building on others' ideas. But how does one maintain composure and inclusivity under stress and with tight deadlines approaching?

One key lesson I've learned over the years is that different people, often subconsciously, have different timelines in mind when they are doing discovery work. Some people are looking at the long term and others are looking a few weeks out. Some engineers have more forward-looking roles and others are more tactical.

During brainstorming, allow people to dream of the future. Establish with the team that, just because somebody relies on an expensive-to-build feature within a story doesn't mean it's going to get built any time soon. This will resolve tension with people who assume you're going to try to cram every last feature into the first release.

And keep up this mindset until you create your first milestone. Your goal is to have a lot of ideas so that you can make sure not to miss the best ones, and to develop a forward-looking roadmap so that each milestone can work toward a longer-term vision.

Brainstorming should be fun! Agile methodologies famously do "sticky note" exercises where people write little stories on colorful Post-it notes, then categorize them into themes and select the good ones. Do whatever works for your team, but it should probably end with a shared document of a few north star scenarios.

Select and Refine the North Star Scenarios

Select the most important and illustrative scenarios that you might want on your product roadmap. Later on, you'll prioritize them further, but the first step is just to curate the most important ideas and flesh out the stories that illuminate those the best.

As presented in Chapter 1, the team should debug the selected stories by looking for plot holes. Are some stories skipping steps in the user journey, or making heroic assumptions about users, or glossing over an important detail? Some engineers on the team may be better at this step than they are at creating the stories, but it's no less valuable.

Personally, I've found it productive and cordial to do this debugging with typed comments rather than verbally. It helps to keep the brainstorming additive and positive.

Remember that these are high-level stories; you're aiming for accuracy but not precision at this stage. When someone writes user flows, they will go into gory detail.

Armed with complete, motivating stories, we'll later spot all of the requirements.

Here is the first north star for Kabletown:

Cable box installation

> Tinker Tia wants to obtain a new cable box for a second TV she's put in her bedroom. She goes to kabletown.com on her laptop and finds Helpy. He agrees to help and asks whether she will require assistance from an installer, and she says she will. It guides her through the changes to her plan, gets her agreement, and kicks off a shipping order. It pings the chat when the order ships, and Tia gets

notified that it's time to schedule the installation appointment. Helpy works with her to establish her time constraints and set up an appointment for after the shipment is scheduled to arrive. Once the technician reports the install was complete, Helpy will check back with her to do a survey.

How did I craft this? My goal was to use stories as a focus for my creativity so I wouldn't miss important requirements.

- I started by thinking of a common user problem, "wants to install a new cable box."
- I kept asking myself "what would Tia need to happen next?" and "what would the Kabletown processes have to be?" until the user's complete problem was resolved.
- I thought about how we would track our value metrics, adding the customer survey at the end.
- I looked for plot holes. When a part of the story seemed too vague or made me fear a certain outcome, I asked myself, "what are the interesting details here that will help guide the requirements?"
- I checked back to see if I was being too prescriptive with specific solutions. My focus should be on the "what" and the "why," but not the "how."

After the brainstorming, the team notices that this scenario shows Helpy going through a complex workflow, and debates whether Helpy will need a high degree of autonomy, or if they can hardcode a workflow to wrap around the assistant. They sketch out a few variations of this scenario, showing the wide range of situations Helpy will confront, and decide that Helpy needs to be an agent, not just an assistant. They go back and update the product thesis/antithesis based on this.

Because north star scenarios are communicated widely, they leave these variations out of the main list so that they are digestible. They create an "appendix" of extra scenarios that are relevant to them, but not that important to communicate to the broader org.

The team sketches a few more north star scenarios that highlight a broad range of requirements, such as mobile versus PC, customer needs of sales versus technical support (or both), and, within sales, upgrades versus downgrades. They want to highlight downgrades because they may be a controversial topic for revenue reasons mentioned in the product brief. Their goal is to call attention to the biggest risks and misalignments early, before changes are very expensive and to make sure all the stakeholders, such as financial folks, feel represented.

Downgrade

Tinker Tia has two cable boxes but never uses the one attached to the television in her bedroom, and she wants to reduce her monthly bill. Helpy searches for a subscription plan that is like hers, but without the extra cable box, and proposes it to her along with the cost savings she will receive. She okays this plan and Helpy tells her that the reduction will be processed as soon as she returns the box. She okays that, so he sends her packaging in which to ship the device. She ships it and he sends her a survey after it's received.

Angry customer with account change
: Tinker Tia never uses the cable box in one of her rooms, and she wants to reduce her monthly bill. She goes to check on her account and finds a link to Helpy. She asks Helpy, who notices she's on a promotional rate and informs her there's no plan she can move to that will save her money. She gets upset and demands to talk to a supervisor. A support rep inherits the chat from Helpy and takes it over. They are able to arrange a small one-time discount for her in return for returning the cable box. She approves and receives a survey.

Outage
: Sad Lisa's cable internet has stopped working. She opens the Kabletown app on her phone—on her still-working wireless plan—sees the Helpy button, and asks Helpy what's going on. Helpy checks her address against the outage map, discovers there's an outage, and sends her an ETA. When it's resolved, it follows up to let her know, along with a satisfaction survey.

Customer hardware problem
: Sad Lisa's internet is slow, and she blames Kabletown. She sees the Helpy "get support" button at kabletown.com and clicks it. Helpy asks her questions about her setup, discovering that she's on a PC laptop on wireless. It figures out there's no outage, so it guides her through a series of diagnostics and suggestions, starting with the ones that have worked the most in the past, including resetting her wireless router, running Windows network diagnostics, and so forth. Resetting her Kabletown-supplied wireless router does the trick. Helpy tells her to contact it if the problem keeps happening (e.g., in case it's a faulty router), then sends her a survey, and she gives strong ratings.

When crafting these:

- I added friction and failures, such as a user that doesn't like bots, so that Helpy would be resilient.
- As I thought of different requirements, I wanted to create stories that included them. For example, I justified mobile support with noting that Lisa's internet was down, meaning she needed to turn to her cellular device. The stories function as sales pitches for those features, and we'll evaluate them when we prioritize.

If I've done my job, these should give a clear, intuitive idea of what we're trying to accomplish. That's because stories are a universal medium of communication that we've learned since we were children. You may conceptualize systems in a different way than I do, but we're probably on the same page about what these stories mean.

It may not be easy to build all that these stories need. That's a good thing. Remember from the Double Diamond model presented in the preface that the discovery phase of the product lifecycle is intended to be divergent and exploratory. Our vision should hold us to a high bar and push us to do things that will have a huge impact even if they are difficult. If it turns out to be hard to, say, give push notifications to Tia when the order ships, we can iterate and come up with alternate stories later on. Or we can sequence our ships to flesh out these stories gradually, as long as our incremental releases themselves provide real value.

Also note that they aren't particularly organized in a way that's easy to divide up and build. That comes next as we write the PRD.

Convert the North Star Scenarios into Requirements

If user stories were put in a database table, it would contain a list of moments ordered by time, attached to a user's persona. This is a great way to think about users' journeys through your product.

It's not as useful of a representation for system designs. Those are more like graph databases— buttons within forms within pages, and clicking those buttons links to API gateways around services that talk to storage systems.

If our brains contain something like these databases, then the process of moving from the discovery phase to the design phase is a *great reindexing* from a time- or story-based representation to a graph- or system-based one. Pictured in Figure 7-2 and Figure 7-3 are two alternative representations of the same product:

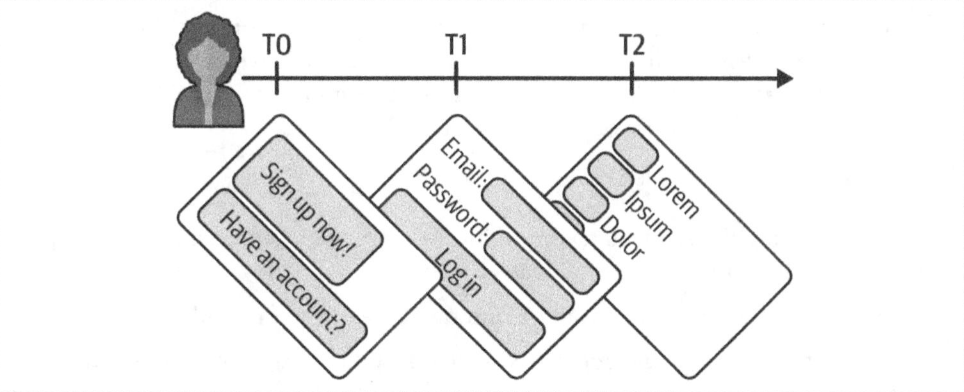

Figure 7-2. The story view

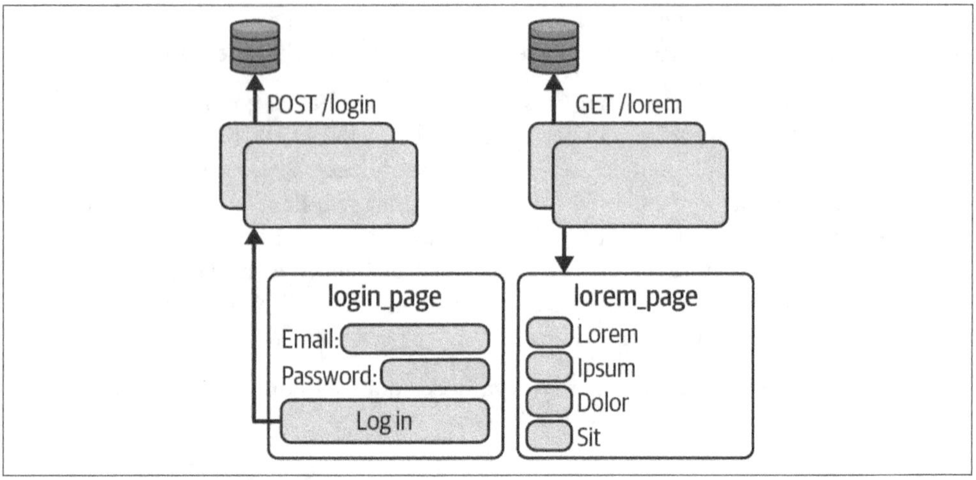

Figure 7-3. The system view

The most versatile engineers are good at building both of these indexes in their brains. If you can only build the first, you're like a Product Manager. If you can only build the second, you're completely reliant on one, and you will struggle to communicate with them.

The translation between the two representations is particularly crucial, and mistranslations are rife, especially when the PM and the engineer can't internalize one anothers' representations.

The great reindexing often starts with high-level requirements and design principles.

High-Level Requirements

The high-level requirements and design principles are a summary that establishes what we're "going for" with our design. Which persona are we prioritizing? Are we going for revenue? Ease of use? This can establish communication and trust with people who won't be able to go through all the detailed use cases.

For Kabletown, it might look like:

- Per the Product Brief, we're trying to increase user satisfaction and lower support burden while being revenue neutral.
- We're focusing on technical support interactions for the first milestone.
- We're going to target the most frequent tasks, such as slow internet diagnosis, first. For example, when Helpy detects something outside its expertise, it will delegate to a human rather than trying to help.

- We'll be focused on safety early to keep Helpy within clear guardrails even if that means sometimes not being as helpful as it could.

Notice how I'm calling out places where we're breaking ties between two different principles. Calling those out tends to be interesting and controversial, which sparks good discussion.

If you put this at the top of a Product Requirements Document, readers will find the rest of the document easier.

The Product Requirements Document

PRD will mean something a bit different at each company that uses the term. For some teams, it may also include the product spec that is coming later in this chapter. Just how much design to include in the PRD is fuzzy and something worth clarifying with your team, especially for larger projects.

For our purposes, the goal of a PRD is to unblock engineers and UI designers to do detailed design work. The Product Spec, covered later in this chapter, will unblock implementation. Thus, we'll be heavy on "what" and light on the "how." We'll include:

- High-level product requirements and design principles.
- Fine-grained product requirements—a *use case compendium* or story compendium that records all the specific interactions users want.
- Milestone definition to select which features will be done for the first release.
- Gather the right teams and stakeholders to work on it. (Out of scope for this book.)

Use Case Compendium

Next, we turn to the product requirements. I call these a use case compendium because each requirement is written from a user's perspective. Common templates for a requirement are:

- "[User] can [action] so that [motivation]."
- "[The product] provides [feature] so that [user] can [achieve value]."

Each requirement is a snippet of one of our scenarios. Let's break down the "Customer hardware problem" scenario—Sad Lisa's internet is slow and she needs to reset her wireless router:

The first requirement is: Sad Lisa can easily find Helpy on the home page without first logging in when she's looking for tech support.

The art to requirements writing is saying what needs to be happening while not being super prescriptive about how. Consider the first requirement. As I authored it, I tried to:

- Be concrete enough to communicate clearly and unambiguously. Helpy is specifically on the home page without needing log in, rather than just "Helpy is discoverable."
- Express intent. We don't just say that Helpy's on the home page, we are clear that it's about discoverability. If putting it on the home page is intractable, an engineer can check back in and look for backup solutions.
- Still allow the engineers some design latitude as they dive into the details. We don't say that Helpy will be in some particular location or menu on the home page, we just say that it must be discoverable and pre-login.

Sometimes it's hard to be clear without being prescriptive, in which case I'll give an example, like "on the home page (e.g., a chatbot button hovering in the lower right)."

Here are the remainder of the requirements for that same north star:

- Helpy can efficiently guide Lisa through diagnostics of slow internet, with causes ranging from software to hardware to outages.
- Helpy suggests to Lisa the most successful interventions that it has learned from our support database.
- Helpy will ask Lisa what worked so it can keep learning as technology changes.
- When its remediations are inconclusive, Helpy can suggest future follow-ups before signing off of the chat so that Lisa won't give up.
- Lisa is presented satisfaction surveys so that we can track our results.
- Helpy can be trained on satisfaction surveys so it can become more effective over time.

We'd break down the remaining north star scenarios similarly, rounding out our requirements. And we can add more that are outside of those scenarios as we think and learn more, and even add new north stars if we missed something big, or remove ones that we decide to de-prioritize.

I've selected a few more from the other north stars that I want to talk about later, relating to delegation of responsibility:

- Helpy can figure out whether a request is for support or sales with 95% accuracy.
- Helpy can detect when a user is frustrated at least 90% as well as a human operator and can delegate to a human.

- A human support agent can consult with Helpy when taking over a conversation so that human support can be at least as good as what Helpy would provide.

The percentages I chose here are somewhat arbitrary, and we may not know exactly what's achievable yet, but we're picking rough numbers. We'll hold ourselves accountable by measuring them with assessments of agent quality called *evals*. If we don't get close to those numbers, we'll rethink our approach.

And here's one final requirement that I'll bring up again:

- Sad Lisa can use Helpy from a mobile device not using her home internet so that she can get support during an outage.

Organize Your Use Case Compendium

Use case compendiums typically guide engineers throughout prioritization, design, and execution phases. And, while it's ideal to figure out all the requirements up front, often more requirements will get added as you iterate.

This makes use case compendiums load-bearing documents, and for a medium-to-large project, it pays to keep them organized and tagged.

If you want, you can turn each requirement into a ticket in your planning system—for example, Atlassian's Jira has a Story ticket type, each of which corresponds to one of these user-centric requirements.

Or you can use a spreadsheet, or an app like Notion with embedded database tables so that compendiums can be sorted, filtered, and managed. They can also be tagged with elements of the original product vision. Here are a few suggested tags or sections:

Persona
: In this case, a section for support requirements for Sad Lisa and sales requirements for Tinker Tia can help focus. We may also make prioritization decisions based on persona, as you'll see below.

North star scenario
: We can query for all the requirements needed to complete the promise of a given scenario.

Edge case
: Edge case requirements are important, but fewer people need to read about them and understand them. Allow them to be filtered out.

Milestone
: This will come in handy as we prioritize and plan our roadmap.

Status
: You can even use this table for project tracking.

Commentary
: Additional info as needed.

Table 7-1 shows the use case compendium.

Table 7-1. A use case compendium for Helpy

Requirement	Milestone	Persona	North star
When she's looking for tech support, Sad Lisa can easily find Helpy on the home page without first logging in.		Anybody	Customer hardware problem, malware
Lisa can use Helpy from a mobile device not using her home internet so that she can get support during an outage.		Anybody	All
Helpy can efficiently guide Lisa through diagnostics of slow internet, with causes ranging from software to hardware to outages.		Sad Lisa	Outage, customer hardware problem, malware
Lisa gets suggested the most successful interventions that Helpy has learned from our support database.		Sad Lisa	Outage, customer hardware problem, malware
Lisa is presented satisfaction surveys so that we can track our results.		All	All
When its remediations are inconclusive, Helpy can suggest future follow-ups before signing off of the chat so that users reengage when they need to.		Sad Lisa	Customer hardware problem, malware
Helpy can be trained on satisfaction surveys so it can be more effective over time.		All	All
Helpy can figure out whether a request is for support or sales with 95% accuracy.		All	All
Helpy can detect when a user is frustrated and delegate to a human.		All	Angry customer with account change, malware causing performance issues
A human support agent can consult with Helpy when taking over a conversation.		All	Angry customer with account change
…			

We're now well on our way to reindexing not only our requirements but our brains. You can start to see how system components can be attached to these requirements, but we haven't lost the original reasons we're tracking them.

But, before we start detailed designs, we need to fill out that blank prioritization column.

Prioritize the Requirements for Your First Milestone

Once we've aligned with the team on long-term requirements, the next goal is to create a roadmap. Which means we need to prioritize.

Prioritization is one of the most challenging and consequential parts of our jobs, and it often ends up being a bit of a mess. Everybody has their own take on what matters, and it's easy to get distracted. Just look at Table 7-1, which is less than half the size of what it would be if I'd written everything out. Combine this with planning a whole sequence of milestones plus organizational and codebase constraints. It's overwhelming.

To make matters worse, there are usually many things to accomplish before we even have something we can put in front of users. This is because of the four "brutal truths" that we'll discuss which show how difficult it is to build something that will make users happy.

We need a strategy.

First, I'll pinpoint, among so many competing concerns, what we should optimize for.

Next, I'll present a prioritization strategy used often in scenario-driven discovery, which is to concentrate on a single north star scenario for the first milestone.

I'll advocate for planning one milestone at a time.

Finally, I'll apply this strategy to the Kabletown case study.

What Really Matters for Prioritization?

The two most fundamental factors behind prioritization are user impact and effort.

> Optimize your bang-for-the-buck; that is, prioritize scenarios and features based on a combination of user impact—bang—and all-up company effort—buck.

This may seem so simple it barely warrants mentioning. But it's easier said than done. In practice, keeping focus is like navigating a maze. Other priorities creep in all the time, borne of navigating interpersonal conflicts and organizational issues, protecting egos, honoring promises to specific customers, or dealing with differing incentives among different employees. Being ruthless means staying focused on the value users will get per unit of effort.

Even measuring bang and buck is challenging.

Most engineers I know are overly attuned to either buck or bang. To caricature, some like to deliver faster, writing less code and keeping the codebase simpler and more maintainable, even if it makes things harder for users or lowers adoption. Others want perfect products and will do whatever it takes under the hood to deliver that. Wisdom means balancing the two properly.

I'll eye user impact and effort separately, as they are each interesting, and then combine them.

Optimizing for buck

As much as I'm tempted to be a purist and say that the only thing that matters is impact on users, the level of effort is important too. If your team spends a thousand hours saving humankind only five hundred hours, you likely haven't made the world a better place.

Engineers, being human, are often well-attuned to the level of effort, so I don't need to say a lot here. But there are two things I want to point out.

First, be willing sometimes to put in more effort than is strictly necessary if it builds an advantage over competing products or if it will delight your users. For example, if you've got a decent-sized user base, spending a little time to save them, collectively, a lot of time, is usually a good trade-off.

Also, consider the all-up costs, not just engineering costs. And this cuts both ways.

When engineers, especially junior ones, are estimating costs to implement, they are prone to just think about the size of the production code in the happy path. But what about defensively coding against the edge cases? Scenario tests? And what about non-coding tasks such as documenting, dogfooding, deploying, A/B testing, and marketing? Even if you don't know exactly how much those things will cost, you can factor them in.

On the one hand, by considering all-up costs, you can avoid scope creep. If you ever think, "this one's easy to add," see what your friendly neighborhood PM thinks. They may counter by explaining everything the company will have to do to get it out the door and in front of users.

On the other hand, think about what all-up costs will be if you *don't* build it. For example, if you decide not to add any programmatic guardrails for Helpy to keep it from saying things it's not supposed to, this could put pressure on user support, the public relations team, and the legal department to have strategies if Helpy goes off the rails.

Optimizing for bang

If you want to get mathematical, user impact multiplies scale or reach and value per user, calculated over a time horizon of your choosing.

$$\text{User Impact} = \text{User Value} \times \text{Scale} \times \text{Time}$$

User impact can be estimated with a *utility function*, which graphs how much value users get out of a product against what functionality is included. As you improve the product, the utility function should increase.

Alas, the math of a typical utility function is absolutely brutal, meaning you've got to do a lot before you make a big impact.

There are four harsh lessons or "brutal truths" about how hard it is to build something valuable for users:

1. Scale is hard.
2. User value is back-loaded.
3. Competitive differentiation is even more back-loaded.
4. Sustaining value over time is hard.

Scale is hard. It's a challenge to make products with high Impact and Scale. Making something deeply useful that appeals to a few people isn't that hard. But appealing to lots of people means making things discoverable, useful, user-friendly, well-marketed, robust at scale, and so forth. On the flip side, you can easily change the font on your home page, which will have lots of reach but isn't that helpful.

User value is back-loaded. The utility function is not linear as products gain features. They're useless until they gain a critical mass of functionality. Bicycles aren't useful until they have two wheels, brakes, can turn with handlebars, and can shift gears for going up hills.

Figure 7-4 shows a utility function for bicycles:

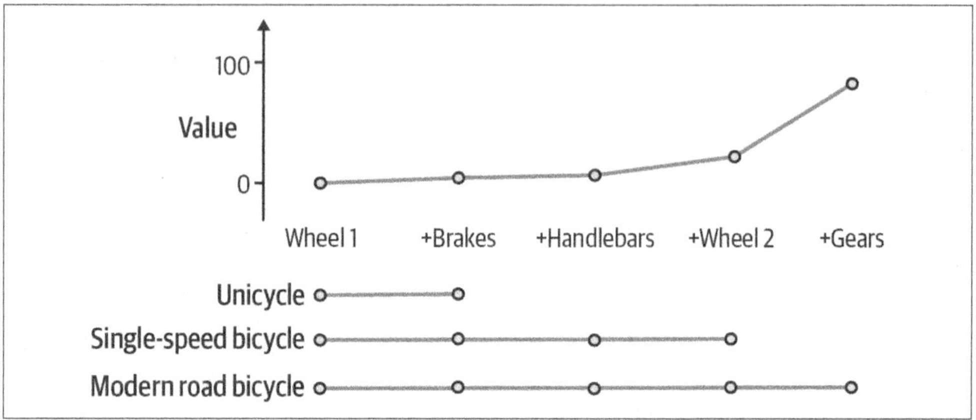

Figure 7-4. The utility function for bicycles as features are added

This flat-until-it-spikes pattern is characteristic of utility functions. Some of first few features may be "checkbox" features that don't need to be great, but they need to be there or the product doesn't work for most users. Unless you want to die, you need brakes. Unless you want to do dedicated balance training on a unicycle, you need a second wheel. Unless you are doing track racing, you'll want to shift gears.

Competitive differentiation is even more back-loaded. The third truth is that competition piles on additional pressure. Unless you're inventing something completely novel, when you enter a market, you often need a certain critical mass of features before anybody will take you seriously. And then you need to add something else, like a new feature or reduced costs. Other times, you're rewriting your product and competing against past versions.

I call this the *Value over Replacement Product* (VORP)[1] To calculate VORP, subtract out the value of existing products on the market, or the previous version of the product you're building, from your utility function. The chart for bicycles would look like Figure 7-5.

As you can see, VORP goes positive later than simple user value. It demands that we build products that are not just useful, but special. In the case of Helpy, we're competing against not only our existing automated system but actual human support agents —a tall order indeed. Later on, the market will have steadily increasing expectations for how well assistants perform as AI technology matures.

1 This term is adapted from sabermetrics, or the study of baseball statistics, where P means "Player" rather than "Product" and refers to the value of a major league player over the top minor league players waiting to replace him.

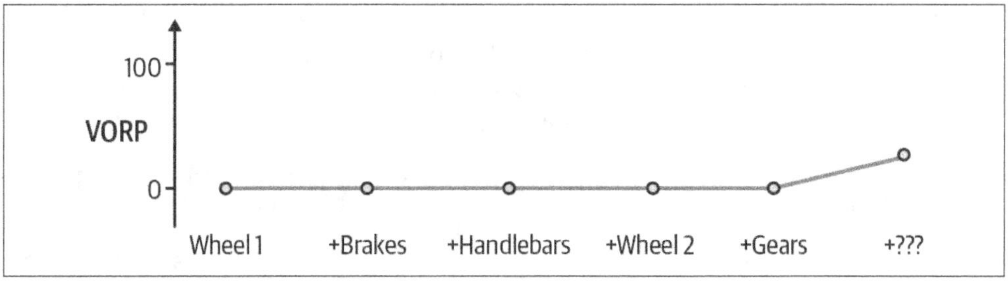

Figure 7-5. The value-over-replacement-product function for bicycles as features are added

Sustaining value over time is hard. The fourth and final brutal truth relates to the time component. It's harder to provide enduring user value than temporary wins. Building a cheap bicycle that breaks down, or one that isn't comfortable enough to attract repeated use, is easier than building one that users stick with for years. Likewise, Helpy will need to stay fed with updated support data and monitored for performance regressions if it's to stay helpful.

Because of the four brutal truths, most products and features fail to make a big impact because they are underbaked— they are missing a critical feature or are not engineered to scale and be maintainable over long periods.

The brutal truths serve as a warning against under engineering, but what about over-engineering? One should also avoid over-polishing, trying to accomplish too many goals at once or picking less important ones, being too slow to come to market, running out of money, or starving oneself of user feedback.

As I mentioned in Chapter 6, we can find a target audience who is under-served by existing solutions and will put up with missing features for something especially for them.

Another standout answer is often to iterate on your product, as discussed in Chapter 5. In iterating, we temporarily ignore one or two of the brutal truths, but we still learn along the way.

In this spirit, let's talk about prioritizing our first milestone.

Combining bang and buck

Many teams start with a *minimum viable product* (MVP). I define MVP as the point on the utility function at which the value goes substantially positive, albeit for a potentially small target audience—ignoring brutal truth #1 (scale) at first.

You may have heard the term *minimum lovable product* (MLP), a term that's growing in popularity as a reaction to MVP tending to be too rough.

In competitive situations, it helps to think of MLP as the point at which the VORP goes substantially positive. MLP ties to VORP because people tend to only love and grow attached to high-VORP products. You won't love a bicycle that only has the checkbox features unless it's your first bicycle.

In brutal truth terms, the MVP focuses on #2 (user value) and the MLP nods to #3 (differentiated value).

As we proceed, I'll show how to target an MVP or MLP using scenario-driven discovery.

Define the Target North Star Scenarios for Your First Milestone

When using SDD, define your minimum viable or minimum lovable product by prioritizing the requirements for one north star scenario, or a minimal set if one's not enough.

Focusing on a north star has quite a few advantages:

- Because north stars are complete stories, we will deliver positive utility.
- Because they include our best product vision, we'll ship something with positive VORP for someone.
- Because they focus only on one persona and story, we can leave out extraneous features and push generalizations to later.

We can narrow our early target audience. The most common example of this is to limit to employees who can dogfood the first release (Chapter 4) or design partners that are willing to tolerate early versions in exchange for having influence on the product or white-glove support. Another option is to limit to users of one platform, e.g., Android users versus iOS users, or to power users who don't need as much instruction.

Thus limited, we may be able to get away without pieces of our north star scenario, at first. For example, say we're targeting employees—if our story contains a discovery step showing how the user discovers the feature, we can substitute for that by emailing our coworkers and asking them to check it out.

Finally, we're ready to prioritize the individual requirements.

Prioritize the Use Case Compendium

We head into a big meeting to discuss prioritization. Maybe the tech lead or the PM has penciled in some as a starting point.

Luckily, we've tagged our table with scenarios and personas, and it will be relatively straightforward to figure out what's in and out.

In my experience, it's much more efficient to focus only on the first milestone. Ratholing on debating whether an item that's not part of your MLP is P2 or P3 is a good way to waste an hour.

Here's a simple format:

P0
: In for MVP. Can't ship or get user feedback without it.

P1
: In for MLP. These are super compelling stretch goals, and they'll be executed closer to ship time. If the schedule slips and you need to be done by a certain date, you won't be happy, but you'll still ship something viable.

Blank
: Everything else. Prioritize it when you plan the next milestone.

If your team works in milestones, here's a handy scheme that allows you to reuse the prioritized compendium as the project progresses:

0
: In for milestone 0.

0.5
: Stretch goal for milestone 0.

Everything else is blank. Then, when planning the next milestone, you add 1 and 1.5, respectively, for milestone 1.

I'll use the milestone format here because it encourages keeping our product roadmap current in a single easy-to-find document.

Most of our employees have Kabletown at home, so we'll limit our first milestone to Kabletown employees, who will be more forgiving and give more thoughtful feedback (Chapter 4). We can roll Helpy out and learn before the product is fully polished. The employee-facing release will thus be an MVP, not an MLP.

Which scenario should we choose? Here are a few considerations:

- We should limit our MVP to a support scenario or a sales scenario, as this will cut out a lot of work in feeding training data to the AI and testing for the one we don't choose.
- Our utility function will spike highest if we pick a common or high-impact scenario. Let's say that most of our existing interactions are for technical support, predominantly when people think their internet is not working or being slow.

- Assume the data shows that most of our tech support volume comes from desktops and laptops as opposed to mobile devices. (I have no clue whether this is true in practice, but let's roll with it.)

The "Customer hardware problem" scenario fits this. It's a fairly meaty support problem, which means we're going to really test our assistant's AI and make sure it's a good direction.

Our narrower target persona is therefore "Sad Lisa, Kabletown employee, who owns a PC." There aren't too many of her, but we hope she will love Helpy and give good feedback.

Unfortunately, there's a website framework refactoring happening at Kabletown, which means we're signing up for perhaps a week of extra work if we start with that. Should we switch gears and do mobile?

In considering all-up costs, a week of engineering is probably not a big deal for a company with as much bureaucracy as Kabletown. That will still be a relatively small part of the effort required to ship.

If PC and mobile usage are roughly equivalent, by all means prioritize mobile. But if 80% of support interactions are from people's PCs, we should probably just deal with the extra week of engineering work.

We focus on value every step of the way. We don't want to assume we're going to get through our entire roadmap—management at Kabletown is easily distracted, and it would be really bad if we got moved onto other efforts before we delivered big hits.

Table 7-2 shows the use case compendium, now sorted by priority, along with some footnotes on why I chose certain possibly surprising priorities:

Table 7-2. A prioritized use case compendium for Helpy

Requirement	Milestone	Persona	North star
Helpy can efficiently guide Lisa through diagnostics of slow internet, with causes ranging from software to hardware to outages.	0	Sad Lisa	Outage, customer hardware problem, malware
Lisa gets suggested the most successful interventions that Helpy has learned from our support database.	0	Sad Lisa	Outage, customer hardware problem, malware
Helpy can send satisfaction surveys so we can track our results.	0[a]	All	All
When she's looking for tech support, Sad Lisa can easily find Helpy on the home page without first logging in.	0[b]	Anybody	Customer hardware problem, malware
When its remediations are inconclusive, Helpy can suggest future follow-ups before signing off of the chat so that users reengage when they need to.	0.5	Sad Lisa	Customer hardware problem, malware

Requirement	Milestone	Persona	North star
Sad Lisa can use Helpy from a mobile device not using her home internet, so she can get support during an outage.		Anybody	All
Helpy can be trained on satisfaction surveys so it can be more effective over time.		All	All
Helpy can figure out whether a request is for support or sales with 95% accuracy.	[c]	All	All
Helpy can detect when a user is frustrated and delegate to a human.	[d]	All	Angry customer with account change, malware causing performance issues
A human support agent can consult with Helpy when taking over a conversation.	[e]	All	Angry customer with account change
...			

[a] Not critical for users in the short term, but user feedback is our lifeblood early in the roadmap.

[b] This is buried behind login in the current product, and we'd like to highlight it to get early dogfooding, since people don't need support every day. Also, logging in when internet is slow could be painful.

[c] For M1, Helpy can just ask the user up front what kind of request they have and send them to our old bot + humans if it's for sales.

[d] Employee dogfooders will be more forgiving.

[e] This will be important to productivity and quality at scale, but not for a limited test.

Now let's see if our north star scenario has held up to prioritization. I'll cross out anything we de-prioritized or made a stretch goal:

Customer hardware problem
: Sad Lisa's internet is slow, and she blames Kabletown. She sees the Helpy "get support" button at kabletown.com and clicks it. Helpy asks her questions about her setup, discovering that she's on a PC laptop on wireless. It figures out there's no outage, so it guides her through a series of diagnostics and suggestions, starting with the ones that have worked the most in the past, including resetting her wireless router, running Windows network diagnostics, and so forth. Resetting her Kabletown-supplied wireless router does the trick. Helpy ~~tells her to contact it if the problem keeps happening (e.g. in case it's a faulty router), then~~ sends her a survey, and she gives strong ratings.

Not bad! The tweaks are minor, and the altered story still seems compelling.

There's now one last step as we finish discovery and enter the design phase. We need to write detailed user flows.

Build Detailed User Flows for Your First Milestone

The stories we told were fairly high-level and glossed over a lot of details, enough so that we might be missing something important.

We also made sure that our stories were more about the "what" than the "how." We still need to audition different ways to let users accomplish those stories. For example, Helpy could run Windows diagnostics for users, or it could just tell them how to do it. It could ask Lisa survey questions inline or it could link her to a separate survey form. And so on.

We now flesh out *user flows.*

> A user flow shows, in detail, a user's sequence of steps in accomplishing one of the requirements, as well as any preconditions necessary to make the simulation work.

In this section, I'll show how to create user flows and then validate them with users.

In doing this task, we transition from discovery (we're learning new requirements as we do these exercises) to definition (we're also starting to define the product itself).

You may have heard of user flows, often called "storyboards," when doing UI design. They can be a series of UI mocks that simulate user clicks.

If instead our interface were code, our flows would be combinations of code listings and command lines, interspersed with commentary.

Here's some high-level advice for authoring flows:

- User flows should contain enough detail that we can argue over important interface questions (Chapter 8) and extract clear system specifications (Chapter 9) out of them.
- As when selecting north stars, weigh different options. Brainstorm, or provide alternative user flows and get your team to help you choose between them. This is a great way to bring in diverse opinions and let people know you're not married to any particular approach.
- Focus your efforts on the first milestone, along with any unprioritized items that you think are critical to understand early so that you can make a holistic design.
- As with any scenario, user flows should tell complete stories, starting from what motivated the user and how they discovered the features.

Let's flow one requirement for Kabletown, namely: "Helpy can learn from our support database what are the most common interventions and suggest those to Lisa."

Our initial results at training Helpy have left something to be desired. Alas, we never annotated our support database in our legacy system, so we have no idea what are the most common fixes for tech support questions. Our best guess is, we need to go through thousands of old support requests and categorize them with either the intervention that worked or that the result was inconclusive. We also want to annotate them with the support person's reasoning so that they can teach Helpy their wisdom.

Here's a user flow for a new persona, Support Rep Sam, who we're going to try to entice into doing a lot of annotations:

1. Support Rep Sam receives email from his boss asking him to annotate fifty of his old chats with customers within the next month.
2. He's pretty busy, but the boss asked, so he opens an internal tool that takes him to one of his old support threads and asks him to look and recall what fixed the issue.
3. He's presented with a dropdown menu of tags, such as "reset router," "scan for malware," "reboot machine," and so forth. He can also add a tag if one doesn't fit, and other support reps will now see that when they categorize.
4. Sam is asked to add commentary about why he chose his sequence of recommendations. He types "I started by restarting the router because two of the users' devices were offline, so it didn't seem device-specific."
5. He submits, and is taken to the next chat thread.
6. Sam gets through a dozen chats before he goes home. A few days later, he receives a nag email reminding him to go annotate more. He clicks on the link and completes a few more.

We could also write up an alternate version that is AI-assisted:

1. An AI scans a thousand chats and extracts what it thinks the remediation and reasoning was for each one.
2. Sam receives an email from his boss asking him to check the AI's interpretations for 50 of his old chats.
3. When Sam opens the chat, he's asked directly if the AI's choice is correct. He can either click *Yes* or modify the AI's choice and reasoning directly inline.
4. When he submits, he's taken to the next chat thread.
5. Meanwhile, the new choices are fed back into the AI. The next night, the AI will be retrained based on the feedback.
6. Sam figures the AI is right three quarters of the time, so he breezes through thirty items in as many minutes.

We'll discuss with the team and settle on an approach. Once we're confident in our approach, we can deliver a storyboard to go along with it. We can also run these flows by a few support personnel to get their takes, like an impromptu usability study. "Would you do this? What features would you want?"

With the user flows sketched and validated, we are finished with the discovery phase, at least until we learn something we missed.

Validating User Flows

For important interfaces, you'll want to validate them with real users to make sure that they are discoverable, intuitive, and address the most important user needs.

I'll talk about two practices: requests for comment (RFCs) and usability studies.

Requests for comment

If your goal is mainly to make sure that the feature does the right thing in the real world, you can create an RFC document that shows prospective users a storyboard, asking if the scenario would be useful to them and requesting feedback on the design.

Given that we're designing a short-lived internal tool for a relatively small number of employees, that's probably what we'd do here. We'd send an RFC over to a few support agents, allowing them to spot feature gaps, highlight confusion, and point out details about their usual workflows that we may have missed. Consulting these support employees early will also help if we're worried about how they might react to being asked to do new work.

With an RFC, we gave them the answer. We'll get more insights if we don't do that.

Usability studies

A *usability study* asks interview subjects to perform tasks based on a working prototype, uncovering many problems such as discoverability, usability, and feature gaps.

Set up some interviews, usually over video chat, and bring a series of tasks you'd like subjects to accomplish,

Your working prototype should seem to accomplish the goals in those tasks while leaving other functionality unimplemented. Many design tools can create such prototypes, and there are even ones that can take existing apps, or screenshots of them, and create modified versions with prototypes of new features.

To begin the interview:

- Help the subject feel comfortable and explain the format.
- Ask them to think aloud as they use your functional prototype.
- Tell them they can ask questions, but that you might not answer immediately.

Then, you give them the task, which is the motive part of a key user flow. Here, you might say, "You've been asked to annotate an old support thread with the type of problem and the remediation that helped fix it. I would like you to share your screen and use this clickable prototype to try to accomplish the task."

Give as little guidance as possible other than presenting the use case. If you do need to answer a question, write that down so you can debug it later.

I highly recommend that you help administer a usability study at your next opportunity. My first, for a C# API I had written for Microsoft, was an incredibly humbling experience. Watching programmers struggle with stuff I thought would be easy to use opened my eyes to how challenging and deep the field of API design was.

Translate User Flows into Jobs to Be Done

The last step in our great reindexing is to write out the components and features we need to build. These are sometimes called *jobs to be done*.

User flows can be translated into jobs to be done in the same way that north star scenarios get broken down into requirements.

For example, if we decide to make Sam manually annotate all of his old support chats, here are a few components to build:

- Internal tool for annotating chats
- An editable database table of tags
- A database table to store annotations with tags and freeform text
- Data pipeline for Helpy to ingest annotations alongside chat histories
- Per-employee tracking of progress toward the goal of 50 annotated chats

The great reindexing is now complete! We've successfully translated a user/timeline-centric view of our product into a system/graph-centric view, at least at a high level.

In Part IV, we'll turn our attention to designing these components and systems.

Feeding Back into the Requirements

Nobody should expect a beautiful waterfall that flows from discovery to design all in one direction. In practice, it's more like a tide pool that ebbs and flows and mixes different waters. We may occasionally need to add scenarios even as we design solutions for others.

That is, the list of north star scenarios and use case compendium should be "living documents" that we keep updating.

Let's say it comes time to add new sales scenarios for Helpy on top of our tech support product. This is going to stretch its capabilities because we need to give it more knowledge and access to new tools.

One of our requirements was:

- Helpy can figure out whether a request is for support or sales with 95% accuracy.

But did we think this through enough?

One of the realities of agent design in 2025 is that complex agents make fewer mistakes when we use a mixture of specialized agents rather than one big brilliant agent. In this case, we could create a tech support assistant and a sales assistant, and then Helpy would act as a concierge agent whose goal is to communicate with the user, plan, and delegate tasks to assistants, as diagrammed in Figure 7-6.

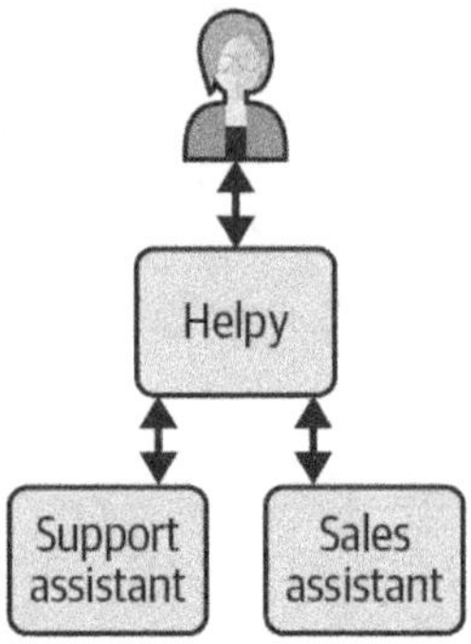

Figure 7-6. A mixture of two specialized assistants and an agent

We now need to look critically at this design and think of stories that could break it. What if a user asks a tech support question for which the solution is to upgrade a device? Rather than Helpy just delegating to one agent in a given chat, it may need to consult both.

If we didn't realize this up front, now is the time to craft a new user story and feed it through the great reindexing.

Chapter Summary

We've gone from a product vision in the form of scenarios to something resembling traditional implementation requirements. But guided by scenario-driven discovery, we're quite confident and set up for success:

- We had good communication because everybody can read stories.

- We're not wasting time because we focused on elements of the north star scenarios.
- Using personas and north star scenarios, we made a long-term vision but executed only an incremental milestone. This gave us a mixture of focused priorities, but in the context of a more holistic strategy so we knew we were building toward something coherent.
- We picked our top priorities based on cost and user value, being aware of the four brutal truths— that Helpy needed to be very strong in a large number of ways before it would deliver value to end users.
- Once we launch, we expect user feedback to not require a big redesign because the team looked for plot holes in our north star scenarios and user flows, and we validated our user flows with RFCs and usability studies.
- As we design and implement, we'll refer back to the use case compendium and user flows when writing scenario tests. We'll make a demo out of our north star scenario.

If you haven't before, I hope you give SDD a try. It's fun to write stories once you get the hang of it, especially as a group. And it could pay dividends tenfold when it takes you fewer attempts to ship the right product.

Exercises

1. In the 2010s and early 2020s, Visual Studio Code won the hearts and minds of millions of developers by providing an excellent discovery mechanism for extensions such as linters, syntax highlighters, and test frameworks. Write a north star scenario for this scenario that really sells extension discovery. If you're not familiar with VS Code, imagine an IDE with an "extensions marketplace" that lets you find the right tools for your needs.
2. Break your scenario—or mine from the previous answer, if you want to compare answers— into high-level product requirements. Try not to be too prescriptive about specific design elements to allow your design more flexibility when building user flows.
3. Pinpoint a couple of edge cases to add to the above requirements that may not have been directly covered by the north star scenario. Again, try to keep it high-level.
4. Write a user flow that adheres to the product requirements for finding well-liked extensions.

Answers

1. Developer Deanna fires up Visual Studio Code on a Python repository. She's new to the repository and has little Python experience. Happily, the maintainer of the repository has checked in a recommendation for a code formatter—she gets a pop-up suggesting she install it. Meanwhile, because her source code is mostly Python files, she is presented with recommended extensions for a Python language server and debugger—these are the most downloaded ones and have high star ratings, so she installs them and immediately gets off on the right foot. Finally, she goes shopping in the extensions marketplace and gets set up with a well-regarded AI coding assistant.

2. Users can author and commit a list of recommended language extensions to help their teammates quickly get up to speed when they clone a repository.

   There is a library or store which has extensions ranked by popularity and ratings so that users new to a language or repository can find the most effective options.

   Users are proactively shown recommended extensions so that new users get up to speed without having previously known about extensions.

   Users can search the extensions marketplace by descriptions, keywords, and names so they can browse for their favorites as well as newer extensions, such as coding assistants that haven't gotten highly ranked yet.

3. Users should see proactive mentions of new recommendations when one of their teammates updates them.

   Users can decline to install extensions, and VS Code should remember their preferences so that they don't get notices about extensions they've already declined to install.

   Users can have per-repository extensions or global extensions in case they have different repositories with different code formatting guidelines.

4. Developer Deanna opens up a new repository. VS Code realizes it's new to her, so she sees a pop-up asking her to have a look at extensions. She can X it out or click "Go to extensions marketplace." She clicks the button and sees a list of recommended extensions, filtered by appropriateness for the languages in her repo and sorted by some combination of popularity and ratings. She can see a name, brief description, downloads, star rating, and two buttons: *install* and *learn more* for each one. She clicks *Install* and up pops a page showing the author-provided details of how to use the extension along with a progress indicator for the download.

PART IV

Define

Now that we have product requirements and know the scope of work, we come to the Define phase of the product cycle, where we rigorously figure out how we're going to solve the problems we discovered. We'll develop detailed system and feature designs that solve those problems in the right amount of generality.

CHAPTER 8

Interaction Design

> *Make every detail perfect and limit the number of details to perfect.*
>
> —Jack Dorsey, founder of Block

Affordances are the ways a product can be used—intended or not. A couch affords sitting, but cats discover it also affords scratching. Both seatable and scratchable are affordances, though only one appears in the manual.

Affordances can be dangerous. Have you ever been to an outdoor concert and noticed that the chairs are tied tightly together? What unwanted affordances of chairs are such ties attempting to prevent? They make the concert safer by keeping the chairs out of people's escape lanes and preventing them from being hurled.

Due to insecure code and protocols, the digital world is rife with unwanted affordances such as spam texts and emails, privacy breaches, money laundering, phishing, and so forth. In some cases, these were inevitable, but in other cases, more forward-looking design could have prevented the abuse.

Don Norman popularized this definition of affordances in his classic book, *The Design of Everyday Things*, alongside the *signifiers* concept that framed the discussion in Chapter 2. If affordances are what a product *can* do, signifiers are the clues we use to determine what we *should* do with it.

Though chairs have an affordance of being throwable, there is no strong signifier that they can be used for this. Items that want to show that they can be thrown can signal it with grips, a ball-like shape that fits into a hand, or an aerodynamic design.

To see the distinction between signifiers and affordances, let's consider public interfaces of classes. In object-oriented languages like Java and C#, public methods are affordances and the `public` keyword is a signifier that they are affordances for callers outside the class. `private` is a signifier only for callers inside the class.

In Python, `def` is the method signifier. Since Python has no private methods, by convention, developers put a _ in front of the name to signify it's not meant to be called externally, but the only enforcement is the "honor system." In a sense, that hides the method from outside callers. I suppose we could call it an anti-signifier, like a "KEEP OUT" sign.

From the perspective of a caller outside the class, methods can be categorized as in Table 8-1.

Table 8-1. Method affordances and whether they are signified as callable to external callers

Designation	Affordance?	Signified?	Note
public method (Java/C#)	yes	yes	Can be called, as users expect.
private method (Java/C#)	no	no	Cannot be called, nor would a user expect it.
normal method (Python)	yes	yes	
underscored method (Python)	yes	no	Can be called, but the leading underscore tells people not to.
publicly accessible method that fails because it's not implemented	no	yes	Seems to be offered, but isn't.

Signifiers and affordances often go hand in hand. In a multiple-choice online survey, a radio button signifies that at most one option can be selected, whereas a set of checkboxes signals that multiple options can be chosen. The different semantics come with standard visual patterns.

As you design interfaces, brainstorm their affordances and think through each one's uses and misuses, leaving out unwelcome ones. This requires a lot of design taste and iteration—at what point does allowing high-throughput use cases become allowing denial-of-service attacks in which someone intentionally spams you to take down your service?

For those affordances you do expose, use signifiers to lead users to the safest and most useful ones.

> Software interface design mostly boils down to choosing which affordances to expose and how to signify them to users.

In this chapter, I'll explore the choices we make when deciding what features to expose and how to expose them. Armed with affordances, signifiers, scenarios, and personas, you'll be able to:

- Call attention to the correct usage of your product and away from incorrect usage.
- Time the affordances you ship wisely.
- Learn when to make your features extensible and when to solve targeted problems.

In my experience, most design debates revolve around these trade-offs, and we could all stand to think about them more clearly. User scenarios and personas unlock a concrete way to do so.

Before we get to the design advice, I'll need to build a little scaffolding for it:

- The role of bias and ideology in software design
- The prerequisites of good design
- A case study to frame the advice

The Role of Bias and Ideology in Software Design

Software engineers bring ideological beliefs and biases to their work.

Here are a few examples:

- Some prefer to design flexible, power-user friendly products while others prefer opinionated, safe, easy-to-use ones.
- Some are pessimists who look at the downsides and negative impacts of features and products. Others focus more on the advantages.
- Some believe that free and open source software is better for transparency, ethics, and security. Proprietary software advocates emphasize intellectual property rights and commercial incentives for innovation.

Ideologies can be a source of strength and purpose, but when designing software, they are mere starting points. The optimal product will always be informed by users and their needs more than the beliefs of the designers.

I'll quickly survey these three examples to show that in practice.

Debate: Flexible Versus Opinionated

Think of the modern smartphone industry. The designers of Apple's iOS and Google's Android started out with very different ideologies, but the products have converged. Apple has exposed more flexible developer platforms, whereas Google and its hardware partners have limited some freedoms and exposed more opinionated experiences.

There are business and regulatory reasons for some of these changes, but also product design reasons. This "convergent evolution" suggests that the companies are listening to similar users and partners who face similar scenarios.

Debate: Optimism Versus Pessimism

Each new wave of technology unleashes a wave of optimism as well as a moral panic over its societal impacts. Last decade, that was social media, and now it's AI. Better software design is often a key part of the solution.

To take one example, people worry about the effect of LLM chatbots on people's critical reasoning abilities and the ability for chatbots to make crime much easier.

As of this writing, it's early, but we're seeing:

Red teaming
: Researchers are crafting adversarial scenarios and then subjecting AIs to them in an effort to harden the AIs against leaking knowledge about threats like bioweapons and identity theft.

Tutoring modes
: LLM providers are developing learning modes to help with student scenarios so as to help students reason critically rather than feeding them the answers.

I'd guess we will see parental controls and other protections for various scenarios and personas over time.

Debate: Open Source Versus Proprietary

In the 2000s, most products were either fully proprietary or fully open source. Many modern software companies have a model that's somewhere between open source and proprietary:

- In open core models, most features are open, but certain corporate user scenarios are enabled by proprietary features.
- In dual licensing models, the licensing terms are based on the user persona, for example by adding restrictions for commercial use.

These modes try to achieve a balance by mixing innovation incentives with openness and transparency.

If we find ourselves arguing only with ideology, we should wonder whether we know enough about our customers and their use cases. Many of the techniques learned so far in this book will unlock better design decisions.

The Prerequisites of Good Design

Much of the design advice in this chapter hinges in part on using scenarios, personas, and in some cases, iterative development. Those prerequisites don't guarantee good design, but they certainly help, and we're going to exploit these foundations built earlier in this book:

- Build the ability to gather feedback and quickly iterate into your development practices. This will give you confidence that if an interface was too limiting, you can enhance it later. This was discussed in depth in Chapter 5.
- Develop a picture of your target audience and what they want, as I covered in Chapter 6. For example, if they all want the same thing, make it the only option. If they want different things, insert those points of flexibility.
- Use scenario-driven discovery (Chapter 7) to think through the details of how customers will use your product. If these scenarios reveal safety gaps, see if you can close those gaps without loss of generality.

Armed with these tools and techniques, you won't have to resort to ideological shortcuts as often, and you'll be able to make design decisions when you have the best information and the most motivation to implement them.

With our foundation in place, here's a case study to help navigate through the concrete design principles.

Case Study Introduction

In the early 2010s, I led the design of Facebook's schema for modeling database objects in the social network's graph. Objects, called *entities*, might be Users, Posts, Groups, Events, and the like. *Edges* are connections such as friendship, membership, or the author of a post. The schema is called `EntSchema`, short for "entity schema."

One of our north star scenarios was:

Schema authoring
: Model creators want to author one representation and have it spit out everything they need—the database schema, the class for reads, and the class for writes.

If that were the only north star scenario, the table stakes version might look like so:

```
class PostSchema(EntSchema):
    def db_config() -> DatabaseConfig:
        return (DatabaseConfig()
            .name("posts"))

    def fields(self) -> dict:
        return {
```

```
            "id": int64_field().primary_key(),
            "text": varchar_field(4096),
            "created": int64_field(),
            # ...
        }

    def edges(self) -> dict:
        return {
            # An author can have many Posts.
            "author": edge(UserSchema, cardinality=EdgeCardinality.ManyToOne),
            # ...
        }
```

This would create:

- A database table with a schema containing `id`, `text`, and `created`
- An edge database table connecting an author to their posts
- A class, `Post`, for read access in Python
- Another class, `PostMutator`, for creating and editing Posts in Python

Here's `Post`:

```
class Post:
    @property
    def text(self) -> str: ...

    @property
    def created(self) -> str: ...

    @property
    def id(self) -> int: ...

    async def fetch_author(self) -> User: ...
```

Note that very little is specified in the schema that is not directly useful at the database layer. It's the bare minimum we needed to solve our scenario.

At the time I introduced EntSchema, there were already many entities in the database and codebase that had been authored by hand. A big advantage of keeping a simple database-level representation would be that we could automatically generate an EntSchema from the database representation we had stored because there's no information in the schema other than what's in the database. A simple script would therefore give us a huge leg up during the migration of a very large codebase.

However, schema authors weren't the only persona. We had to think about the people reading and using schemas, too. For example, engineers often used object inspectors to help debug production issues.

Suppose we asked the Post author for rich type information, and they specified that the `created` field was a timestamp, not just an integer. Now their users could see a human-readable time pretty-printed when debugging Post objects.

But was this just scope creep? An incremental strategy was risky. If we did the easy thing and just shipped the low-level version, we'd struggle to retrofit richer type information later.

This case study will walk through how we picked which additional information authors should provide into their EntSchemas, and why. By the end of this chapter, we'll have transformed the PostSchema that I showed previously into something suitable to more scenarios.

Ents in Go

A popular open source Go framework called ent is based on EntSchema. Check it out to get an overall feel. However, the type system for fields is not as rich as in the internal Meta version.

Call Attention to the Correct Usage of Your Product and Away from Incorrect Usage

A well-designed product signifies and defaults to the productive and safe affordances while making sure people don't accidentally use the riskier ones.

Affordances can be signified as more or less welcoming just as traffic lights signal how safe it is to go. Green affordances should be safe and generally effective, whereas yellow lights are cautionary, and red are forbidden.

> Divide your affordances into green, yellow, and red colors based on how recommended they are, and then signify them accordingly.

To illustrate this, let's think about clicking a link to a possibly suspicious web URL:

Green
: The link navigates to another page within the same site.

Yellow
: The link sends the user to a page outside of the same site. They may be shown an "are you sure you mean to go to this external site?" warning to make sure the user isn't going to go to a site that's impersonating the origin site.

Red
: The user clicks a link that leads to a suspicious site without a valid security certificate. The browser puts up a tall hurdle before the user can navigate there.

Green, yellow, and red affordances are all available, but you can also eliminate affordances entirely. Perhaps the webpage they click into is known to be malicious. The browser could completely prevent this.

Products that make green scenarios very discoverable and yellow or red ones less so are a pleasure to use. The user proceeds with confidence, building up enough trust in the product to operate without second-guessing.

Here are a few common techniques to guide your users to the most useful affordances:[1]

- Choose safe, predictable defaults.
- Optimize your path of least resistance.
- Give affordances to the right persona in the right scenario.
- Perform validations.

I'll elaborate on each of these.

Choose Safe, Predictable Defaults, or None at All

Mix flexibility with ease of use by providing proper defaults for the masses but allowing customization for the pickier types. The people who don't spend time looking at detailed settings should get reasonable behavior, while those willing to invest the time in customization can find more power.

Users trust and pay product developers to pick good default configurations.

As a convenience, EntSchema assumes that users want to have the same database column name as what's specified for users, but it can be customized. Suppose the `Post Schema` maintainer figured "posted_at" was a clearer name than "created" and decided to change it. They could do:

```
"posted_at": integer_field().db_config(name="created"),
```

This is flexible without requiring every schema author to redundantly specify the database name, or to do a database migration just to change the name used in code.

Defaults are more than just a convenience. The consequences of choosing improper defaults can be politically fraught or even disastrous:

1 In 2003, Rico Mariani coined the term *pit of success* to describe the practice of helping users to "fall into winning practices." I love this.

- Operating System companies such as Microsoft, Apple, and Google have faced litigation for defaulting users to a particular browser or search engine.
- Early versions of Internet Explorer enabled ActiveX controls by default, creating significant security vulnerabilities that allowed various viruses and worms to spread.
- In 2009, Facebook began defaulting users' new posts to "Everyone" privacy, causing substantial blowback and loss of trust with customers that lingered even after they gave users more explicit control.

The Facebook example brings up one of the most overlooked defaults: *no default*. Developers get used to providing default arguments to everything to keep callsites small and product surfaces slick, but this can be a false trade-off. Users should make conscious decisions when either alternative might be unsafe, unexpected, or ineffective. A self-driving car wouldn't default to turning left or right—it would insist that the navigator input a destination to help the car choose. And social media companies should prompt their newer users to make informed choices about their audiences.

> The quality of a product interface can be measured by the relevance of the questions it asks of its users.

Let's see this in practice. PostSchema has a major database problem. The database has many shards, and yet a common query is "get all the recent posts for this author." If they aren't all on the same shard, this will be incredibly expensive because it will require fanning out to every shard to find and retrieve the posts.

If posts are all in the same shard, the query performs well. Therefore, the `PostSchema` creator should specify a colocation in their database config:

```
def db_config() -> DatabaseConfig:
    return (DatabaseConfig()
        .name("posts")
        .colocateWith("author"))
```

If EntSchema defaulted to assuming there was no colocation, since none was specified, posts would have been spread randomly. The creator wouldn't have realized the error until they hit production and not even until they hit scale.

Therefore, there should be no default. The user should be forced to make a choice, and we did our best to inform them of the trade-offs.

Next, I'll generalize this maxim of picking good defaults.

Optimize Your Path of Least Resistance

Users are not perfectly premeditated when exercising products. They often naturally take the path of least resistance.

A *malfunctioning traffic light* is where the relative discoverability or ease of use of two features is inverted from what it should be. If you like, picture the traffic light as upside down, with red affordances below green or yellow ones when they should be at the top.

For example, when the designer defaults to a yellow affordance—public posting on Facebook—when they should have defaulted to a green one—sharing with friends—that's a malfunctioning traffic light.

This is a case where the *relative* ease of use and strength of the signifiers between different affordances matters more than the absolute ease of use and discoverability of the product. And this is common.

When we designed these application-level EntSchema field types, we created string subtypes like emails, natural language text, enums, and phone numbers. Developers typed these as `email_string_field` and so forth.

But we had a problem: I knew we couldn't account for all possible types of strings. Users could add them over time, but that seemed burdensome, so I added `string_field` as a catchall fallback.

Alas, the least helpful option was also the most discoverable! Many schema authors began to overuse `string_field`. It had an attractive signifier—it looked just like what they'd expect in other systems. I'd bet many engineers didn't even notice there were other options. Others maybe knew, but meant to come back later and figure it out, then forgot.

That is, yellow affordance `string_field` is easier to find than green affordance `email_string_field`. It was as if our traffic light had yellow on the bottom rather than green.

`string_field` was also easier to specify—it was shorter to type. It required no extra thought, whereas those other types required developers to look through a menu of string types and choose thoughtfully.

Green affordance `enum_string_field(MyEnum)` is harder to use than yellow affordance `string_field`. Again, our traffic light is malfunctioning.

Each individual declaration was straightforward to use, but due to the relative usability and discoverability, the system as a whole didn't work.

To fix this, we removed `string_field` and replaced it with something more overt: `custom_string_field`. This put it on an even playing field with the other string subtypes and signaled to users that it wasn't the mainstream option.

That tackled the discoverability inversion, but busy developers still might overuse it anyway. Perhaps they copy/paste it from somewhere or put it in as a placeholder, forgetting to come back to later.

So I added a little friction: I forced them to add a validator. Suppose a schema author wanted to accept a regular expression as input. They could do:

```
'my_regex_field': custom_string_field().validator(lambda x: is_regex(x))
```

They could always add an empty validator, but I felt I'd nudged enough to get most engineers thinking. Failing that, I'd given a signifier to code reviewers—they could notice the lack of a validator and flag it.

`custom_string_field` was much less tempting than `string_field` and dramatically improved the accuracy of schema specifications.

Give Affordances to the Right Persona in the Right Scenario

Put careful thought into who you're giving choices to and when. Start with who:

In setting those three `Post` fields, `id`, `posted_at`, and `text`, what could go wrong for a developer who is creating a post?

```
post = await (PostMutator()
    .set_id(rand())
    .set_posted_at(now())
    .set_text(some_user_input)
    .create())
```

Here are a few gotchas:

- The database should be allocating IDs from its ID space to avoid duplicates and ensure fair sharding, not letting the user do it.
- `id` could be inadvertently left out.
- `posted_at` could be left out, or set to 0. (If you've ever seen Dec 31, 1969 as a timestamp, you may have seen this bug.)
- `posted_at` could accidentally be set to some other integer that is clearly an invalid timestamp.

How can a schema author create a pit of success so that people creating and editing objects don't get into trouble?

With little effort, the schema author can pack more meaning into their field specifications, and all these scenarios can be prevented:

```
    def fields(self) -> dict:
        return {
            "text": natural_language_string_field()
                .db_config(type='varchar(4096)'),
            "posted_at": timestamp_field().at_creation(),
            # ...
        }
```

We made several changes here which widen the pit of success by reducing engineers' decisions:

- `id` is left out completely—we're just going to create it automatically for all our schemas at creation time.
- `posted_at` is specified as a timestamp, allowing certain range checks. It's also marked as a special `at_creation` timestamp so the `PostMutator` will automatically set it without requiring input.

More precisely:

- We shifted the decision over the `id` from a persona who didn't know what they were doing—app developers—to one who did—database engineers.
- We shifted the decision for `posted_at` from the person creating a `Post` to the person who authored `PostSchema`.

Think carefully about which persona should be making choices.

Multipersona Onboarding Flows

Purchasing flows for SaaS users are often multipersona. If you're building products for individual contributors but selling to companies, imagine the IC, who's excited to adopt the product, being confronted with the payments screen. They won't have access to the company's purse strings, and the people who have them probably won't want to text the company's credit card information to them.

Asking the IC for the purchaser's email may be an easier lift. The IC can let them know to look for the email, and then the finance person can click and fill out the form.

Beyond targeting the proper persona, we should provide the affordances to them at the right time, that is, when the user has the information they need to make a decision and when they're motivated to do so.

I mentioned colocation for EntSchema. When should the schema author decide their database layout? Do they need to think about that up front?

One of the key scenarios we kept in mind during development was the "hackathon scenario," for when the user was doing rapid prototyping. They wanted to quickly sketch their product model, maybe wire it up to some UI, and demonstrate a product idea.

To this end, we built a draft mode for prototyping users. Users could remove this mode when they were ready to productionize. Until then, many production-readiness checks are turned off, including the checks to make sure you'd chosen a colocation. This both deferred the decision until they had a better idea of what they wanted and deferred the extra work until the author was even sure they wanted to productionize.

Once the right person is deciding at the right time, it's time to validate their decision.

Perform Validations

Validate users' decisions. Let's add some validations to the `text` field:

```
"text": natural_language_string_field()
    .max_length(4096)
    .user_input(),
```

First of all, I've up-leveled our `varchar(4096)` declaration to a `max_length` in the schema. This means I can validate the input length earlier, in our API tier, rather than in the database tier.

As discussed in Chapter 3, I have:

- Shifted left, validating earlier and reducing load on our database
- Validated at the interface layer so I could provide a clearer application-level error

Secondly, I marked this field as `user_input`, as opposed to something our internal engineer is choosing—meaning we can screen for malicious URLs and other security vulnerabilities, rather than relying on each callsite that creates a post to do so.

Now that we've talked about feature design and various techniques for digging pits of success, let's talk about whether we should even include features at all.

Time the Affordances You Ship Wisely

People say technology can be used for good or for ill, and the safest affordance is one that doesn't exist. Even something as seemingly benign as allowing users to specify their names on a social network opens up vectors like profanity and abuse, and so we have to harden most things we expose.

Therefore, we gamble when we expose a feature we haven't thought through.

In an ideal world where we are iterating and listening to users, the question surrounding a prospective feature is not: "should we add it?" it's "*when* should we add it?" If you leave out an important feature, simply add it later.

In such an environment, it pays to be a bit conservative about what you expose. You can always add later when you have more details from users about what they need.

> When in doubt, leave it out.

If you're too aggressive and ship a feature too soon, there are many bad things that can happen:

- You don't have enough data from users. You therefore make ill-informed design decisions because you resorted to ideological defaults.
- Poor testing produces shoddy results.
- People struggle to use it because you didn't spend enough time on design.
- You could have built something more valuable.
- It may require maintenance or long-term ownership that you won't have time to prepare for.
- If you're building software like an API that needs to be stable, users won't like when you revise and break compatibility.

Note that you're much more likely to cut these sorts of corners when the feature is not one of your team's top priorities. So here's a corollary:

> Build features when you can give them enough focus to do a good job.

The other corollary to "When in doubt, leave it out" is: "don't remain in doubt." Building conviction about whether a feature is needed can require as little as a couple of conversations with users, of the sort I introduced in Chapter 6, or a look at the metrics. Either you'll get the feature built or see that it wasn't as important as you thought. Both of those are good outcomes! We engineers like to be the ones who "had the idea," but our managers love when we verify our assumptions and learn from data, and users love the results.

Let me retreat from the ideal, iterative world and let practicality enter my thinking. In practice, there are certain overheads in shipping features, such as code review, deployment, knowledge transfer, management, and documentation costs. So we may want to bundle certain lower-priority nice-to-haves with critical features out of expedience or to put a little extra love into our products. But our meta-goal should be to minimize these trade-offs by reducing the overhead of shipping. This more neatly aligns our goals with those of our users.

Here are a few useful maxims for shipping a feature that work well both in theory and in practice:

- If it's worth building, it's worth validating.
- Be neither an optimist nor a pessimist.
- Apply the rule of three.
- Build it in stages.
- If necessary, start with an experimental version.

If It's Worth Building, It's Worth Validating

Don't ship unvalidated features. Many engineers love to slip in extra affordances just in case users want them.

That's great, but if you can't find time to write even a test, it may be a bad smell.

In Chapter 4, I surveyed various ways to learn whether your features were working. Writing a test should be a bare minimum.

Don't just test the happy path. Look for negative affordances that you're exposing and test those. What if users pass in bad data? What if there are race conditions?

Be Neither an Optimist nor a Pessimist

Another ideological default is optimism versus pessimism. Some engineers are naturally optimistic builders, thinking only about the happy path. However, other engineers are pessimists, instinctively testing ideas and looking for the downsides. They are skeptical of complexity.

These mindsets can be sources of strength— a pessimist could become a brilliant security engineer, for example, and an optimist could start a company without realizing just how many challenges there will be.

But when designing software they can be weaknesses. How can we each progress beyond our innate personalities and become the balanced designers that our products need? Scenarios can help us build confidence in designs.

Every feature has downsides, ranging from cluttering the interface to causing users direct harm. Designers should generate adversarial scenarios to break their ideas. In security, this is called *threat modeling* during the design phase and *red teaming* after the code is written.

On the flip side, building hard things on behalf of your users is part of how your product will add value in the world. If it's easy, others can easily replicate it. Brainstorm the good scenarios that could come of your feature.

In considering both the optimistic and pessimistic views, we can find solutions that maximize green affordances while limiting red ones.

Simulate both green and red scenarios regardless of your personal biases. You could even pair with an engineer who is the opposite of you—perhaps somebody you find yourself disagreeing with a lot about these things.

Apply the Rule of Three

When building consumer software, you'll often get quirky feature requests from power users or friends. Business software feature requests are similar. Some enterprise that is paying you lots of money may put pressure on you to fulfill their unique needs.

It doesn't pay to say yes to everything. You can't maintain a zillion features at quality, and customers don't want bloated, labyrinthine interfaces. Even the customers requesting features don't want to be the only ones using them, as they don't want to be an afterthought in your test matrix.

But if you receive three pieces of feedback from different customers that can all be resolved with the same feature, there are probably many more who will use it over time. It's probably worth building.

Just make sure you understand the users' underlying scenarios well enough to make these judgments.

You can also try to come up with three user simulations to justify a feature. In EntSchema, we had to decide whether to make descriptive comments part of the schema, like so:

```
    def fields(self) -> dict:
        return {
            "text": natural_language_string_field()
                .description("What the user wrote, in plain text"),
            "posted_at": timestamp_field().at_object_creation()
                .description(
                    "When the user posted this.  If they put it on a schedule, "+
                    "this is when the post was scheduled to go live."),
            # ...
        }
```

It would be extra work for schema authors to write these, and we could have simply let them place inline comments next to the fields in the schema definition. But there were several scenarios for incorporating formal descriptions:

- Comments could get placed in the code-generated read interfaces so that users who go to the definition in their IDEs could see a comment.
- Similar for write interfaces.
- We planned to one day generate web docs (which we later did).
- Production object inspectors could show descriptions inline or in tooltips to help users understand and debug their objects.
- We could validate that people were adding descriptions, increasing coverage beyond what comments could do. I'll talk more about this shortly.

This passed the rule of three with flying colors, so we added them.

> If you can think of three compelling scenarios for a feature, or if three users ask for it, strongly consider it.

Sometimes features can't be completed all at once, so you have to figure out how to stage them, or create a series of ships.

Build It in Stages

Sometimes, there's a user scenario you want to target, but it's not the highest priority. But it will be much harder to add support for that scenario later unless you build something now. You face a "trapdoor decision," meaning it may be difficult to undo or recover from the decision later.

Other times, the feature is too complex to ship all at once. You need to ship an early version, get feedback, and then finish.

In such cases, set up a perimeter as you build. Think of a chain link fence surrounding the hard hat zone of a construction site: it keeps people out while tradesmen build the house inside. You're going to invite people inside eventually, but only after putting in all the walls, fixtures, and safety features. Since civilians are outside the perimeter, you still have a lot of options on what you build and how you apply the finishing touches.

Such a perimeter will buy you time to add the feature later.

Here are some examples of building in steps, setting up a perimeter during the first step:

- You'd like to have a free tier for your service, but to enable that, you need anti-spam protections and efficiency optimizations. Your perimeter is a paywall until you have time to add them.
- You want to provide a good default, but you're not sure what it should be, or you need to do more work to make it suitable for everyone. Force users to make an informed choice, and then stop requiring that choice when you know what users prefer or when you're ready with the needed polish.
- The future feature will require collecting data. If you don't get the data up front, it'll be hard to go back and get it for existing users. So you ask for the data even though that might deter some initial users from using your product. You can stop requesting the data later if it lowers growth or if users complain.

The EntSchema descriptions are in the last category. Our highest priority was improving the speed of authoring new models, but we knew we also wanted great descriptions for users of models as well. If we didn't require the descriptions up front, we were pretty sure most authors wouldn't write them, and a migration process would be needed to add them later. It was a quick feature to add, so we did it.

But we were also worried about turning off schema authors by adding too much friction. There was probably a "best of both worlds" balance, but we had other problems to focus on.

Our perimeter was to forbid descriptionless fields for starters.

In response to feedback, we quickly followed with a `.self_explanatory()` tag on fields and edges for people who wanted to skip descriptions. However, this was a yellow affordance since it could easily be used to skip important documentation. So we required at least some of the fields on a schema to be described. This forced users to do at least a sparse commenting pass. (We also didn't perform this check in draft mode to avoid bothering prototypers.)

Later, I noticed lots of useless descriptions such as "the text of the post" on `Post`'s `text` field, so during a hackathon, I added a heuristic validation to flag meaningless comments. If your entire text only consisted of the name of the class and the field, plus some filler words like "of" and "the," I would flag it as a useless comment and ask for elaboration or `self_explanatory`. (I was worried this would be considered annoying, and it probably was, but I received a few nice, smiling "you got me!" notes from some engineers who were glad to be nudged toward being more thoughtful.)

We started simply but decisively, then refined the feature and lowered the perimeter over time, ultimately balancing ease of use with limiting yellow affordances. It would have been premature to be so thoughtful up front at a moment when we had no user feedback and were still figuring out a lot of other basics.

If Necessary, Start with an Experimental Version

At Facebook, we had a phrase: "code wins arguments." This meant that working, demonstrable code is more persuasive than abstract debates, scenarios, requirements documents, and so forth.

You can't always be perfectly confident and researched when you ship features. Sometimes the best way to research is to build something and test your assumptions.

In such cases, you can gather more information by dogfooding the feature (Chapter 4) or shipping it as an experiment (Chapter 5). Use feature flags rolled out to a small percentage of users, even run A/B tests. Send out a request for comments. Get beta users to test it.

You may unship it, but that's fine.

For EntSchema, we didn't have the ability to run experiments, but we validated it by dogfooding it and learned what we didn't know. We built the first few schemas ourself and experienced the pains and joys of building them before users did. We also migrated some old battle-tested models to EntSchema to make sure we were handling real production use cases and not just toys. Testing our design against real usage helped us prioritize the important features early.

Once we've decided whether and when to ship a feature, we need to decide how broadly and generically to expose it.

Narrow Versus Extensible Features

Should we build the extensible version of the feature to unlock more use cases, or a narrow one that caters to a specific scenario? How should we make these decisions?

You may have a personal bias, either toward flexible or opinionated interfaces. Scenario-based design can help move beyond your defaults.

When we decided whether to use database-level types like `varchar_field` and `int64_field`, or use the application-level types such as `timestamp_field`, `string_enum_field` and `email_string_field`, we were able to generate three compelling scenario motivations:

Input validation
: Object creators want to ensure that inputted enums are valid and have been specified before corrupt database objects are created. Emails should be valid email addresses, and so forth.

Readability
: Users want to know what the fields and edges are for by glancing at types.

In-production object inspectors
: Engineers would see pretty-printed data from `timestamp_field`, make the web address in a `url_string_field` clickable, render links to User objects from an ID field, and so forth.

Netted out, these use cases sold me because they unlocked another version of the "rule of three" heuristic.

> If the extensible version of a feature unlocks three distinct, powerful, near-term scenarios, build it. If not, start with a specific, targeted thing for the one or two scenarios your users care about.

When you're costing out building the extensible version, keep in mind a few things:

- If it's worth shipping, it's worth testing. If you're building for three scenarios, write a scenario test (Chapter 4) for each one. This makes sure that your feature is as extensible as you think it is.
- Extensibility adds complexity and often comes with more red and yellow affordances. Make sure you're discovering and mitigating those as well.
- Be wary of when the use cases have vastly different priorities. In my preceding list, the scenarios decreased in priority, with runtime validations being easily the most urgent. We could have built something specific such as validators. However, even the last one was quite compelling, and we simply waited to build the object pretty printer until we had time. In other words, up front we laid a foundation for building it, but didn't actually build it until later.

Here's an example of premature extensibility. Suppose you're at a studio building its first video game. The studio's dream is to build lots of games, and so you're tempted to scaffold out a platform for creating games along the way. But since you aren't even sure you have enough funding to complete the *first* game, perhaps it's best to keep the generality to a minimum. Wait until you have money to build a second and third game. As a bonus, by then, you'll start to see the common and contrasting elements between games, which will help you choose the right abstractions.

Chapter Summary

EntSchema benefitted from our use of scenarios in affording a safe and productive developer experience. And the rule of three didn't lie: it evolved into a general development platform powered on the knowledge it captured from schema authors. Over the years, this has supported many features, such as web docs, object inspectors, data migration tools, data integrity checks, GraphQL schema generation, and so forth. Though it started as a developer productivity improvement, it eventually became required for all entities because some of these features were mission-critical.

This chapter was all about crafting usable, safe interfaces. Here's a recap of some of the advice:

- Don't be dogmatic. Get into the details of user personas and scenarios to decide what to build.
- Pay attention to your signifiers and how they highlight the best affordances and lowlight the bad ones in an effort to create a pit of success.
- Make sure any decisions you give users are important, validated, and are handled by the right persona.
- Be neither an optimist nor a pessimist. Generate scenarios to accentuate your feature's benefits and its unwelcome downsides.

And here are some that add an element of thinking about time and iteration to the usual focus on scenarios and personas:

- You do your best work when you're focused, so make sure to build features at a time when they are high priority and worthy of focus.
- When you need to avoid a trapdoor decision, build a perimeter, collecting data and limiting access to features in a way that preserves your options for future development.
- Cutting against that, remember the rule of three: don't spend time on features and points of extensibility that aren't backed up by several compelling scenarios.
- Finally, if you still can't decide: when in doubt, leave it out. Hopefully, you can add it later when and if the case becomes clearer.

I hope you enjoy applying these techniques. They are just rules of thumb, but in my experience, thinking through tough product choices in these terms gives me and my teams clarity and conviction.

Exercises

Let's build a password manager together. (Think: LastPass, 1Password, or Bitwarden.) Your target persona are digital natives whose goal is to securely store high-quality passwords for all their apps and websites without having to remember all of them. Of course, they want it to be easy to use for creating, modifying, and storing passwords as well as hard to misuse. They are willing to pay a small monthly fee for the privilege of never having to think about passwords again.

For these exercises, I want to choose a topic familiar to everyone, so let's focus on traditional passwords. I'll put aside passkeys—while more modern and secure, they are less widely used.

1. Let's make sure users have good password hygiene. List some green, yellow, and red affordances when creating passwords in our manager. Think of two broad scenarios. First, creating credentials for new accounts, and second, when inputting logins for accounts they created in the past.
2. Look at the answers to the first question. Think of at least two ideas for designing our password manager to signify the green affordances at the expense of the yellow and red ones. Think about a scenario of a user creating an account on a standard signup webpage.
3. You're considering building a database of website domains along with updated security information for those domains to help protect your users. This is a big investment because you'll need to create ways to ingest data from the security community and from users, so it needs to be justified. Suppose the only alternative plan is to rely on a third-party database that provides a list of domains that are suspected of phishing attacks. Considering the "rule of three," see if you can think of enough important scenarios to warrant building your own, more general, database.

Answers

1. Here are a few affordances with scenarios to illustrate how recommended they would be.

   Green
   : The user selects a strong, automatically generated random password that is unique to the specific app.

   Yellow
   : The user types their own memorable password which is guessable by an algorithm trained on common passwords. Or, the user types a password that we detect is shared with another site or app that they use, exposing them to a

potential "credential stuffing" attack where leaked email/password combinations are tried on other sites.

Red

When entering an existing login, the user creates a password and email combination that is known to be compromised via a data breach.

2. It's quite easy to type one's own password, especially a short and familiar one. That means it needs to be even easier and more discoverable to use the autogenerated password feature. The password manager I use, 1Password, publishes a browser plugin. This plugin does a few key things:

   - It automatically detects password forms and pops up a dialog to use the password manager, preventing a discoverability inversion.
   - It presents a one-click option to generate a strong password that's easier than typing, avoiding a usability inversion.
   - Some websites have password constraints such as symbol and length requirements. The plugin allows users to configure these policies, making users less likely to drop into creating their own inferior password.

3. Our own database could have information about verified-safe domains, domains with data breaches, as well as the phishing domains already provided by the third party. And it could map domains to lists of compromised passwords. As a bonus, thinking about the password requirements mentioned above, it could even keep track of which domains have which restrictions. Here are a few possible use cases:

   - When users are asked for username and password for a suspected phishing domain, pop up a red dialog to warn them.
   - Pop up an extra warning when they are about to pass credentials to an unverified domain that is not the domain for which the credentials were originally stored within our password manager.
   - Warn users when their username/password may have been leaked in a data breach, including when they shared such a password with other websites and apps.
   - When enough users generate passwords with certain restrictions on a given domain, it could record that and infer that this site has such restrictions. For future users, it would automatically autogenerate passwords with such constraints.

   Of course, this analysis isn't enough to make a decision, but given these several scenarios, it seems worth at least considering whether we want to build an extensible database of our own and making it a core competency of our company.

CHAPTER 9
Product Architecture

> *In software, we rarely have meaningful requirements. Even if we do, the only measure of success that matters is whether our solution solves the customer's shifting idea of what their problem is.*
>
> —Jeff Atwood

Functional requirements are the set of goals for the affordances of our product that do what users want. Chapter 8 was all about fulfilling functional requirements, though we didn't call them that at the time.

If that's all we think about, we end up with the software equivalent of a Potemkin village—a nice interface that doesn't work. So when we think about *Nonfunctional requirements* (NFRs), we consider key attributes that engineers design for, including cost, scalability, latency, throughput, data consistency, elasticity, and availability. And don't forget privacy and security, though those are not covered here.

NFRs are a means to an end rather than enabling user goals in and of themselves, and sometimes represent things users only notice when they're not working.

I love this topic because it's the most engineeringly subject in the book, and yet it still benefits from product thinking. Designing a system architecture for these factors is a pure synthesis of user-centric and system-centric thinking, and it's also the area that Product Managers and other roles are least likely to be able to help design.

This synthesis is sometimes dubbed *product architecture*—system design in the context of users and business constraints. I like the term because it shows the full range of thinking required to do it well.

In this chapter, I'll show how to apply product thinking to system design.

I'll start by laying some foundations for bringing the mindset of an editor to your product architecture.

Then I'll pivot to the usual case study to frame the following sections.

Next I'll bring product thinking to two different categories of NFRs.

NFRs in the first category provide a quick, reliable user experience—factors like latency, availability, and data consistency.

The second are scalability factors such as throughput and isolation that only kick in when many users are using the system simultaneously.

I've omitted a final important category of data governance requirements like compliance, security, and privacy, although those also showcase the power of product thinking.

Finally, I'll talk through how to communicate to customers so they know what system characteristics they can depend on.

The Foundations of Product Architecture

Product architecture is related to interaction design. This is because internal abstractions are miniature products in their own right, to which most of the same lessons from Chapter 8 apply around use cases, the rule of three, iterative development, and so forth.

But product architecture is uniquely challenging because nonfunctional requirements are pesky. There are a lot of them, and they are often difficult to satisfy, meaning we usually don't have time and money to address them all. Worse, even if we had all the time in the world, they often trade off against one another—think: robust data replication leading to increased latency, or security hurdles hampering availability.

Thus, we must bring an editorial mindset to product architecture: what do users really care about?

To that end, I have four techniques I use when considering an improvement to avoid the most common misprioritizations, each of which I'll flesh out in turn:

- I zoom out and look at the big picture.
- I avoid the "streetlight effect."
- I communicate the user impact.
- I investigate the impact using technologies that bridge the "system-product gap."

These little tricks can help you avoid *premature optimizations*, which are code changes that improve NFRs before we have good reason to spend the effort. They are wastes of time and can even cause harm to other requirements.

They come up a lot, so I'll go over each one.

Zoom Out and Look at the Big Picture

Suppose you can do some caching and reduce an algorithm from O(n) to O(log n) or O(1). This seems like a big deal, but it will take work and make the solution more complex.

Zoom out and consider the context. This algorithm's runtime may be tiny compared to other problems. We can say that one problem *dwarfs* another when it's the same type of problem but it's an order of magnitude more important.

Shaving microseconds from the execution time of your function hardly matters when that function is always called by your customer behind a network round trip. In turn, optimizing that network round trip hardly matters when it's kicking off a package delivery that's going to take a week.

These are cases when you can easily prove that an optimization is premature, but let's generalize that.

Avoid the Streetlight Effect

Many engineers are trained to think about system problems and gravitate toward solving them. They are prone to ratholing on unnecessary hardening and premature optimizations.

This is known as the *streetlight effect* (Figure 9-1). The story goes that a drunk man is searching for his lost keys under a streetlamp, even though that's not where he dropped them. When asked why, he explains, "Because this is where the light is."

Our lit area is our training as a software engineer and the corner of the codebase we've become most familiar with.

Don't be the drunkard. If you are reading existing code and notice a database access isn't hardened against race conditions, before deciding the priority of the fix, simulate in your mind how likely it is to happen in practice.

To help yourself look beyond the light, draw a line between the problems you're solving and the "why"—the user scenarios that necessitate you thinking about them.

A handy way to keep yourself honest is to write down the justification in terms of user impact.

Figure 9-1. The streetlight effect

Communicate the User Impact of a Proposal

How would you sell your proposal to a user? They wouldn't be sold on "O(log n) algorithms" even if they knew what that meant. But they might be sold on "pages will load twenty-five percent faster."

Take throughput. If you told a user, "we should scale our system to process a million requests per second," their eyes would glaze over. But suppose you calculate that a typical active customer fires off a request every five seconds. Thus, in user-ese, you'd say, "our system supports five million concurrent customers." The first statement was abstract, but the second one primes us for good decision-making. We can now project user numbers based on growth rates to decide when we need to invest in scaling capacity.

Such an analysis isn't always cheap, and I don't want to encourage you to overthink when getting that product context is expensive. It's perfectly legitimate to improve your NFRs using best practices. Take data consistency. Ensuring strong consistency with a database transaction "just to be safe" is quite reasonable for some low-scale applications. It may also make the system easier to reason about, leading your team to be more productive. If your product later reaches scale and that fully consistent transaction becomes a bottleneck, you'll think about loosening your consistency guarantees then.

Judging when you need to gather product context and when you should fall back on standard practices is a key skill for a product architect.

Once you do want to gather product context, how do you do it? It's often quite challenging. It helps to select a toolchain that helps you hop to different levels of abstraction, from low-level system abstractions to user-facing ones. By tying them together, you can understand how your system architecture will affect users.

Use Technologies That Bridge the System-Product Gap

The *system-product gap* is the chasm between low-level abstractions that are built around computing primitives and high-level components built to facilitate user actions. It's about the limitations of our system components and what we need to do to make them debuggable and reliable in the context of the whole product.

The gap comes up in two ways:

First, take observability. When the system-product gap is wide, we can't easily determine the impact of our low-level decisions on users. This makes the streetlight effect worse, because we're not empowered to think big-picture.

- If I own a microservice that has certain latency, how much does the latency affect the product flows? Maybe it happens in parallel with other services and doesn't matter at all, or maybe it's a critical path. An observability tool could let me know.
- If I'm building a frontend, how much does excessive memory usage on my web page component contribute to the peak memory usage of my app, which is the point when users would be most affected? A memory profiler could help.

Second, consider reliability. Components have fundamental limitations that we must account for when placing them into a product. For example, there will always be network failures. Any time I'm confronted with a system problem, I need to decide whether to fix a low-level system component directly or put it in a context that compensates for its limitations. For example:

- If I'm building an agentic AI, Large Language Models (LLMs) are flaky but powerful. I could use a framework that uses retries to account for failures and uses guardrails to make sure the LLMs don't do things they shouldn't.
- If I'm serving static content via a web page, I can't have every user hitting my data center or it would melt. I need to use a content-delivery network to cache the content and bring copies closer to my users.

Being aware that we can make fixes at multiple layers in the stack is important. With the right technologies, we can either make the low-level limitations irrelevant or, when they are relevant, I can understand their impact and which ones to focus on.

Case Study Introduction

Stripe processes online payments at extreme scale. The scale and reliability requirements of money movement make this a good candidate for thinking about product architecture.

I'm going to modify and simplify the object model that was used when I worked there. Customers purchase things online from Merchants. Merchants have a Balance which tracks how much money they have in their account. This money will be paid out to them periodically and should not go negative, such as when processing refunds to Customers.

Figure 9-2 shows a simplified data diagram, wherein a cross on a line represents the "many" side of a one-to-many relationship. The boxes represent a fairly standard ecommerce data schema. Customers make Payments to Merchants. Merchants have Balances to store all the money they've received and to make refunds as necessary.

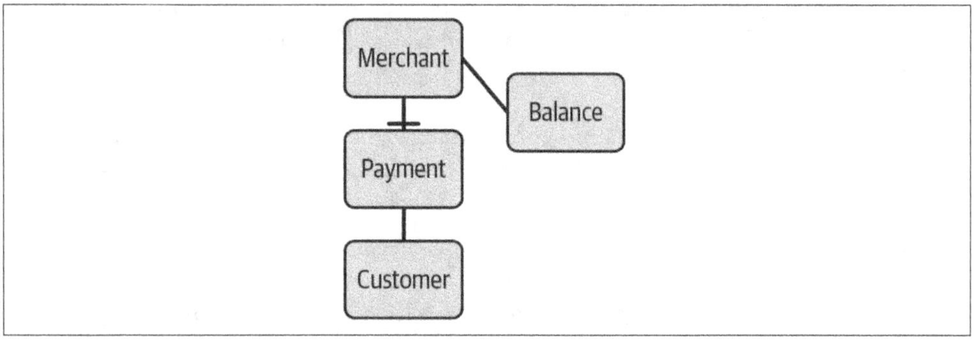

Figure 9-2. A simplified data model diagram for Stripe Payments

This setup offers some interesting product architecture challenges; so in this chapter, I'll bring it with us as we visit a few design trade-offs.

Reliable User Experiences

Let's explore some of the most common reliability and speed concerns through a user-empathetic lens. This will help us be more strategic in our product architecture.

Always remember that latency, availability, and data consistency are really proxies for what really matters, which is: do users engage with your product and successfully complete their tasks? In this section, I'll consistently advocate for bringing your thinking closer to the root goal, and tracking metrics "closer to the user."

Latency

I'm going to mention a bottoms-up, system-centered way of thinking about latency, then I'll cover how to figure out where latency really matters to users. As you'll see, these two involve very different techniques, and so I'll finish by illustrating how to bridge the system-product gap that divides them so you can view the entire problem holistically.

The most straightforward way to measure system latency is to time an operation such as endpoint, function, or remote procedure call. Stuff the results into a metric in your favorite observability system and you obtain numerous advantages:

- Time all of your operations and you get a comprehensive set of metrics.
- If you've identified a slow user interaction, knowing detailed data about each operation will help you find culprits.
- When optimizing the latency of an operation, you can track improvement in its metrics.
- Alert your team when there are major regressions.

This is useful data to have, and you should generally instrument your product in this way if latency is a concern. At Stripe, for example, each separate API call was instrumented, as were latencies for databases and individual services. But be aware that each of these metrics is like a streetlight, tempting you to spend too much time bathed in its light. Ultimately, it's the user experience that matters, and increased latency on a single operation may or may not be visible to users.

How do you figure out where latency is a problem? First, I'll help with building an intuition about this, and then I'll discuss more rigorous approaches.

Here are a few litmus tests with examples:

- Which operations are users or upstream systems actively awaiting, and which are happening in the background? Which content do users want to see right away, such as the first few paragraphs of text on a web page, and which can be delayed?

  When accepting payments at a company like Stripe, one divides requests into the synchronous portion—validating that the funds were there and that the payment could go through—from the asynchronous portion—logging the transaction in audit logs, actually moving the money to the target account, and so forth.
- Which user flows are the most common? Optimizing those will reduce the most user time.

  At Stripe, it was more important to optimize the latency of payment flows than Merchant signups because the former happened a few orders of magnitude more often.

- In which circumstances are users going to be most sensitive to latency? Times when users aren't sure if they're going to continue reading/buying/browsing are called *low intent* times. Users may get distracted in pauses during low intent times.

  For example, when a user is browsing and putting items into their shopping cart, they could get distracted during delays. They will likely be more focused when completing a purchase.

  But what if the user's credit card is declined? If it takes a while to tell them that, maybe they tab away from the page and not even realize the payment didn't succeed. We should complete any validations as quickly as possible.

These intuitions can help, but sometimes we need to be more rigorous. Let's turn our attention to optimizing payment flows on an ecommerce site. Typically, a customer goes through three phases:

1. Shops and adds items to their cart.
2. Loads the checkout page.
3. Makes the purchase, after which the payment processes.

Let's say we're deciding which of those three phases to focus on. We have some ideas in mind that will improve each phase by a few hundred milliseconds, but they aren't cheap to build and we want to start with the most impactful one. We're not even sure if latency is one of our biggest problems.

What do we really care about here? The key user metric we are driving is conversion rates—from the moment the user adds something to their cart to the payment, we want to know what percentage of users make it all the way through. Our product thesis (defined in Chapter 6) is that reducing latency will improve conversion rates.

Conversion rate is an example of a *scenario metric* because it tracks the outcome of a user's progress through a scenario.

One technique I've seen work is to A/B test. Introduce artificial delays for a small percentage of users at each of the three phases. Add a second of delay, then compare conversion rates with our control group who didn't have the delay. Turn to optimizing the phase where the conversion rate is most adversely affected.

Another scenario metric would be the elapsed time from adding to the shopping cart to checkout. This is a great metric to track because we have a lot of options on how to improve it. If, in the checkout page, we add better JavaScript code validating the user's credit card number, such as via a checksum, we can speed up the flow when users make a typo. We're probably not going to track this with an individual metric, but the end-to-end flow's metric will catch it.

What if this metric spikes up after a code push? How do we figure out the culprit? We need a technology to bridge the product metric with the detailed system metrics we're collecting.

Distributed tracing is such a bridging technology. Each user flow gets a "trace ID" which is threaded through all the various operations. Those operations log events with that ID, and we can query for all the events for a given session and find out where the big delays were. Then you can visualize with a flame graph or a waterfall chart.

Figure 9-3 is a rudimentary chart showing time spent at different layers of the stack for the first two phases of the checkout flow.

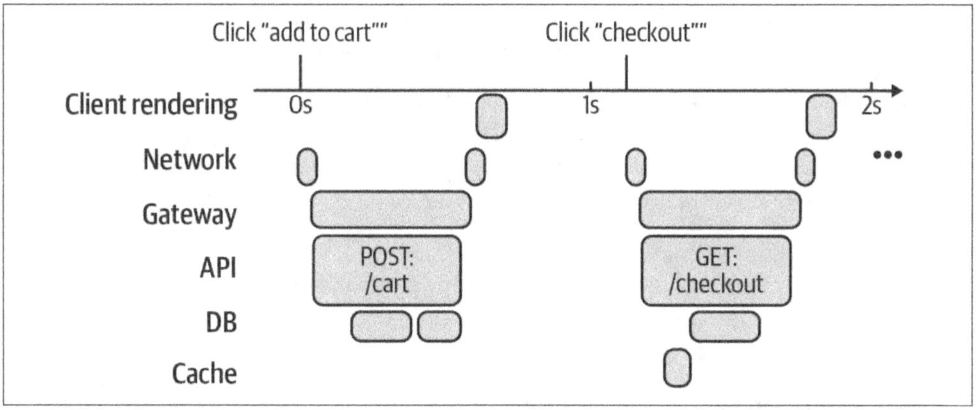

Figure 9-3. A waterfall chart of latencies for an ecommerce checkout flow

While viewing various layers of abstraction in one image, we are at our most powerful. We can "zoom in" from the whole trace to a problematic piece or "zoom out" when something specific fails to see the trace that it's part of. It's easy to put off investments in technologies like distributed tracing because it's not something we use every day. But on those occasions where it's needed, it's a 100× productivity win.

Another attribute that can affect conversion even more than latency is availability.

Availability

As with latency, you want to optimize for availability of operations from the user's perspective while also understanding the behavior of the underlying system.

Consider a common setup—a website with a frontend team and a backend team to run the service. The backend team may know the percentage of requests to their service endpoints that succeed. They may even track volume to alert on unexpected dips in traffic.

There are many parts of the user experience that these metrics don't capture:

- Are network requests getting to the service?
- Are client-side retries compensating for blips in service, turning availability problems into increased latency?
- Is the web page that loads the button that calls the service even rendering the button?
- Are users getting errors on the client that prevent them from calling the server?
- Are users confused due to a recent change to the UI and can't find the button anymore?

Working together, these teams can develop a holistic picture of the product experience. Instrumenting the client brings your insights closer to the user, while tying those metrics with backend metrics can help you pinpoint availability issues.

Client monitoring is easier with a technology that spans the system-product gap, such as *real user monitoring* (RUM). These tools capture issues users experience, including page load times, client-side errors, network timeouts, and so forth, and can correlate those errors with user factors such as browser or app versions, geography, and so forth.

Here are some technology ideas that help compensate for system availability problems:

Workflow engines
: A workflow orchestrates a user flow across various stages while also giving us a top-level view of what's happened. It's accountable to completing the entire flow, which it accomplishes by retrying individual stages and managing parallelism, making it resilient to availability problems.

  Workflows help with observability too. Workflows typically represent product features or product scenarios, and can track each step. Thus, if one step fails or is slow, you can pinpoint both what's the impact on the product as well as exactly where it went wrong.

Content delivery networks (CDNs)
: Data wants to be stored and managed centrally in a cloud service, but users want it close to reduce the chance of network problems and delays. CDNs replicate and cache static data around the world, literally bridging the gap between the database and the user.

Data Consistency

Data consistency is one of the tougher challenges to unpack from a user perspective, as there are different levels of consistency you can offer, and they can present stark trade-offs. As Martin Kleppmann says in the excellent *Designing Data-Intensive*

Applications, "[Consistency guarantees] don't come for free: systems with stronger guarantees may have worse performance or be less fault-tolerant than systems with weaker guarantees."

Data consistency guarantees come in flavors like strong, causal, and eventual consistency. These are useful, if abstract terms. For our purposes, I'm going to focus on a spectrum that ranges from immediate consistency to eventual consistency. (Systems with no consistency guarantees are usually not user-facing.)

You will also see terms like *read-your-write* consistency, which I prefer for product architecture thinking because it incorporates the user—"your"—into the term. In this section, I catalog different sorts of consistency guarantees in terms of who benefits from them. I'll break down the actors in a given product into three groups: you, the user; other users; and the system.

Table 9-1 shows a catalog of the different immediate consistency guarantees you can provide, starting from the most commonly seen guarantees and getting stronger.

Table 9-1. User-centric consistency guarantees

Guarantee	Meaning
Write your Writes (WyW)	All future writes are informed by previous writes.
Read your Writes (RyW)	When users read data, it accounts for all previous writes they have done.
Write after system Writes (WsW)	Updates caused by automations and agents immediately take effect.
Write after others' Writes (WoW)	Other users using the product can't do writes uninformed by your writes, and vice versa.
Read others' Writes (RoW)	You'll immediately see the results of others' writes once they've had a confirmation that their write succeeded.
Read after system Writes (RsW)	Edits by automations and agents are immediately propagated once those actions are confirmed to the system.

Note that these guarantees are the properties of product features, not databases. Databases usually have no concept of who's reading, meaning it's up to the application developer to carefully choose the semantics.

In fact, you can cobble together stronger guarantees atop a database with weak guarantees, and you don't automatically get strong consistency even if you're making strongly consistent queries to a database. You'll make decisions at multiple layers of the product architecture.

For example, suppose we're building endpoints for a group food order, where different users may be simultaneously editing the cart, and then the creator of the order will submit the order. Here's a layer-by-layer look at designing it for consistency:

Database
: We could use a transactional database so that everyone's writes are consistent, or solve the problem higher up.

System design
: Let each food orderer append to a list in the database rather than making overlapping writes to the same table. This will prevent an entire class of RoW and WoW consistency concerns.

Endpoint inputs
: We don't want repeated identical requests from the client to cause extra orders to be added to the cart. We can allow clients to provide *idempotency keys*, checking whether those keys have already been committed before allowing an identical request through.

Endpoint outputs
: Provide the updated data back to the client. Clients can now use that to see the updated state of the cart without requerying and getting a possibly stale database replica.

Clients
: Use cookies or local storage to keep the data, to make the app responsive, and refresh it periodically.

Product decisions
: Lock the cart when the account's owner goes into the checkout flow, preventing race conditions between adding orders and submitting payment. The owner will need to unlock if somebody complains about the lock as they try to add something late.

Bridging frameworks that close the gap between what the databases can provide and what the product demands can help. For example, here are a few technologies that help when users want atomic, transactional semantics but the underlying databases don't support it:

Event sourcing
: These frameworks essentially keep track of everything that has happened as "events" and then replay them and continue them in case of an outage. They can, for example, be used to populate a new database starting from a checkpoint. Effectively, an entire chain of operations is grouped together into a sequence, and so the user perceives eventually consistent behavior for the whole sequence.

Saga pattern
: This pattern, which can be layered on top of event sourcing, provides all-or-nothing guarantees for a product feature atop operations that can't use transactional databases. If you're authoring a series of steps, you give each step an "undo" that kicks in when something fails, and the system ensures that either everything happens or nothing.

Data integrity checkers
: Check databases for consistency with each other based on user outcomes you care about, like ensuring after a financial transaction that the payer's and payee's records match.

We saw how a combination of thinking of consistency in a user-centric way and thinking holistically about our product design helps create consistent experiences. Now let's talk about trade-offs between the three NFRs we just explored.

Latency, Availability, and Data Consistency Trade-Offs

Martin Fowler noted that "Architecture isn't about building the perfect system; it's about making trade-offs." So let's turn back to our Stripe case study to explore how product thinking can help us navigate these dilemmas.

Commonly, companies like Stripe use a sharded database to store their models. Each shard is replicated several ways to guard against data loss. One of those replicas is the "leader" which takes writes. Reads from that replica are immediately consistent, but reads can come from other replicas. Such reads may be out of date before the data propagates, and are often called *secondary reads*.

In short, primary reads are less available but with stronger consistency guarantees, while secondary reads are more available but with weaker guarantees.

In the early years, Stripe reads were generally from the leader, which made the system easy to reason about and provide correctness. However, as the company scaled, it needed to get more formal and let engineers around the company choose primary or secondary reads based on the product scenario they were enabling.

For practice, let's choose between semantics, and then how to achieve them, for a few Stripe scenarios.

Onboarding Merchants
: An applicant is progressing through a form inputting their details in order to get verified and become a Merchant. The flow should branch appropriately depending on, for example, whether they are a sole proprietor or a corporation. And they should be able to review their submissions at the end. RyW and WyW semantics are called for.

  Primary reads will be the most expedient way to achieve this. This use case is not nearly as high-scale as payments, since the average onboarded Merchant will be associated with orders of magnitude more payments. So we can get away with more expensive reads and writes.

Payment balances
: When a Customer pays a Merchant, what do we really need to enforce in their balances? For one, the Customer's balance should not be allowed to go negative,

so we should provide WyW semantics for this object in case they pay for two different things in quick succession. To achieve this consistency, we'll do primary reads from the Customer's balance.

In contrast, the receiving Merchant need not get the funds immediately—the customer doesn't often care when they get the money, and we don't need to enforce a maximum balance. Therefore, the Merchant will not need RoW semantics—when they check their balance, they'll perform secondary reads and their view might be slightly out of date. This will only be awkward if they're directly talking to the Customer, which is surely quite rare.

Blackholing Merchants

Once a Merchant is discovered to be a fraudster or a terrorist, we'd want to turn off the ability to pay them with all haste. A simple approach is to write a "blackhole bit" to the Merchant table which is checked each time a Customer attempts to pay the Merchant.

Given the seriousness, should users get RsW semantics, doing a primary read of the Merchant's table each time there's a payment? This could cause availability and performance problems. But with secondary reads, security updates might take a long time to propagate in times of heavy load, though generally within a few seconds.

It depends. If marking the Merchant as fraudulent was done as part of a manual review process wherein a Stripe analyst needed to make a decision and click a button, surely a few more seconds to propagate is not consequential compared to the overall flow. However, if this action is done automatically and is used to fight off fast-moving, coordinated threats, that extra propagation delay might be a big deal. This situation will require a lot of thought and perhaps should use a solution specifically optimized for countering this kind of threat—perhaps we can use a different data architecture or give priority to propagating auto-triggered security remediations.

The consequences of being inconsistent can have a dramatic impact on the user experience, but consistency can have catastrophic impacts on availability. As I mentioned above, Stripe evolved from an "everything is consistent" mode to a mixed mode over time.

One of the key moments in this transition was sparked by an outage a few years ago.

One thing I didn't mention earlier was that Stripe also serves platforms such as Shopify to power online stores, and marketplaces like DoorDash, which serves restaurants and couriers. They bundle Stripe payments along with other services for their own customers. To accomplish this, they onboard Merchants, in the thousands or millions, and provide them with Stripe payments.

The outage arose from a detail: each time the Shopify or DoorDash Merchant takes a payment from a Customer, it must pay its platform a small fee.

We were recording this fee in the platform's leader database in every payment request. Unfortunately, we were doing it synchronously. This provided RyW consistency to callers, who would immediately get back the details of the fee. Which was fine until the database shard that housed one of our largest platforms went down for the better part of an hour, meaning the payments requests failed for every single Merchant attached to it!

After a review of the incident, my immediate task was to move the platform fee write to be asynchronous, eliminating the bottleneck and preventing such a widespread outage from happening again. The team then did a wider evaluation of our consistency posture which necessarily led to analysis of many product scenarios.

Careful reconsideration of data consistency is an important part of how Stripe worked to consistently achieve 99.999% reliability in recent years.

Scalability

In any internet-backed product, with scale comes problems. Your system may have limited throughput, and the consequences of users exceeding your throughput limits can be dire, as illustrated by successful denial-of-service attacks. This is due to a lack of *isolation*, meaning that some users of the product can adversely affect the experience of others.

There are two categories of problems that limit throughput, bottlenecks and elasticity. *Bottlenecks* are choke points that prevent the system from supporting more simultaneous users, and *elasticity* problems mean that you *could* support more throughput but are insufficiently reactive to changes in user demand—perhaps scaling your number of machines is too slow.

Problems in each category can be pinpointed in advance with testing, which is the focus of this section. We can simulate scenarios like users vying for contended resources, sudden changes in demand, and deliberately go above our throughput limits to assess how badly we degrade.

Testing for scale is a deep and wide topic that I couldn't hope to cover here. I'll dwell on how product thinking can help you design effective simulations and feel confident that it's worth fixing what you found.

Scale Simulations

Throughout this book, we've simulated individual users interacting with our products and systems. Sometimes, we do it in our head, through user scenarios (Chapter 1). We've done it in code through scenario testing (Chapter 4). We've asked users for their stories (Chapter 5) and to simulate their stories in Customer Discovery Interviews (Chapter 6).

Scalability dynamics are too big for our heads. We'll need sophisticated scripts to test load, sudden spikes in traffic, and capacity.

Instead of the terms "test" and "injection," I prefer "simulation," as one of your primary goals is to build a test environment and inputs that match the real world as much as is reasonable. To an unseasoned engineer, "load test" makes it sound like I can just spin up a script that calls the same service a few million times and call it a day.

Therefore I'll use these terms, collectively called *scale simulations*:

Load simulation
: A test that simulates a certain amount of realistic production traffic to determine if we can scale to a certain point.

Capacity simulation
: A similar test that sends increasing amounts of such traffic in an attempt to find the limits of our system and find out how gracefully it degrades once it hits those limits.

Spike simulation
: A test that quickly ramps up traffic to simulate realistic spikes in user requests, making sure our system is elastic.

> Aim for high production fidelity with your scale simulations.

Let me first paint a picture of a high-fidelity scale simulation for an internet infrastructure company like Stripe. Imagine you want to find out if you'll scale to double the load with your current system and to find how much capacity you have to scale further.

- Instrument your code with metrics, logging, sampling, and distributed tracing so that you'll be able to debug anything you find.
- Record every request you initiate, along with its timing, so that you can replay the simulation and reproduce issues.
- Make a complete replica of your entire production cluster; call this the "shadow cluster." The shadow cluster is as similar to prod as possible—the only difference is that it doesn't interact with the outside world.

- Each time a request comes in to your production cluster, double it into two similar synthetic requests, differing only in IDs, and send both to your shadow cluster.
- Be able to increase the replication factor for capacity simulations.
- Run it for a long time to catch slow-building issues due to "state buildup," such as memory leaks, growing database indexes, and so forth. These can cause dramatic performance degradation.
- Be able to ramp the amount of traffic up further to pinpoint when issues will occur.
- Measure scenario metrics to understand the impact on typical users when the system is under load.

If instead you're trying to simulate adding a big new customer to your mix, make the same setup, but then instead of doubling traffic, add synthetic traffic carefully based on what you think the customer's planning to do. That will test the customer's traffic in context of the broader existing usage.

Such a test architecture would provide these benefits:

- It would find issues that will come up in practice, avoiding the streetlight effect.
- Engineers would feel confident in prioritizing investigations and fixes.
- Engineers would understand how urgent such fixes are based on the scale at which the problems occurred and projections as to when traffic will reach that level.
- The team can test performance improvements against this same setup.

This vision is fairly expansive and will be quite expensive to build and run. Many teams will need to make do with less.

Let me break it down into smaller suggestions that you can choose from.

Scale simulation tips

Full production fidelity in your scale simulations is a lofty goal. In reality, many teams try to get as close to that as they can within the time and budget they have.

A simple load test, like hammering a single endpoint that is known to be a scalability bottleneck, can provide a good return on investment due to its simplicity, especially before you have user traffic to simulate. But it shouldn't be mistaken for comprehensive, and it will likely find false positives or false negatives if the traffic is not realistic. Even when you're taking a quick-and-dirty approach, try to feed it production-like scenarios.

A combination of high-fidelity simulations and simple, targeted load test scripts can work well, too. The former can find bottlenecks and the latter can make them reproducible and testable.

First, you'll generally have a test harness that issues requests, and an environment that takes those requests. Be careful here:

- Make sure your harness doesn't have limitations that prevent it from simulating production. For example, issuing requests in a simple loop could be problematic because each request gets backed up depending on the timing of the previous request. In the real world, users don't wait in line.
- Make your simulated environment as much like production as possible. You could even have all the normal jobs running in the background.

Think also about motivating your teammates to actually fix issues that your harness finds:

- Think about reproducibility. For example, make the harness deterministic and use random seeds, so that there is less variation.
- Spend the extra time to make the simulations believable. Let's say you had two testing approaches, one with a 25% false positive rate because it used realistic traffic simulations, and another with a 90% false positive rate because its traffic had little bearing on reality. People will be much more motivated to investigate issues flagged by the first one, even if it were otherwise harder to use.
- Show the real-world impacts of the degradations in terms of scenario metrics.

How to simulate real-world usage? Shadowing production traffic, or recording it and replaying it, is a great practice. But what if the traffic you are worried about is different from what's happening today? Then you'll need to predict the details of what customers will actually do.

- If you're working with individual large customers, work closely with them to do the load test.
- Generate full scenarios, not individual calls. For example, at Stripe, a customer might load a credit card form and then submit a payment soon after. Write a scenario that does those two in sequence and randomizes the amount of time in between.

Finally, be aware of time:

- The real world doesn't stop, so run extended tests. You'll find state buildup issues such as memory leaks that trigger garbage collection events and many more.

- Predict calendar effects. Example questions might be: Do you expect spiky traffic or smooth traffic? Will it peak at certain times of the day, and if so, what peak do you expect? Or days of the year? At Stripe, much preparation is done each year for the U.S. traditions of Black Friday and Cyber Monday, during which traffic goes through the roof.
- Record performance profiles in a database so that you can detect regressions over time as the product evolves.

Scale simulation truly benefits from full-stack thinking.

Bridging technologies

There are many load simulation, traffic capture, and fault injection tools out there, and which ones you pick will depend on lots of factors. Make the ability to model production a goal when you choose a tool and approach, while also making sure you have enough instrumentation to debug bottlenecks once you've found them.

Communicating Nonfunctional Requirements to Users

Customers of online platforms don't just want reliable, scalable systems—they also want guarantees. Often, organizations will negotiate with any companies that they take dependencies on, inking certain quality bars into their contracts. Your job as an engineer is often to figure out what guarantees that you can offer, to communicate accurate information to customers, and to make engineering changes such that you can achieve your reliability goals.

The two chief goals of customer communication around NFRs are to align incentives and to build trust with customers. I'll start with the former.

Guarantees are provided in contracts called *Service Level Agreements* (SLAs), which most commonly govern:

Availability
: What is the uptime of your service, measured as a percentage.

On-call response times
: How quickly must engineers respond to incidents?

Latency
: How responsive are critical endpoints?

I'll cover availability, the most common SLA. A typical contract might stipulate that at least 99.9% of your API calls over a certain time period will succeed. If your company doesn't live up to that standard, your customer will be owed something, perhaps refunds in the form of credits. Such contracts are important because they incentivize your company to obsess about reliability.

An SLA isn't the goal, it's a lower bound, and typically customers want higher availability in practice. A platform company will have a higher *Service Level Objective* (SLO) that they are trying to achieve. This is typically kept internal because it may confuse or mislead customers.

Therefore, companies need other ways of building trust with their customers that they're not just going to do the bare minimum for the SLA.

What does build trust is being honest and transparent:

- Showing uptime at a site like *https://status.stripe.com* which reports honestly about availability over an extended time period.
- Posting Root Cause Analyses (RCAs) to customers or, even better, on the internet when an incident does happen.
- Keeping folks up-to-date during the incident response, showing what steps you took and how quickly.
- Listing the remediations you've done or are doing to prevent the problem from happening again.

Don't succumb to the temptations of hiding information or making excuses, perhaps by throwing your own infrastructure suppliers under the bus. This doesn't build trust.

For example, if Amazon Web Services (AWS) is your cloud compute provider, if you blame them for an outage in a region, customers will hear that you don't plan to do anything about it in the future. If instead you talk about adding another region or cloud provider to prepare for disasters, they will understand that you are learning and getting better and will be more interested in being long-term customers.

Before you can be transparent with customers, you must be transparent internally. This is because if individual employees or their managers aren't comfortable speaking up about what happened—maybe they fear getting fired or giving up on a promotion—they will hide the facts, and they will never bubble out to customers. This is part of why Stripe encourages a culture of "radical transparency."

A related cultural practice that massively accelerates infrastructural improvements at both Facebook and Stripe is the "blameless postmortem." With this philosophy, when teams get together to figure out what happened during a production incident, they focus primarily on the systemic failures that allowed the incidents to happen rather than blaming individuals for failures. When individuals did make mistakes, they are expected to learn rather than be punished. I love attending these types of postmortems—they are constructive, creative, and collegial.

For example, if an engineer misconfigured a knob when rolling out databases, which caused an outage:

- How might the individual validate their rollouts better in the future? They might bounce some ideas off of their manager or their tech lead in a private conversation.
- Why wasn't there a sanity check in place to prevent that? This is a great topic for a group postmortem.

Since every bit of infrastructure is a product, blameless postmortems are exercises in blaming the product rather than the user. That's a fine note to end the chapter on.

Chapter Summary

This chapter synthesized system design with user-centric thinking into the domain of product architecture. With product architecture skills, you'll make more strategic and confident choices, and your users will be happier for it.

I'll highlight a few key takeaways:

- Don't just look under the streetlight. Lean on knowledge about users and their behaviors.
- Your life will be much easier with tools that bridge the system-product gap. Choose tools like workflow engines, distributed tracing frameworks, and load simulators that let you model your product behavior holistically while also keeping track of the system details.
- Look beyond low-level metrics. Track and goal on behaviors that matter directly to users, such as concurrent users, scenario completion rates, and client-side availability.
- Look at data consistency not just in terms of databases, but from a user's-eye view through consistency concepts like "read your writes" and "write after others' writes." Consider whose reads and writes does each person need to be synced with? Creatively consider solving problems at different layers in your product's tech stack.
- Trade-offs dominate thinking about reliability and scalability. Learn what users want to pick the right balance.
- When doing scale simulations, replicate how users will hammer your product in the real world.
- If you work on a platform, build trust with your customers honestly and transparently while setting up mechanisms to align your incentives with them.

Here are some exercises, and then I'll wrap up the book.

Exercises

You're adding collaborative editing to your online spreadsheets, similar to Google Sheets. You want to support up to 50 users simultaneously editing to support use cases like team brainstorming sessions and hackathons in which people can sign up for tasks by dropping their names into spreadsheet cells. To pull this off, you'll need to think about scalability, data consistency, race conditions, and availability.

I suggest you read the answer for each question before moving on to the next one.

1. What category of consistency guarantees would users want you to provide for each cell if they want to play it safe and not lose data?
2. What could you do if you wanted to provide this level of consistency at the database level in the scenario mentioned in the previous answer? And how would you handle that in the product?
3. Google Sheets doesn't actually enforce strong consistency guarantees, perhaps because of a lack of demand, or because they couldn't come up with a design without heavy trade-offs. Instead, it uses a simple "last writer wins" policy. What work-arounds could provide an as-consistent-as-possible experience without actually providing WoW semantics? Consider at least two ideas. (One of my answers will be something Google does already, and one won't be.)
4. Name a few latency metrics or traces you would collect to give you a picture of how your product is performing while also allowing you to narrow down the problem when latency regresses. Name at least one metric related to the edits we've been discussing and one unrelated.
5. How would you approach load testing of simultaneous users editing a document to achieve high real-world fidelity?

Answers

1. Cautious users would want Write after others' Writes (WoW) consistency—they don't want to accidentally clobber someone else's entry into a cell without being aware of it.
2. Google could use a standard conditional writes approach. Each client could keep a sequence number for each cell showing how up-to-date their copy of the data is. Every time a user commits a write, the global sequence number for affected cells would be incremented. All writes would be conditional on the sequence number matching. So, if during a write, the global number is "ahead" of your client's number, you won't be allowed to perform the write.

What should you show the user when this happens? Perhaps you'd show a pop-up with the latest value alongside their own edits and give them some conflict resolution options.

What about edits that affect multiple cells, for example via a copy/paste? My best guess is that users would want atomicity—apply all or reject all, then show the conflict resolution screen. Otherwise, the inconsistent data across cells would quickly get confusing and hard to manage.

3. Google assigns each user a color, and collaborators see a box of that color any time a user clicks into a cell. This sends a powerful visual signal that conflicts are possible, allowing users to police themselves, and it was likely relatively simple for Google to build. This reminds us that it's not all about databases when it comes to data consistency—the closer our solutions are to the users, often the more cost-effective and targeted they can be.

   Google could also do the same kind of sequence and history tracking I mentioned in the answer to the previous question, but instead of throwing a hard error when a cell conflict is detected based on the sequence numbers, they could display a warning icon next to the affected cell. Users would click it to resolve the conflict. To facilitate this, Google would need to keep a history of the edits to provide context so that users could effectively resolve conflicts.

4. I'd start by measuring the timing of each server call so that we can narrow down issues to client or server problems, and likely measure key database calls within the server.

   I'd also track loading and rendering a spreadsheet, separately and together, as that will be an exceptionally common scenario and also a user's first impression of the product. I'd measure starting from when the user enters data into the cell to when it's stored in the cloud and propagated to others.

   The colored boxes approach to consistency will fall apart unless the boxes show up quickly, so I'd measure how long it takes after a user clicks into a cell before other users see the colored box.

5. As a first step, I'd come up with a high-scale real-world scenario toward the top of what seems reasonable, and I'd get a bunch of users in a room to hammer it. Or, I'd identify some high-scale sessions that have properties I want to test based on real-world usage. In either case, I'd record all of the actions—anonymizing the data, of course—so that I can replay them in load simulations inside of "headless" browsers that can replay user actions without a user in the loop. Or if I want to focus my load tests on the server only, I could cut out the browsers and just record the server requests.

   One concern about simply replaying real-world data is that a lot of factors go into it. For example, if I improved some client-side rendering delays, that could cause users themselves to speed up, thus putting more pressure on the database. So I might want to resimulate after making major changes.

Once I've figured out where there are problems based on the real-world data, I can home in on specific parts of the system and build more targeted load tests to execute those bits. That will give me a tighter feedback loop as I optimize, and then I can test my optimizations using the original simulated traffic.

Wrap-Up

Like a sea otter, the product-minded engineer possesses a rare combination of skills. Thinking in terms of scenarios, personas, signifiers, and affordances alongside your technical skills gives you a sort of "structured empathy." This is a great fit for the engineering discipline because it helps to navigate trade-offs.

To gain these powers, the most important thing is just to practice focusing on users:

- Constantly ask "why?" Why are people behaving in this way? How are they going to benefit from what you're building?
- Validate your software. Dogfood, test, simulate, and expose yourself and your team to customers and their feedback.
- Build iteratively, in part to gain more frequent exposure to users.
- Practice simulating user journeys. In the same way that a chess player learns to look ahead more and more moves, you can improve your ability to tell longer and better stories about users.
- Align your personal and team goals with those of your users, which will help you to pay attention.

Thank you for reading! I hope that this material makes a difference for you, and I'd love to hear your feedback—if there are errors, you think I missed an important trade-off, or something was confusing, I can still make edits.

You can find me on LinkedIn or on Substack at *https://drewhoskins.substack.com*, where I write about software engineering and product management.

Index

D

E

F

G

H

I

J

K

L

M

N

Q

R

S

T

About the Author

As an engineer, Drew Hoskins has helped design and build a wide range of innovative products and platforms for Microsoft, Meta, and Stripe. Throughout his career, he has carried a passion for empowering developers, starting with a passion for API design and then broadening from there. Highlights include founding and designing Meta's main ORM, EntSchema, as well as the workhorse of Stripe's asynchronous services, Workflow Engine, and helping to rearchitect Oculus VR's services stack. He also contributed to Stripe Connect, Stripe's APIs, Facebook's Graph API, Windows 7, and Visual C++.

He has most recently joined Temporal Technologies as a product manager in charge of improving the developer experience.

He lives in the San Francisco Bay area, plays a lot of competitive bridge, and loves to learn about technology and its history.

Colophon

The animal on the cover of *The Product-Minded Engineer* is the northern sea otter (*Enhydra lutris kenyoni*). A subspecies of the sea otter, the northern sea otter is a marine mammal that can be found near the coastal waters of the north Pacific Ocean, primarily found along the shores of Alaska, British Columbia, and the Pacific Northwest. Although the northern sea otter can walk on land, it is so well adapted to aquatic life that it can live entirely in the water.

Unlike most aquatic mammals, which rely on a layer of blubber to stay warm, the northern sea otter keeps warm using its incredibly dense fur—up to a million hairs per square inch, the thickest of any mammal. This fur consists of two types: long, waterproof guard hairs and a soft, insulating underfur. The guard hairs keep the underfur dry, while a layer of trapped air forms between the fur and the otter's skin. This pocket of warm air, heated by the otter's body, creates insulation that keeps cold water from reaching the skin, helping the otter stay warm in its chilly ocean environment.

The northern sea otter is one of the smallest marine mammals, typically weighing between 50 and 100 pounds and measuring about 4 to 5 feet in length. Its diet includes sea urchins, crabs, clams, snails, and fish. It is one of the few mammals that uses tools—often using rocks to crack open its food. Northern sea otters have a very high metabolism, which, along with their thick fur, helps them stay warm in cold water. Because of this fast metabolism, they need to eat a lot—up to 25% of their body weight every day.

The cover illustration is by José Marzan Jr. based on an antique line engraving from Lydekker's *Royal Natural History*. The series design is by Edie Freedman, Ellie Volckhausen, and Karen Montgomery. The cover fonts are Gilroy Semibold and Guardian Sans. The text font is Adobe Minion Pro; the heading font is Adobe Myriad Condensed; and the code font is Dalton Maag's Ubuntu Mono.

www.ingramcontent.com/pod-product-compliance
Lightning Source LLC
LaVergne TN
LVHW080040210926
848481LV00011B/3240
* 9 7 8 1 0 9 8 1 7 3 7 3 9 *